DEDICATION

This Letter Tracing Journal Log book is dedicated to all the kids and children out there who love to learn how to write their uppercase and lowercase letters and want to practice.

You are my inspiration for producing books and I'm honored to be a part of keeping all of your letter practicing notes organized.

This journal notebook will help you record your details about learning new letters to write.

Thoughtfully put together with these sections to record:

You can trace the uppercase and lowercase letters to learn how to properly write them. Plus at the bottom, there is a blank dotted line space for you to try it on your own!

HOW TO USE THIS BOOK

The purpose of this book is to keep all of your Letter Tracing notes all in one place. It will help keep you organized.

This Letter Tracing Journal will allow you to accurately document every detail about trying new letters. It's a great way to chart your course through learning to write properly.

Here are examples of the prompts for you to fill in and write about your experience in this book:

Each page has one letter for you to trace (uppercase and lowercase) many times and write on your own. At the bottom of the page is space for you to practice writing on your own. You could even put your own words in there if you wish.

Enjoy!

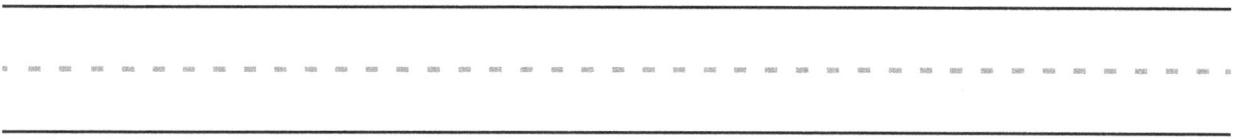

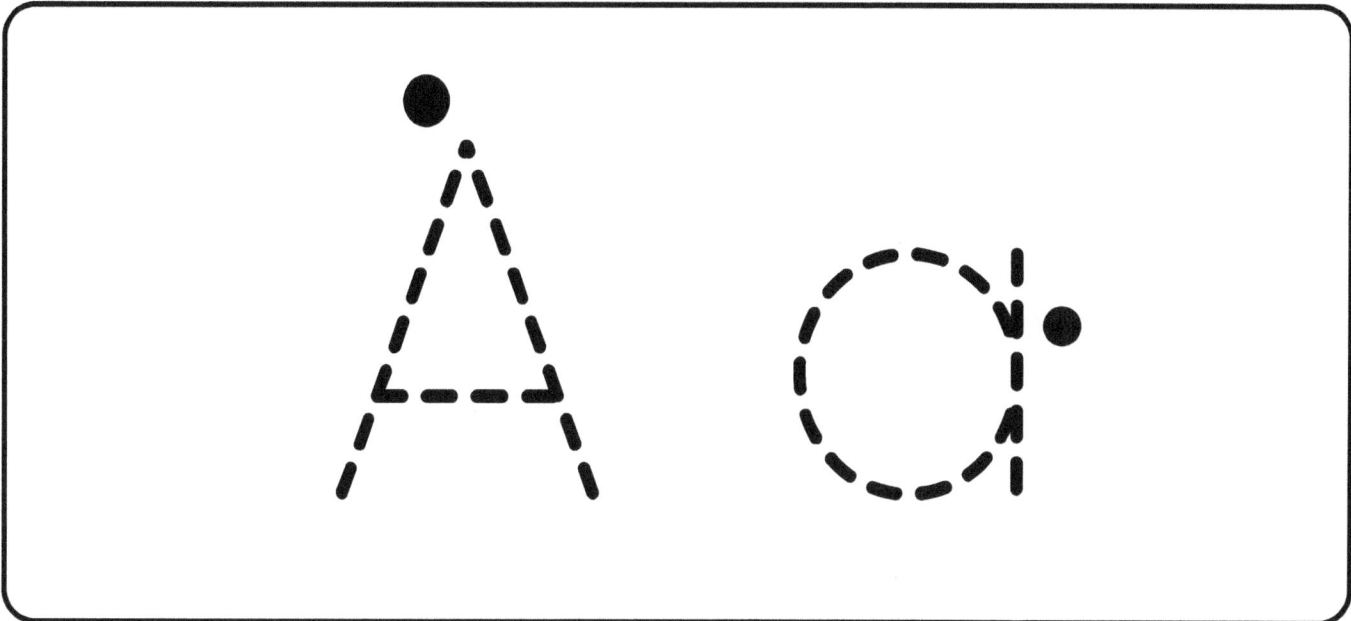

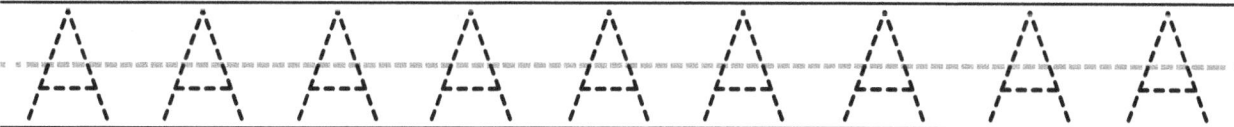

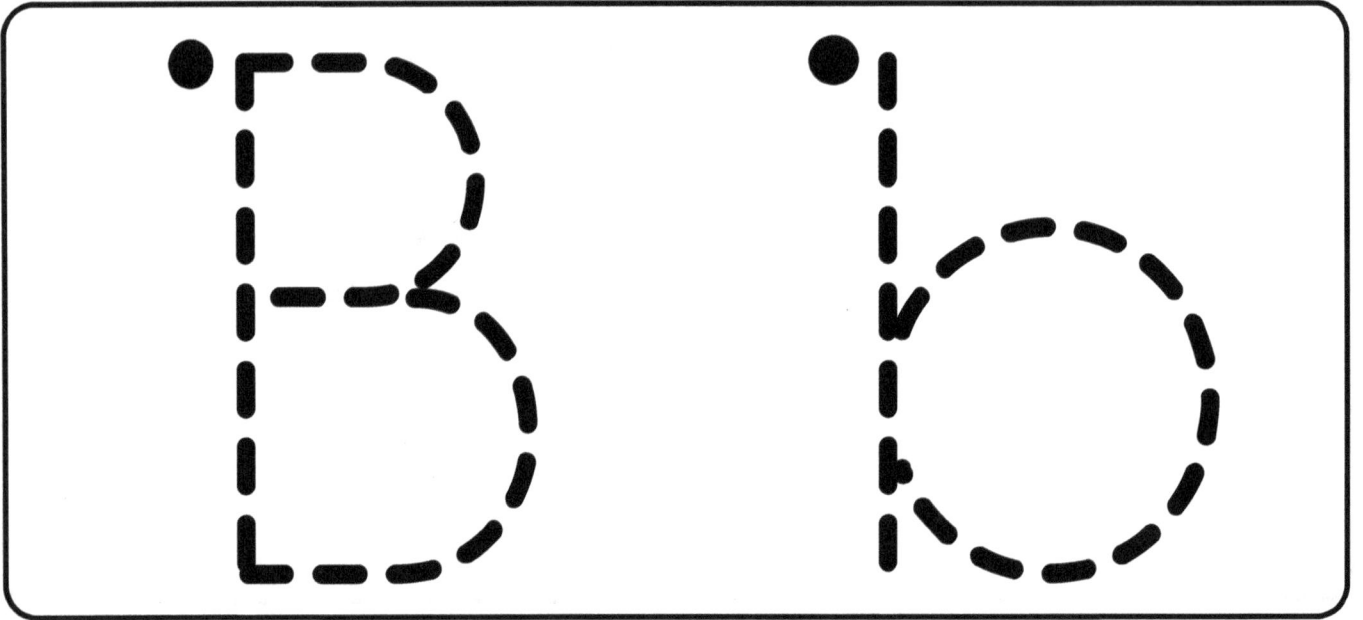

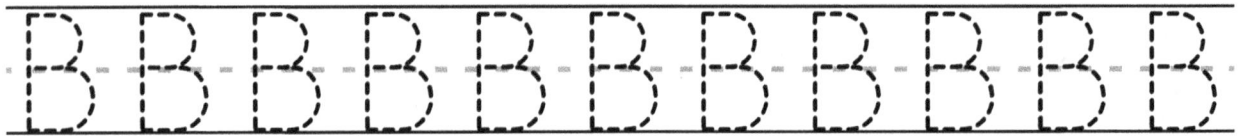

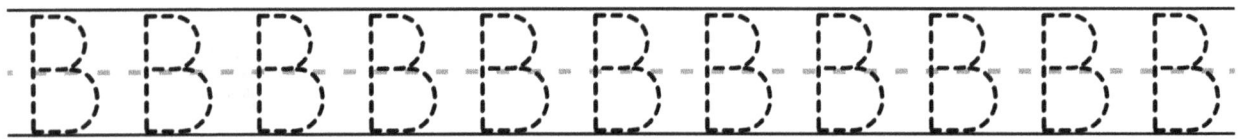

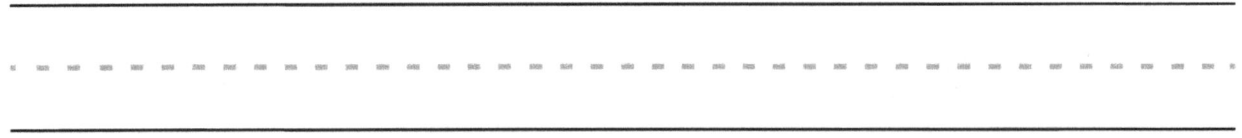

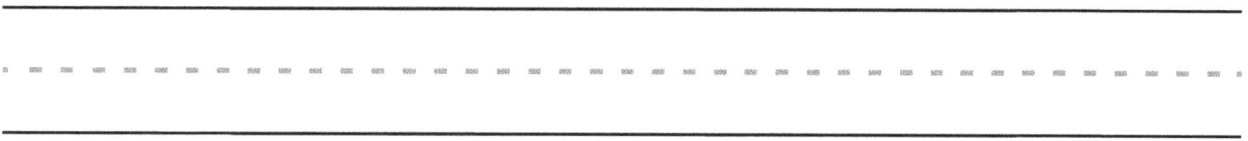

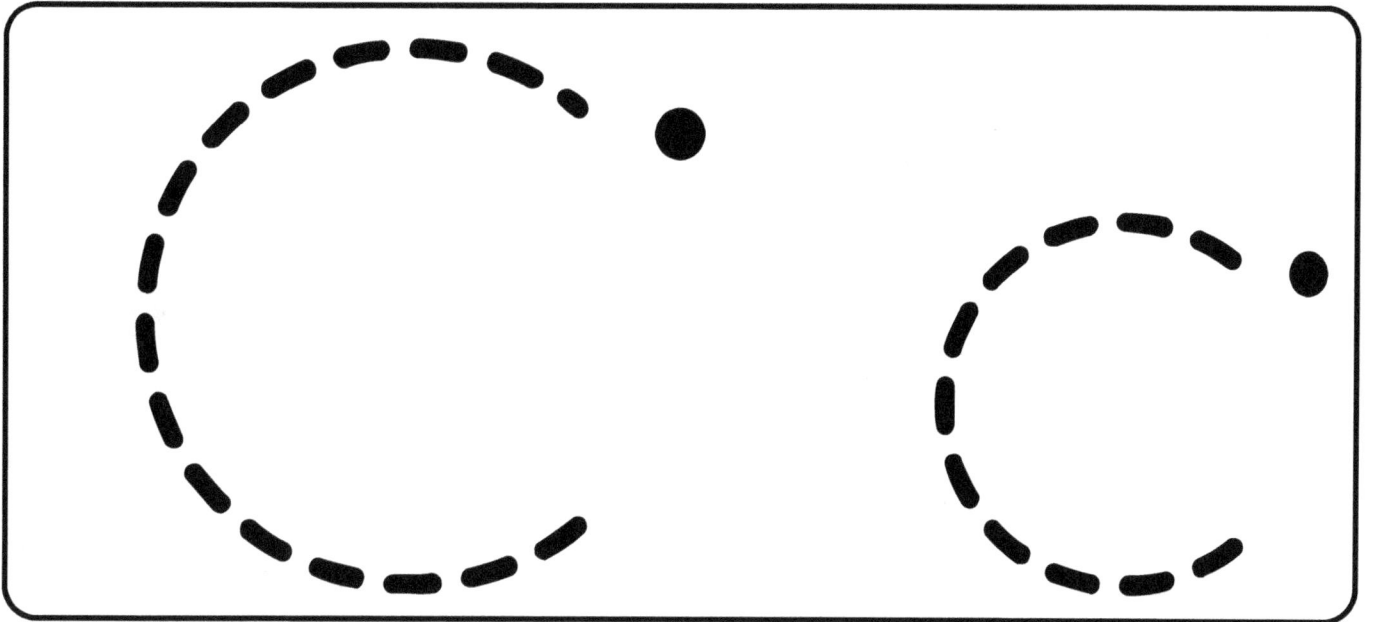

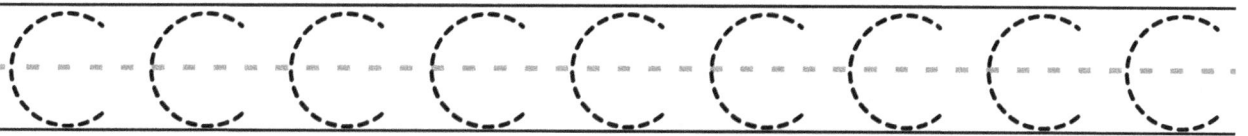

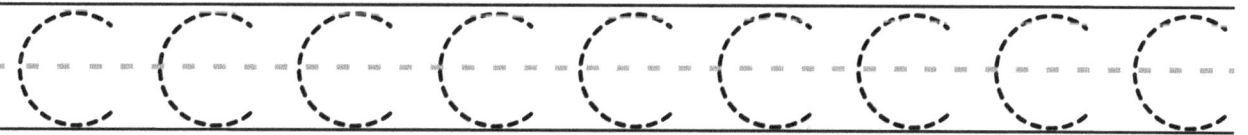

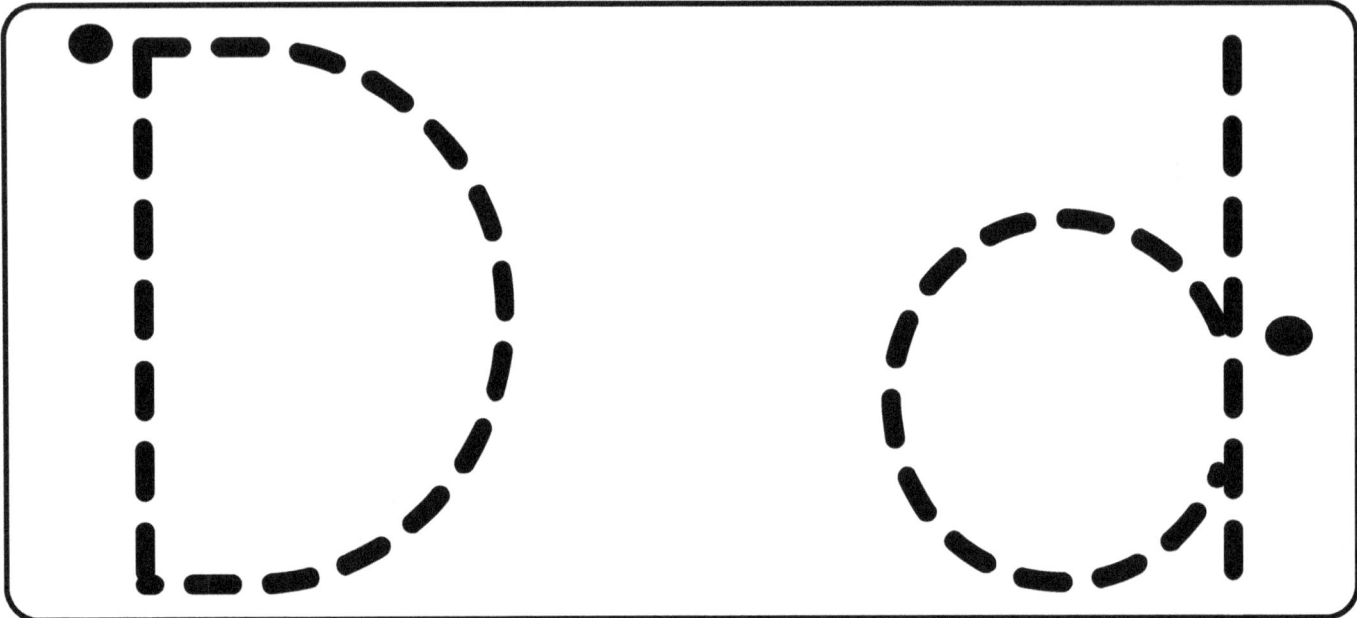

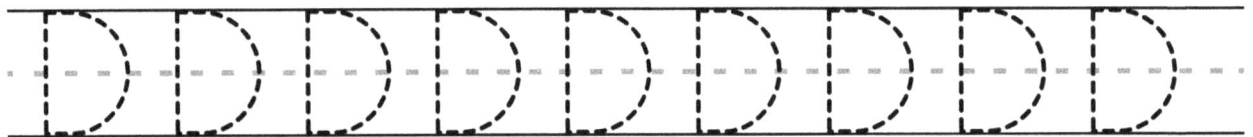

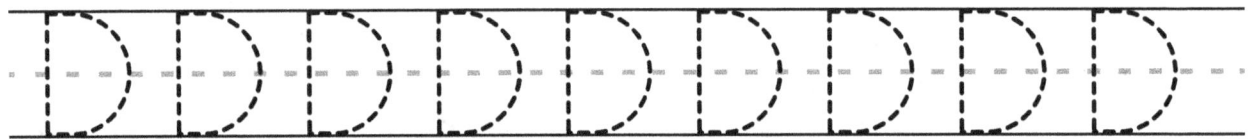

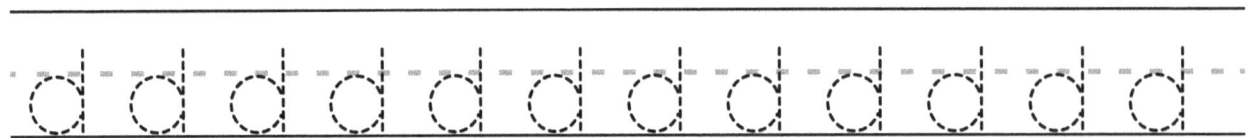

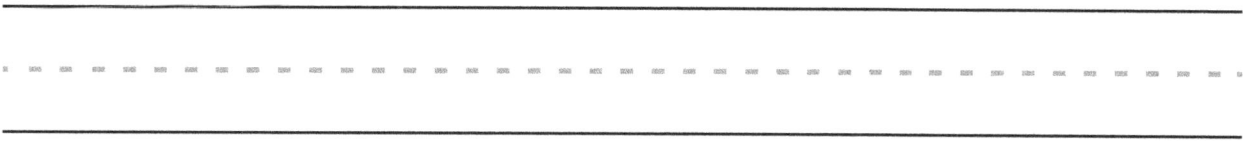

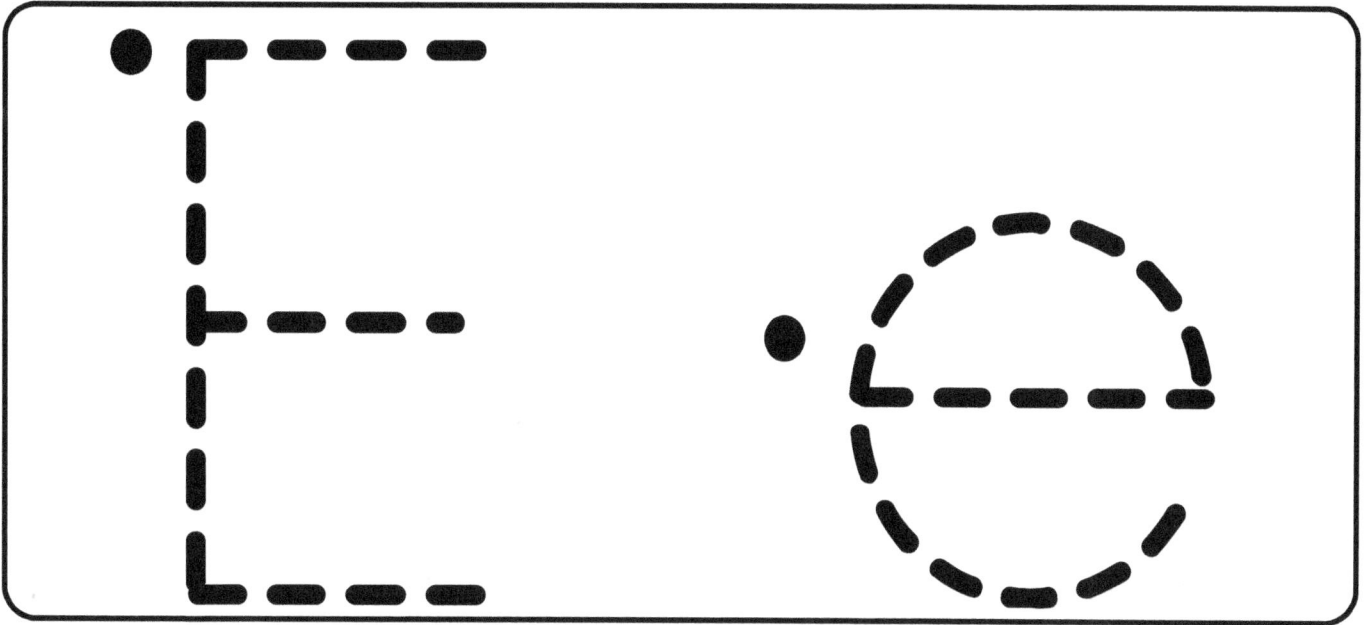

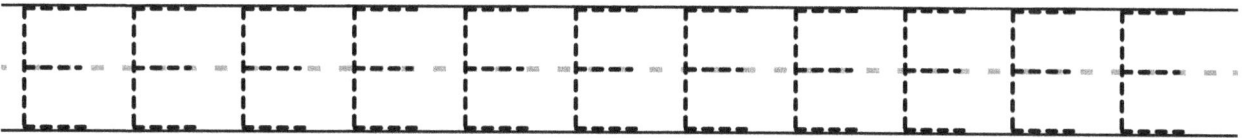

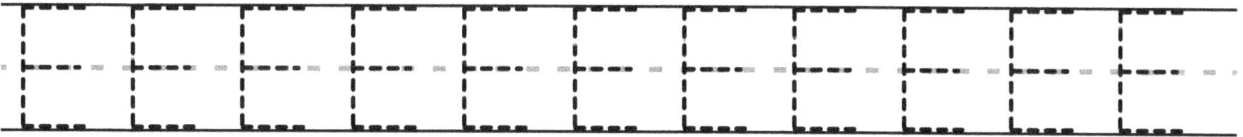

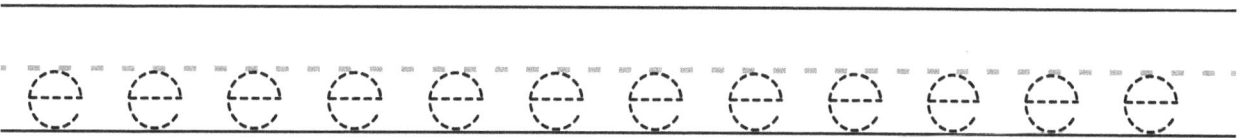

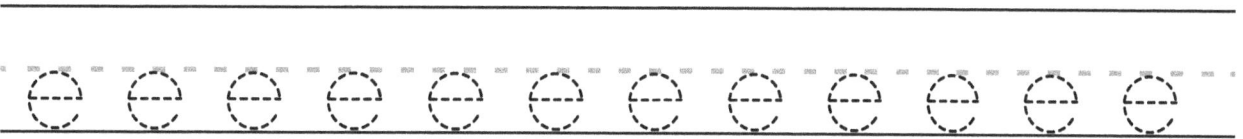

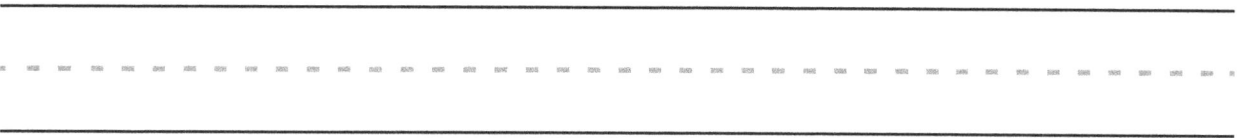

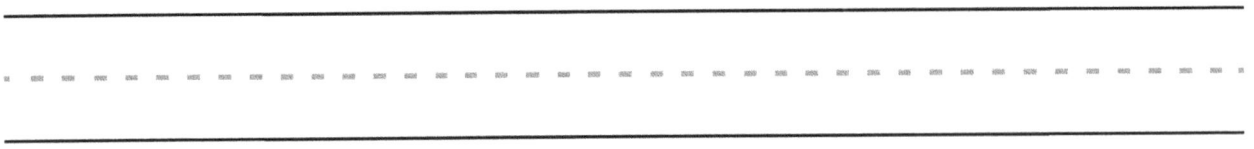
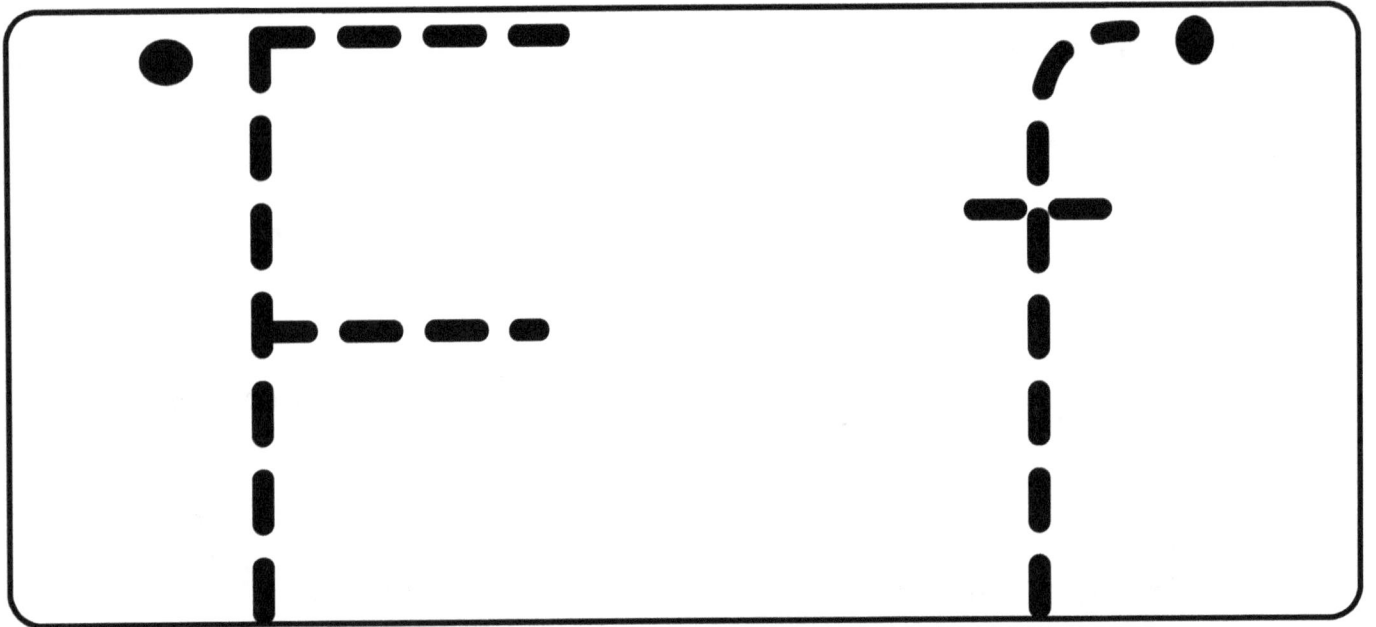
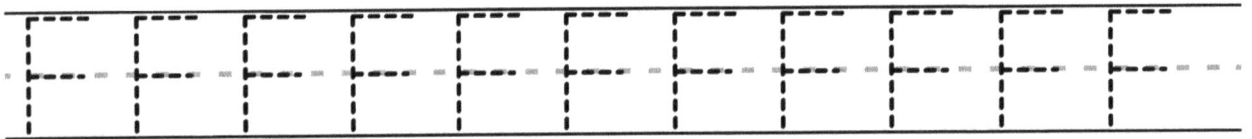
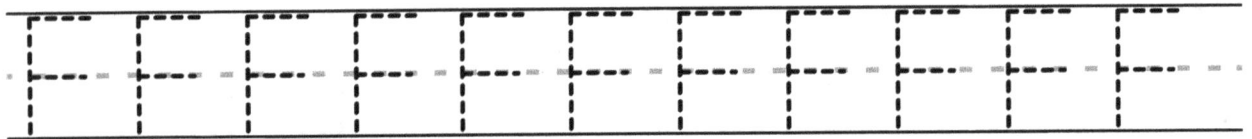
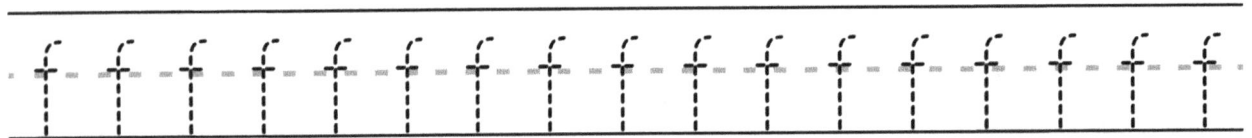
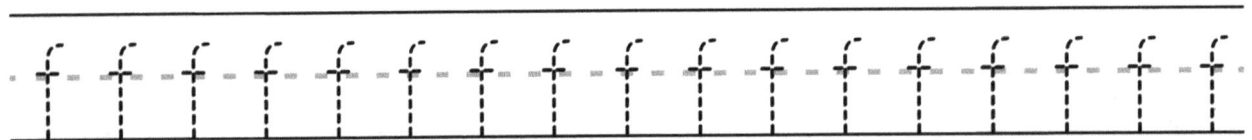

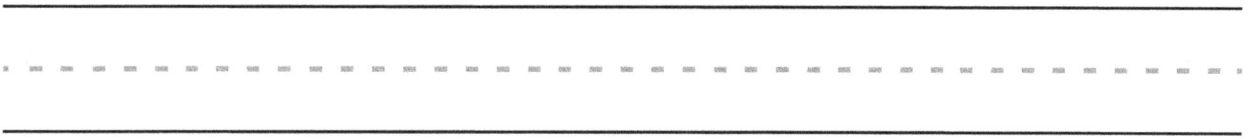

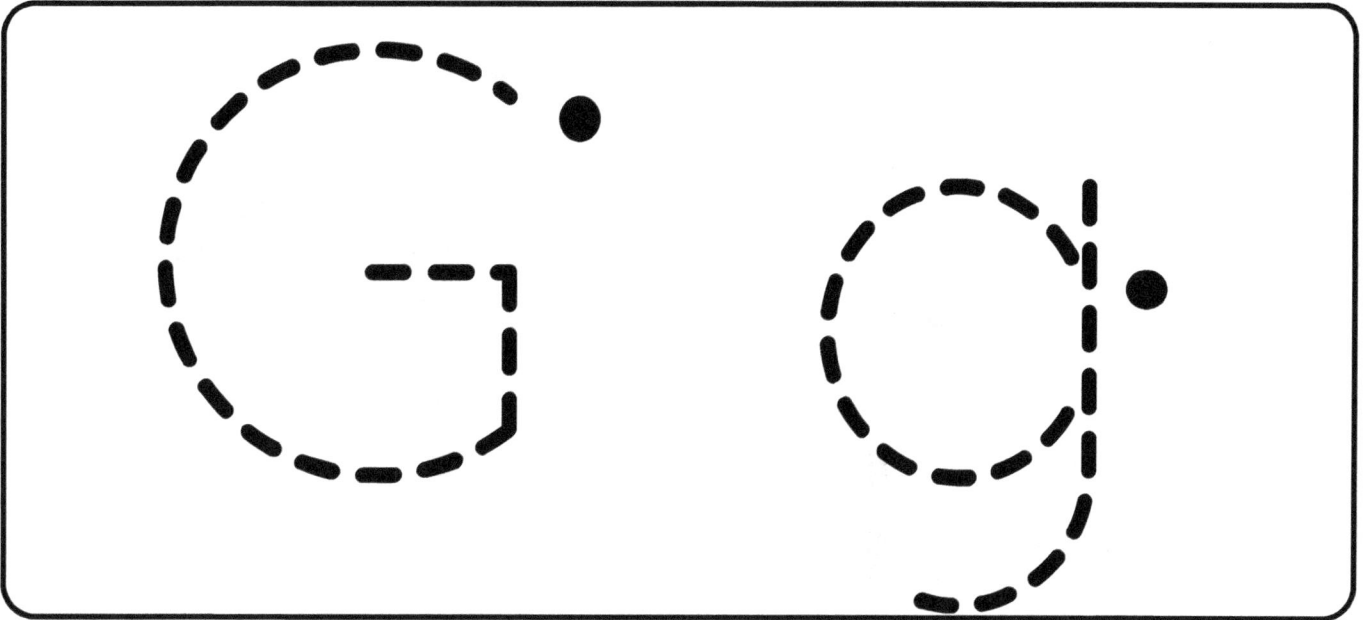

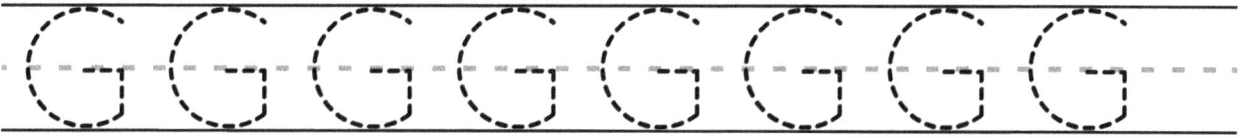

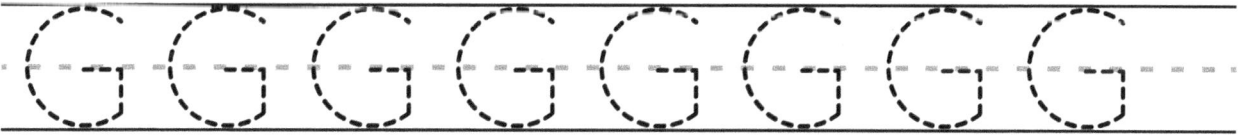

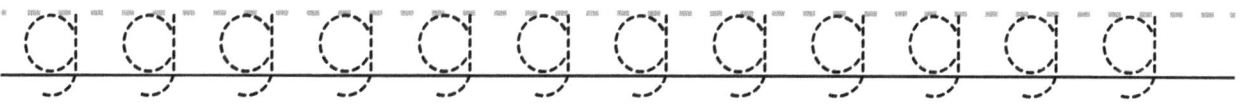

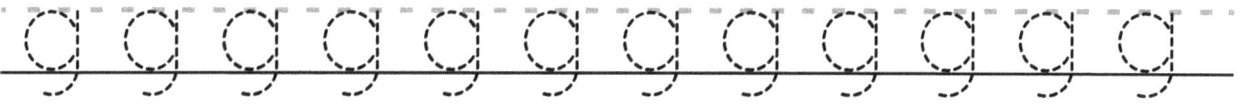

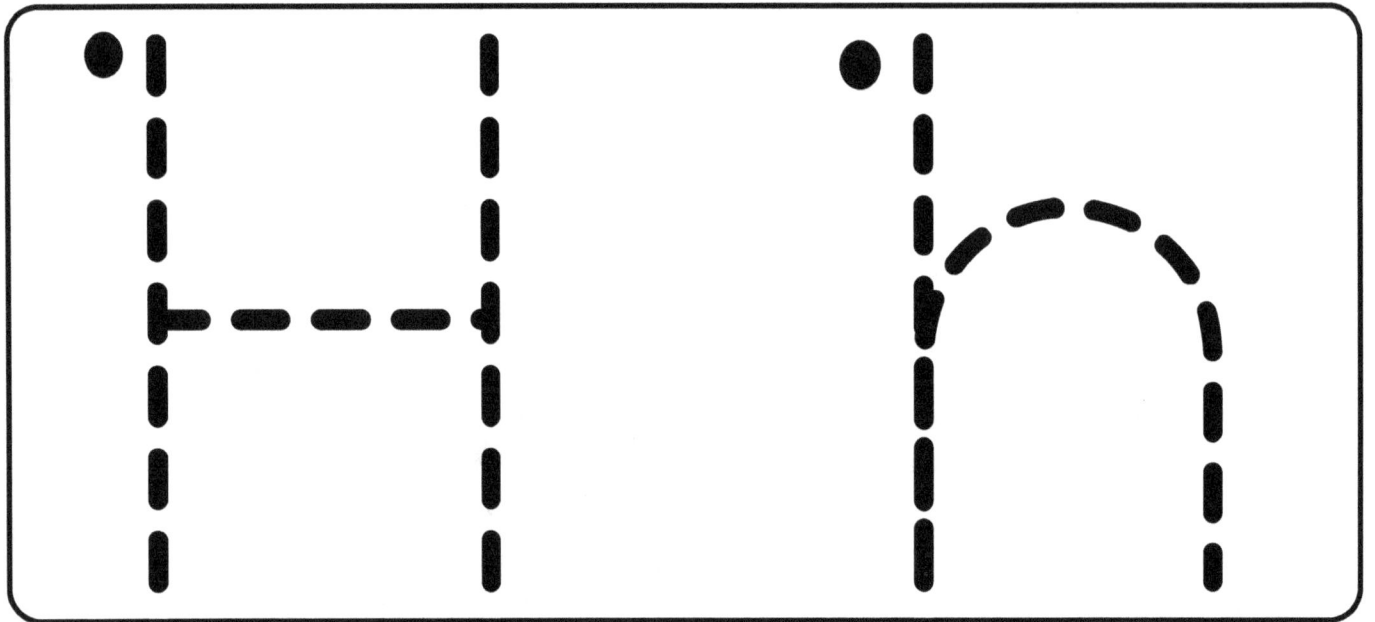
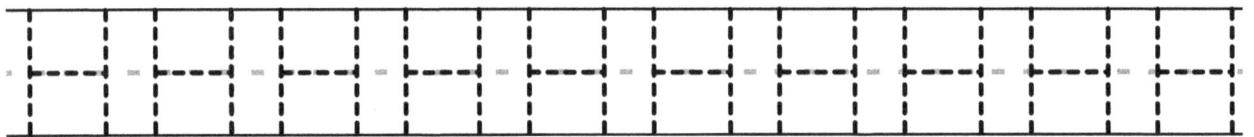
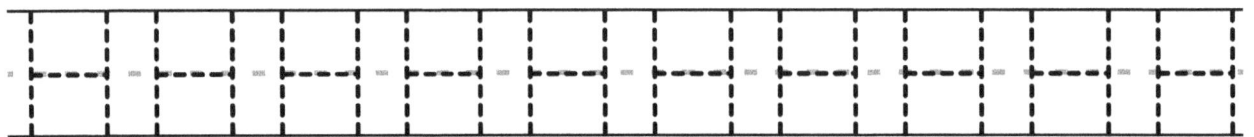
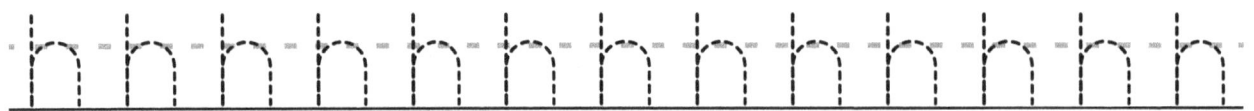
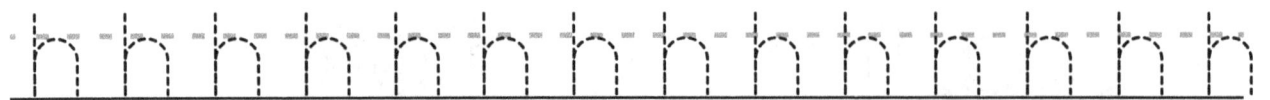

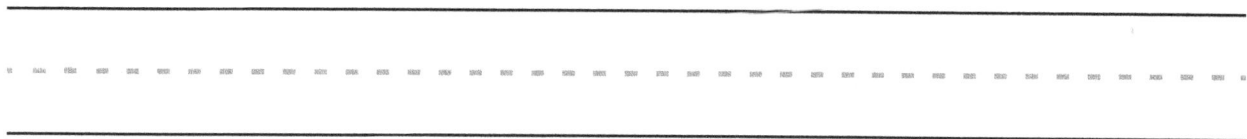

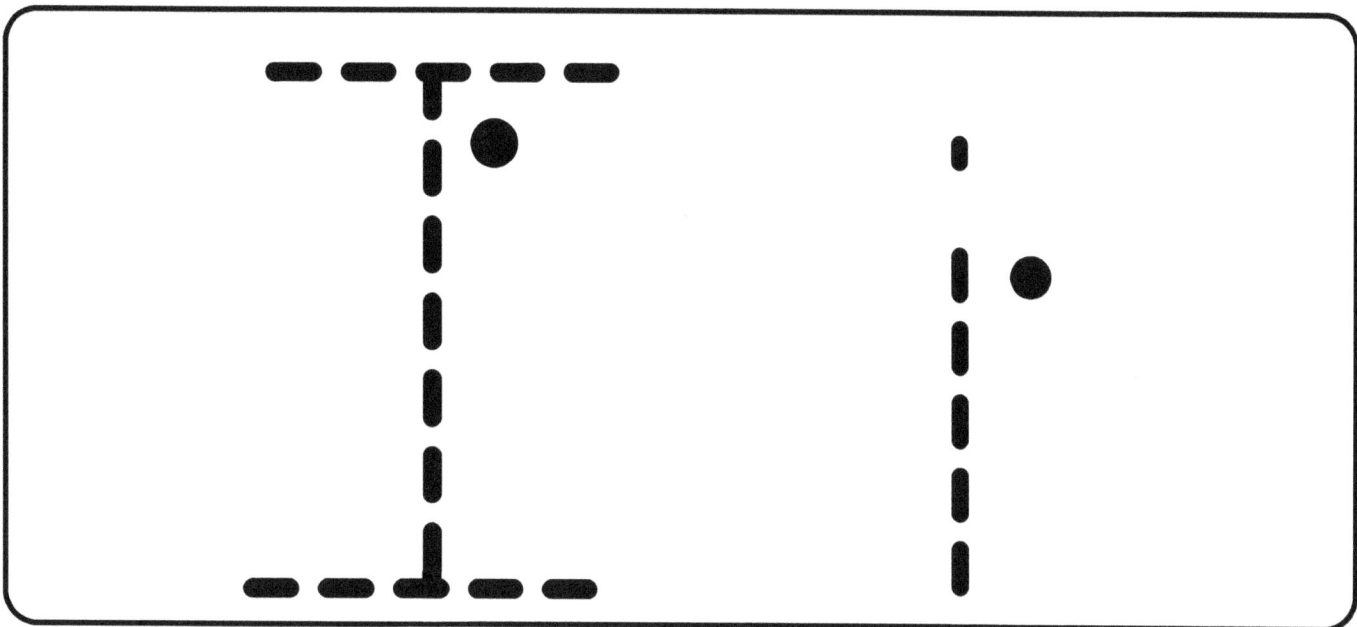

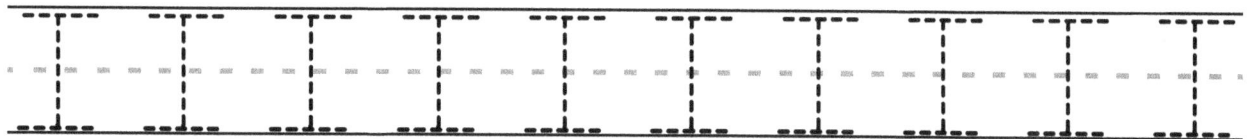

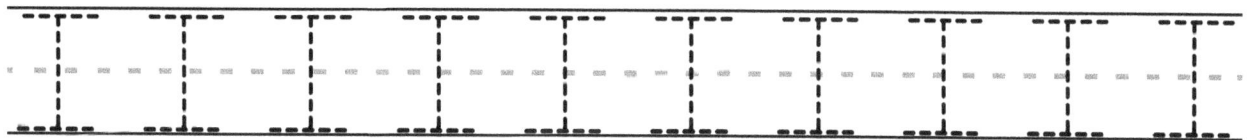

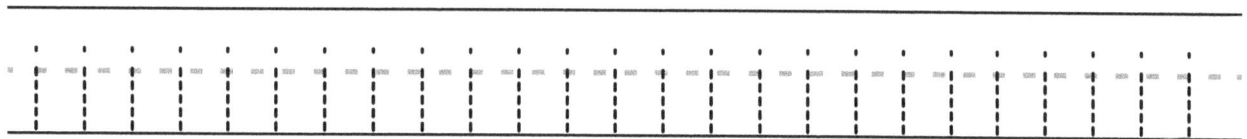

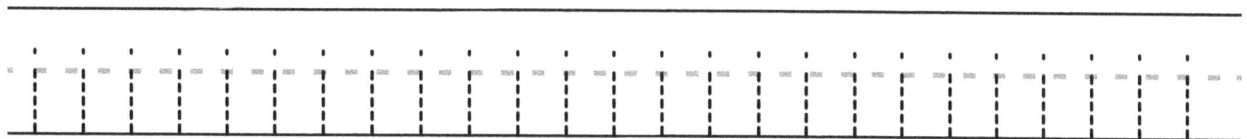

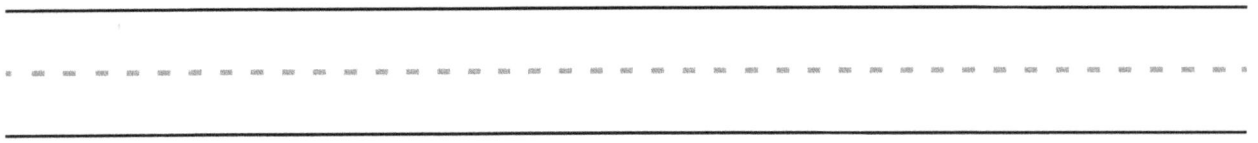

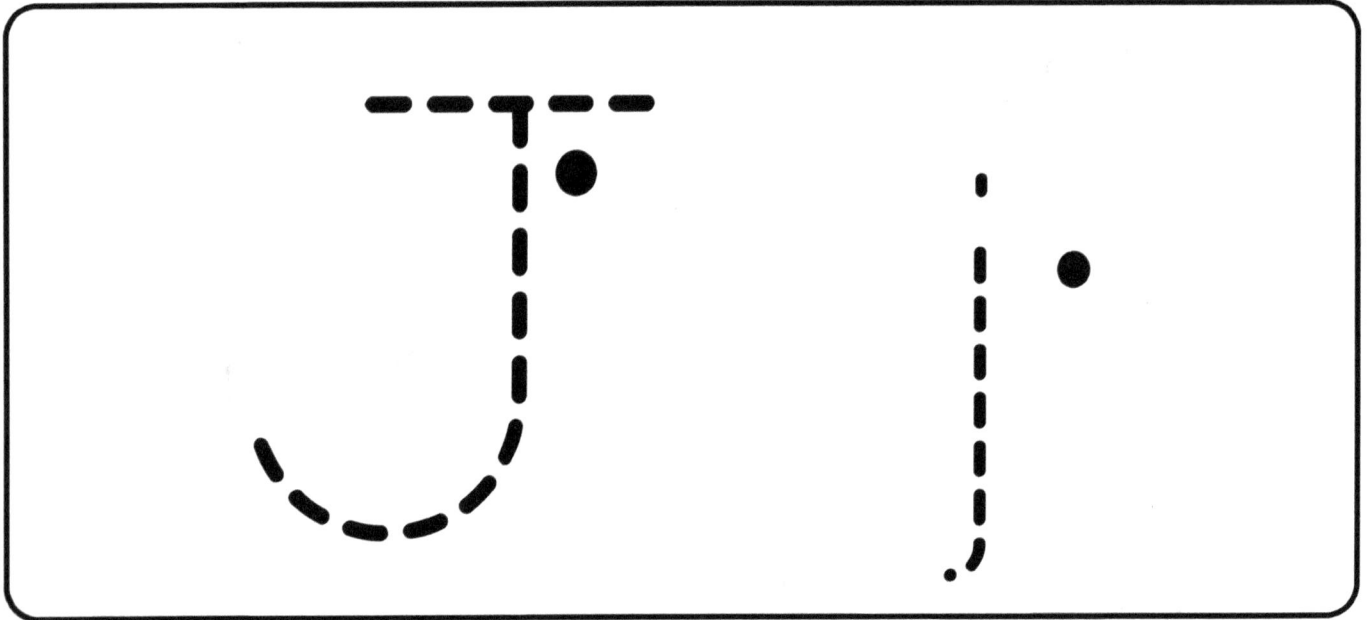

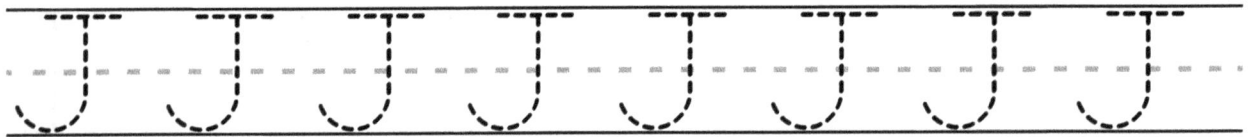

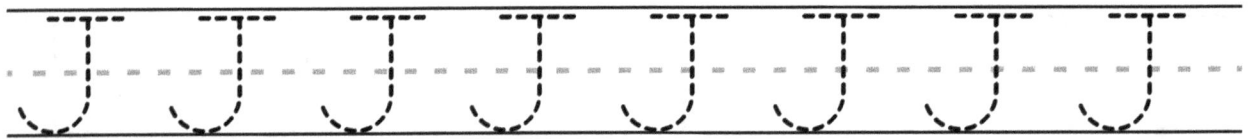

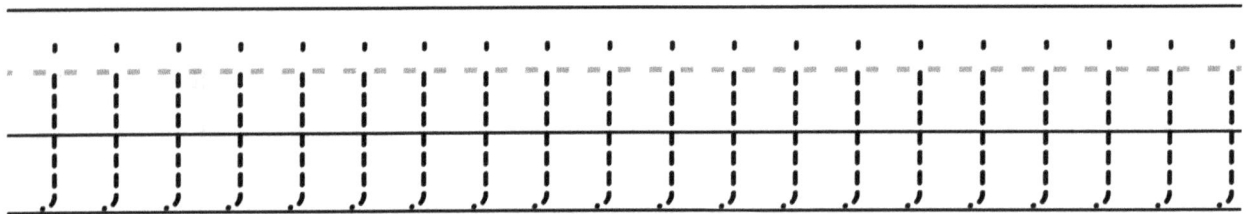

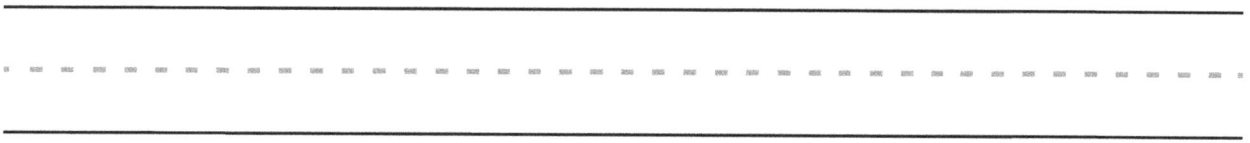

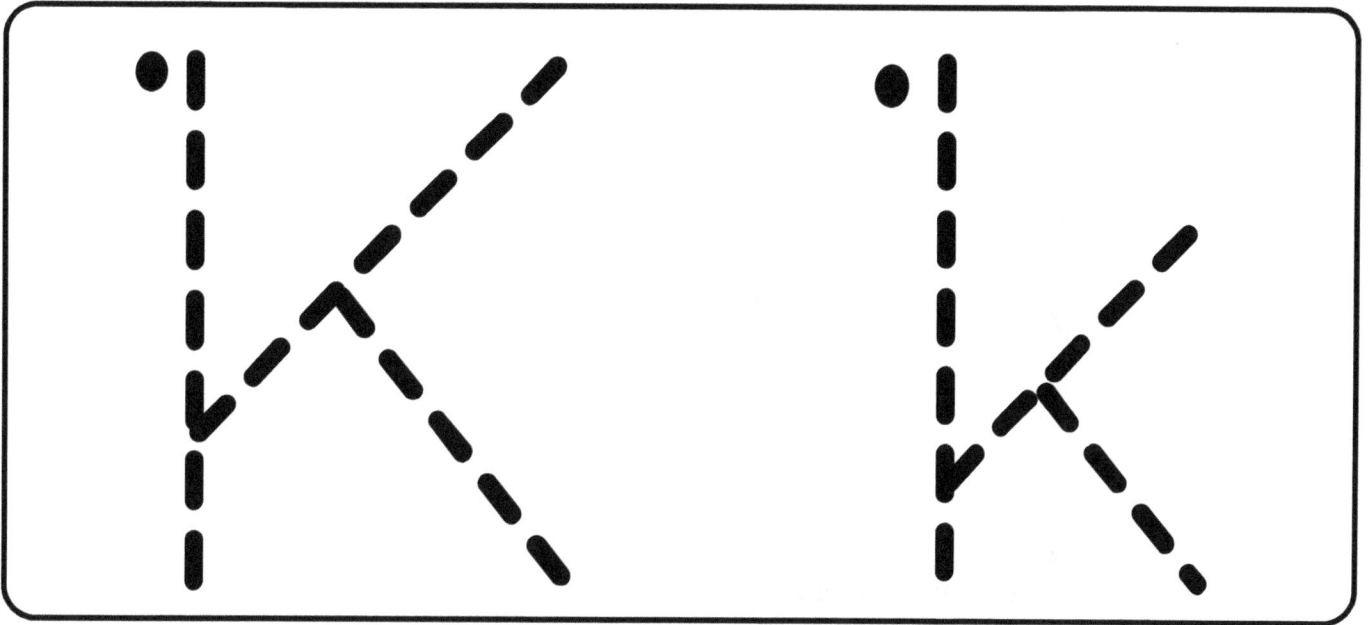

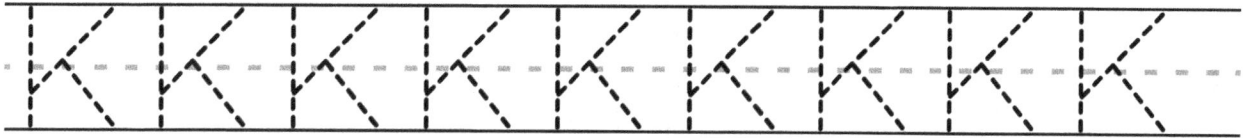

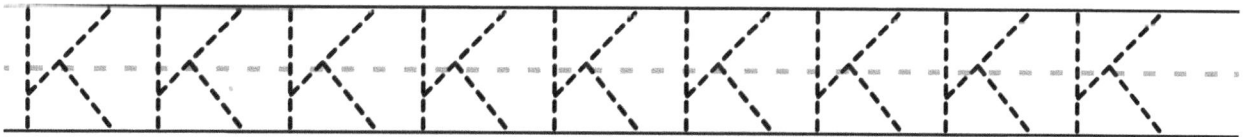

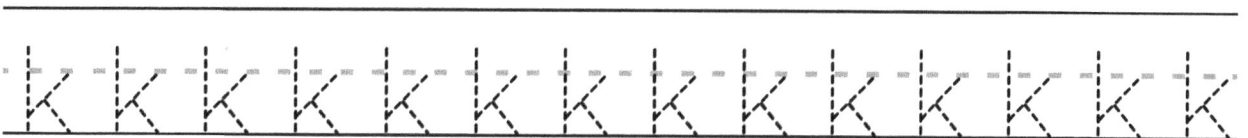

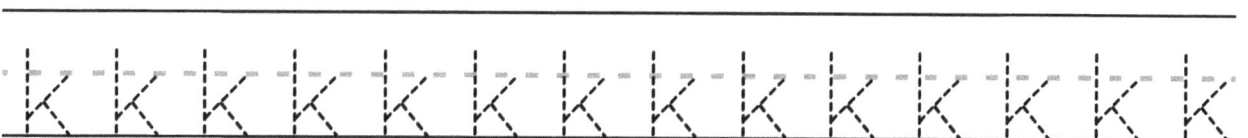

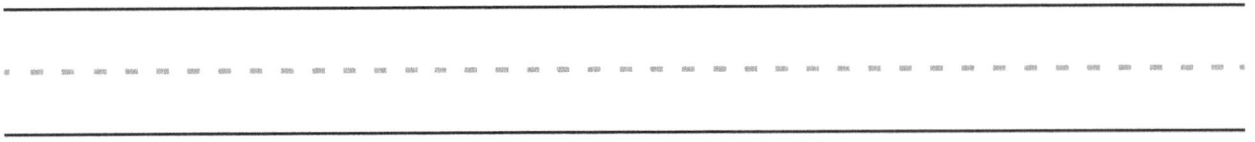

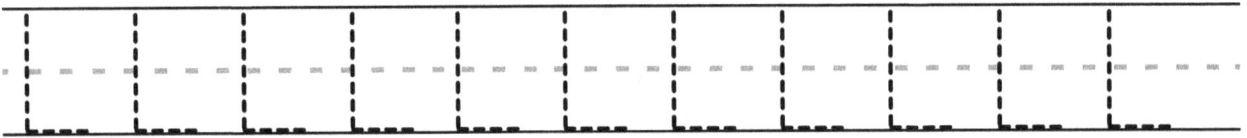

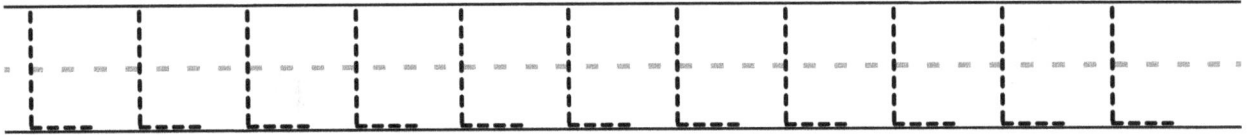

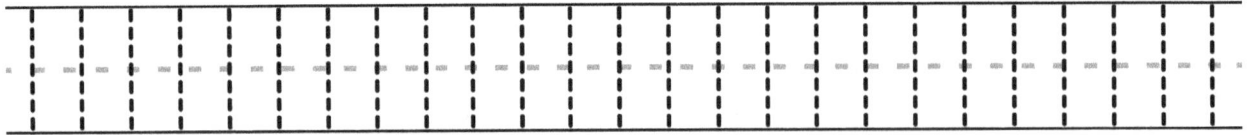

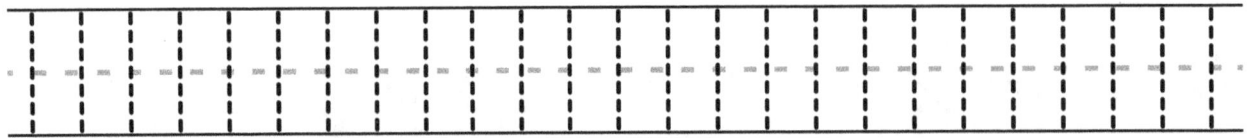

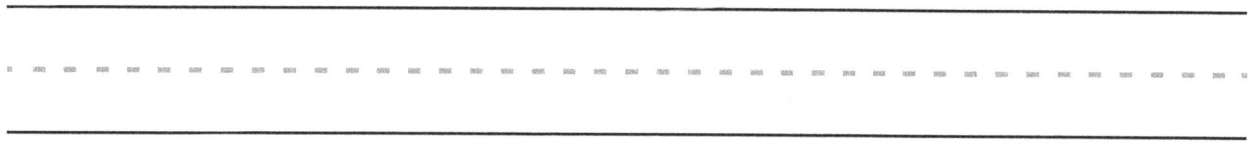

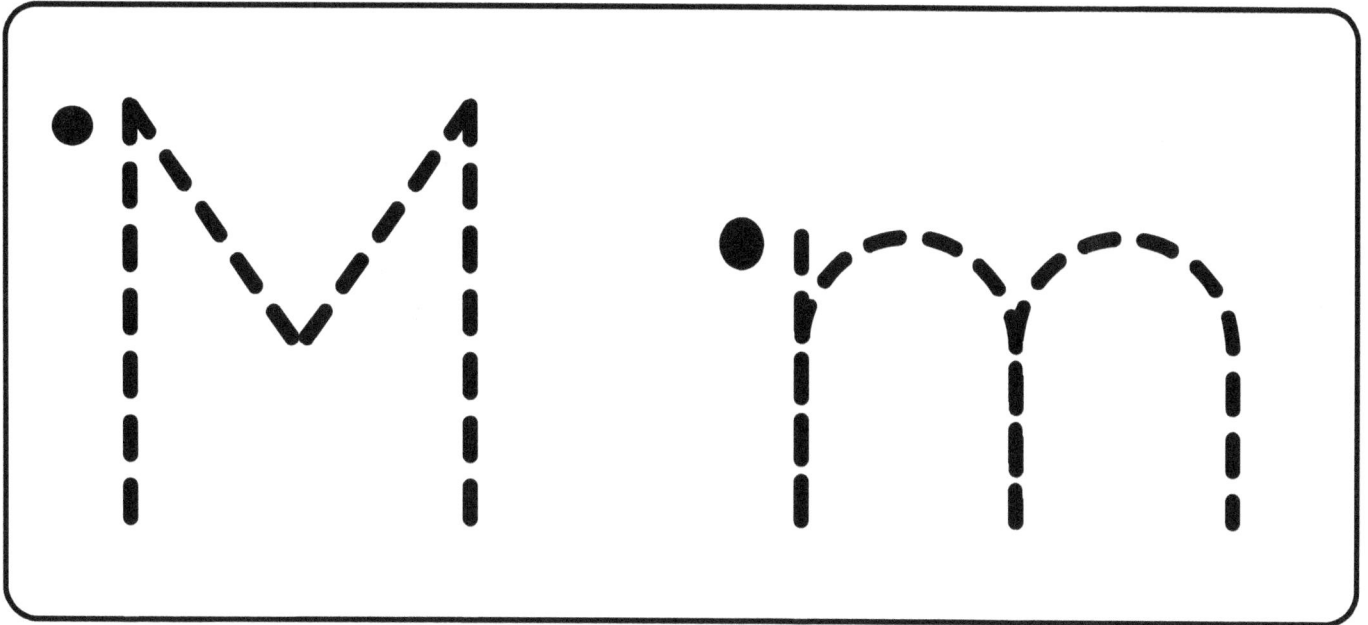

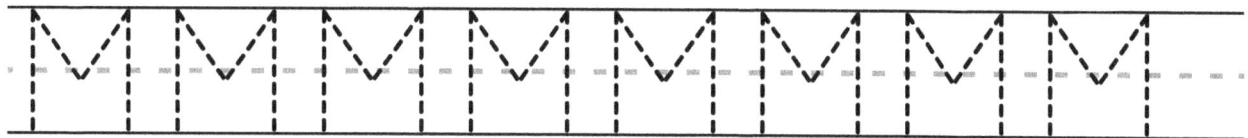

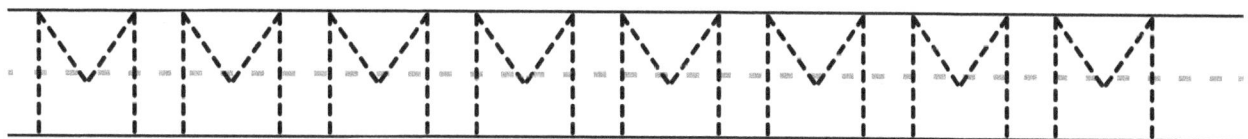

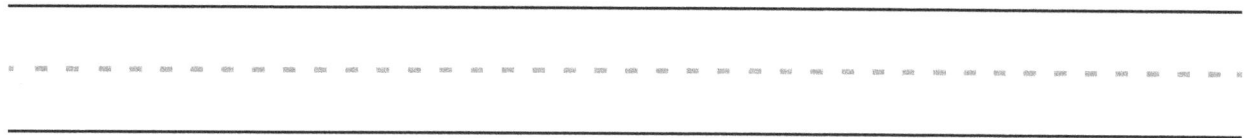

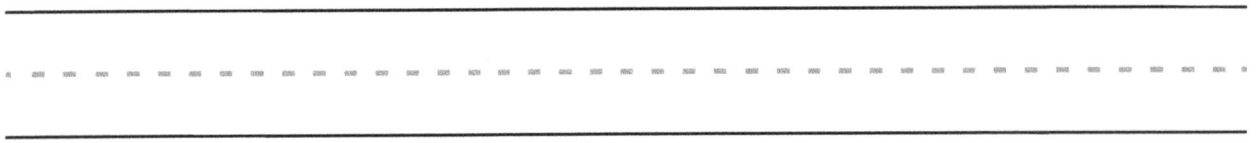

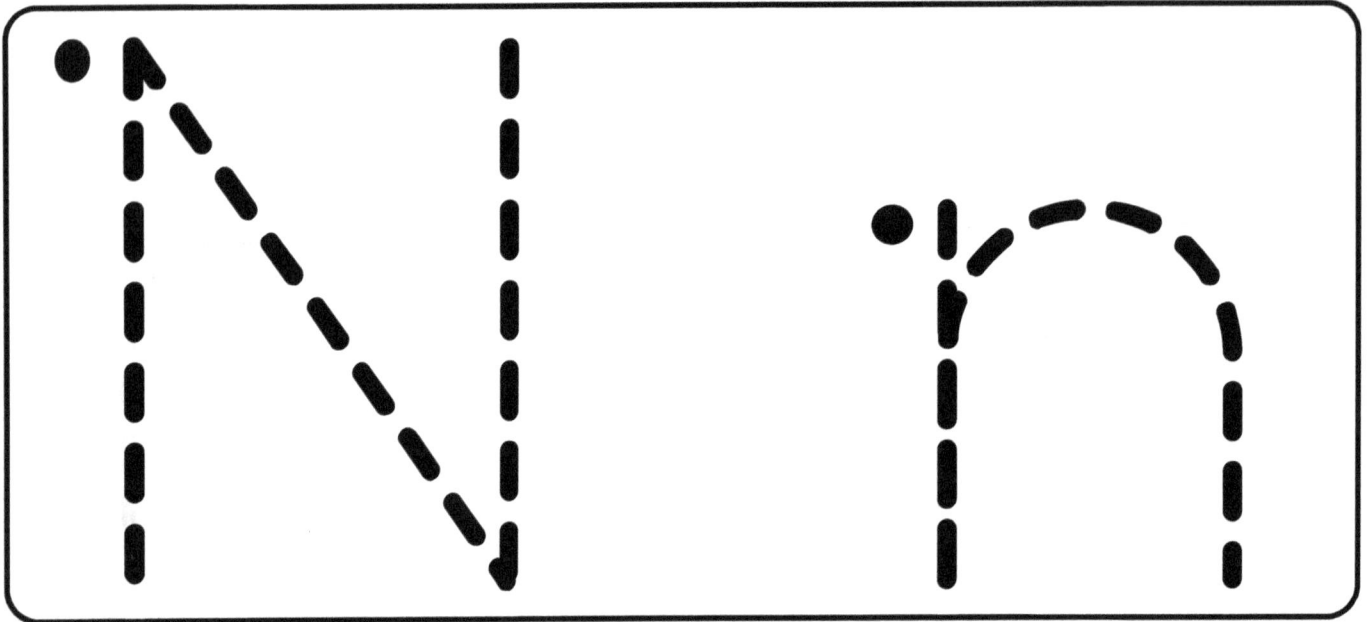

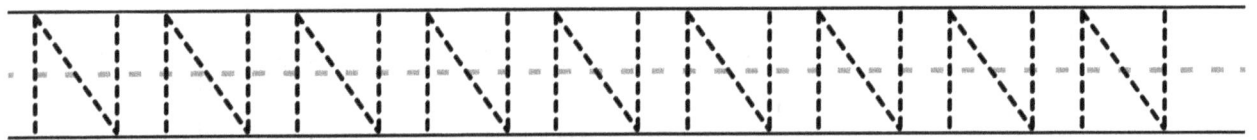

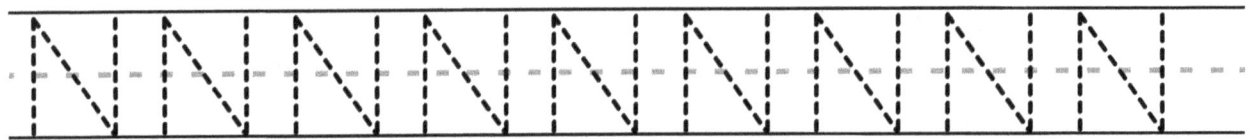

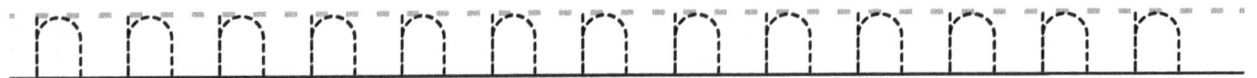

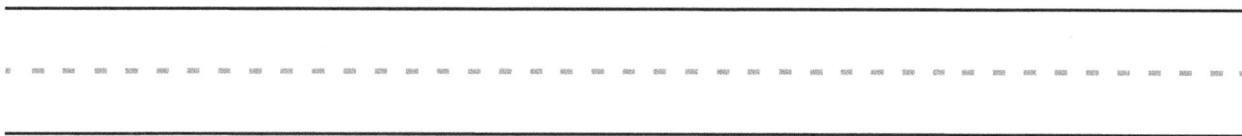

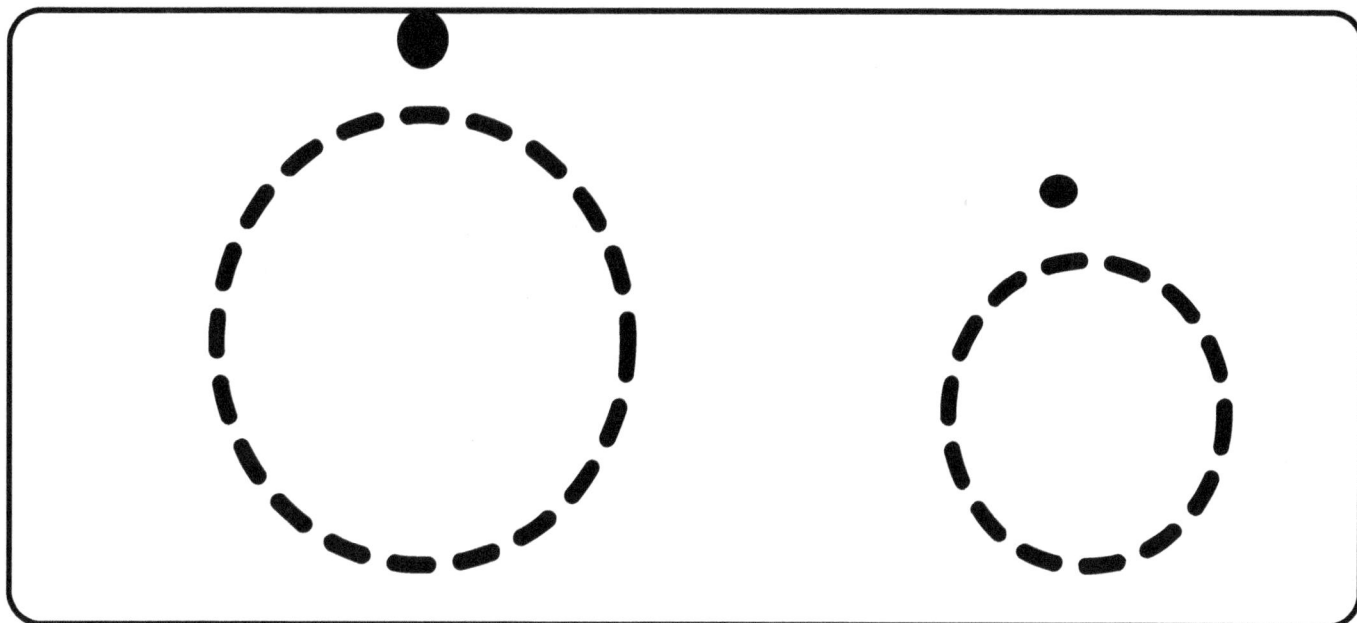

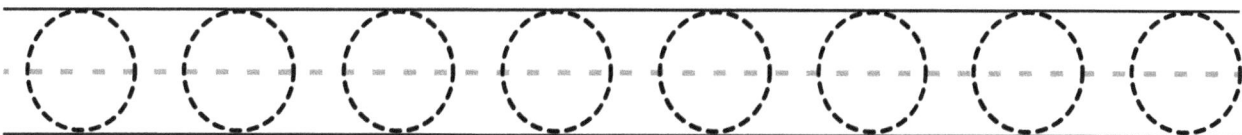

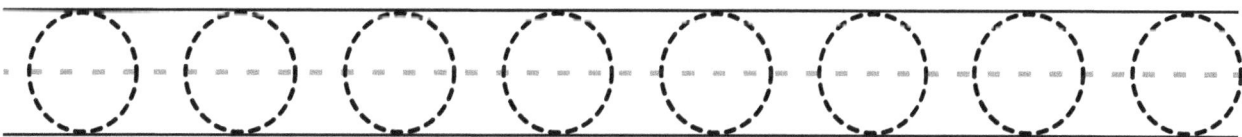

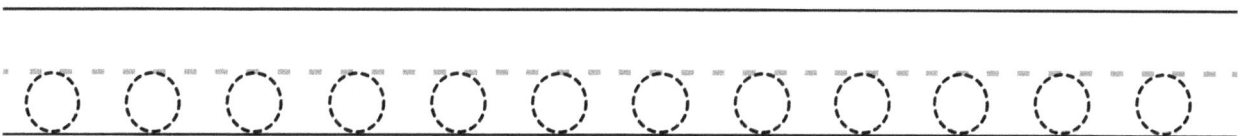

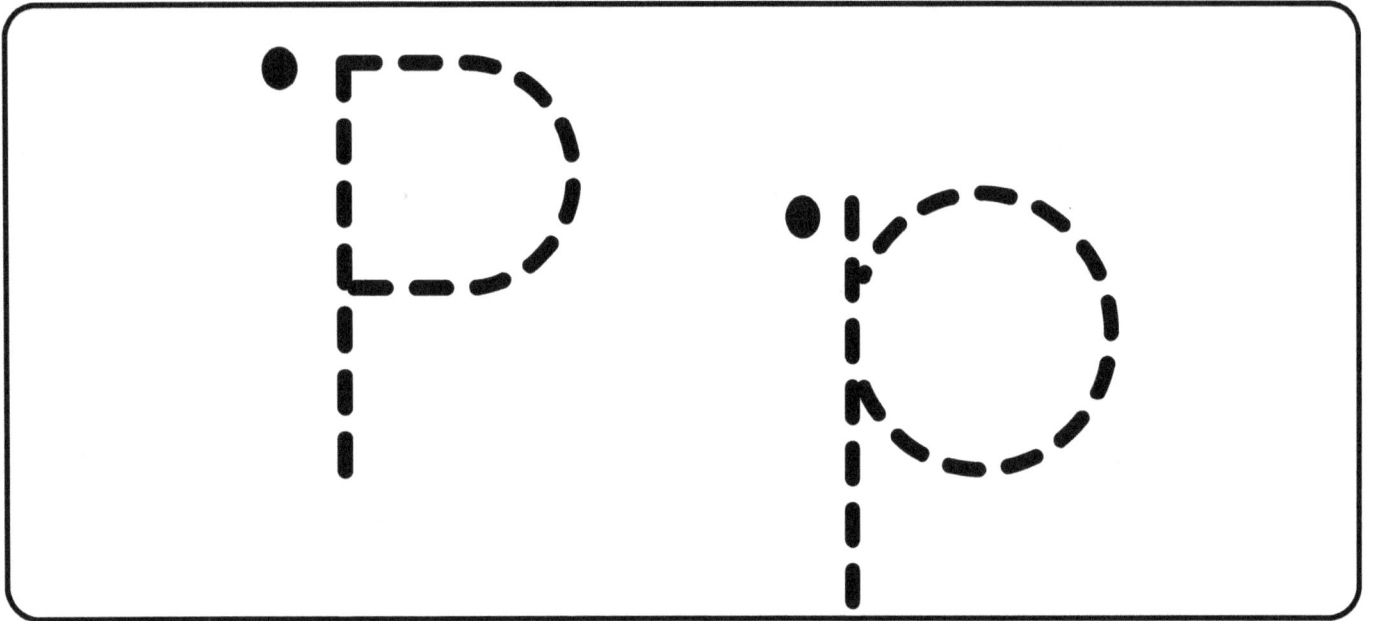

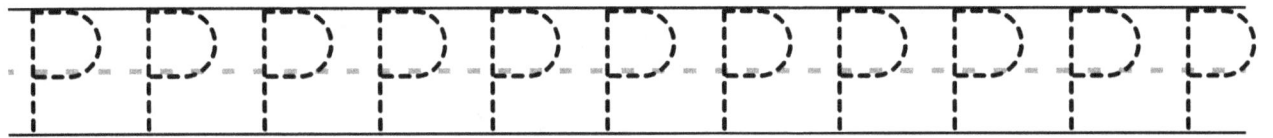

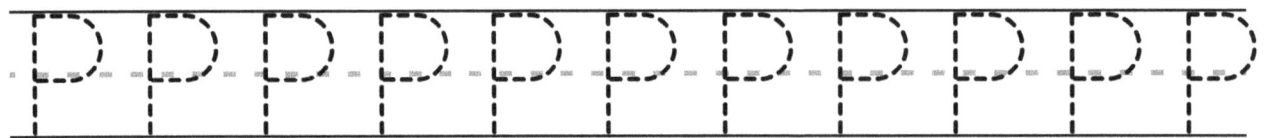

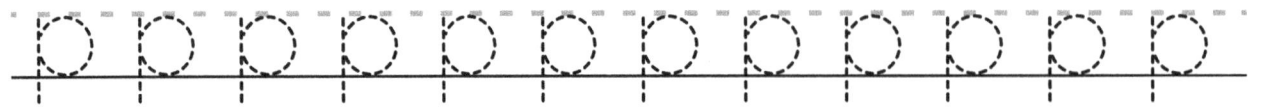

Q q

Q Q Q Q Q Q Q Q

Q Q Q Q Q Q Q Q

q q q q q q q q q q q q

q q q q q q q q q q q q

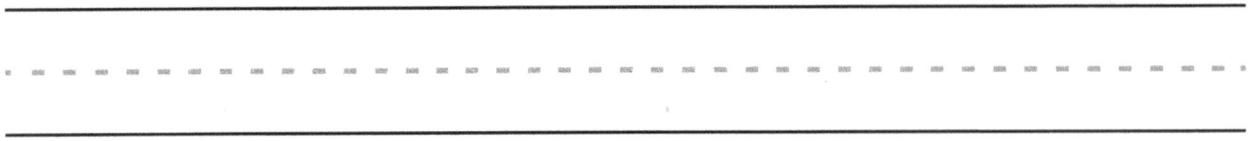

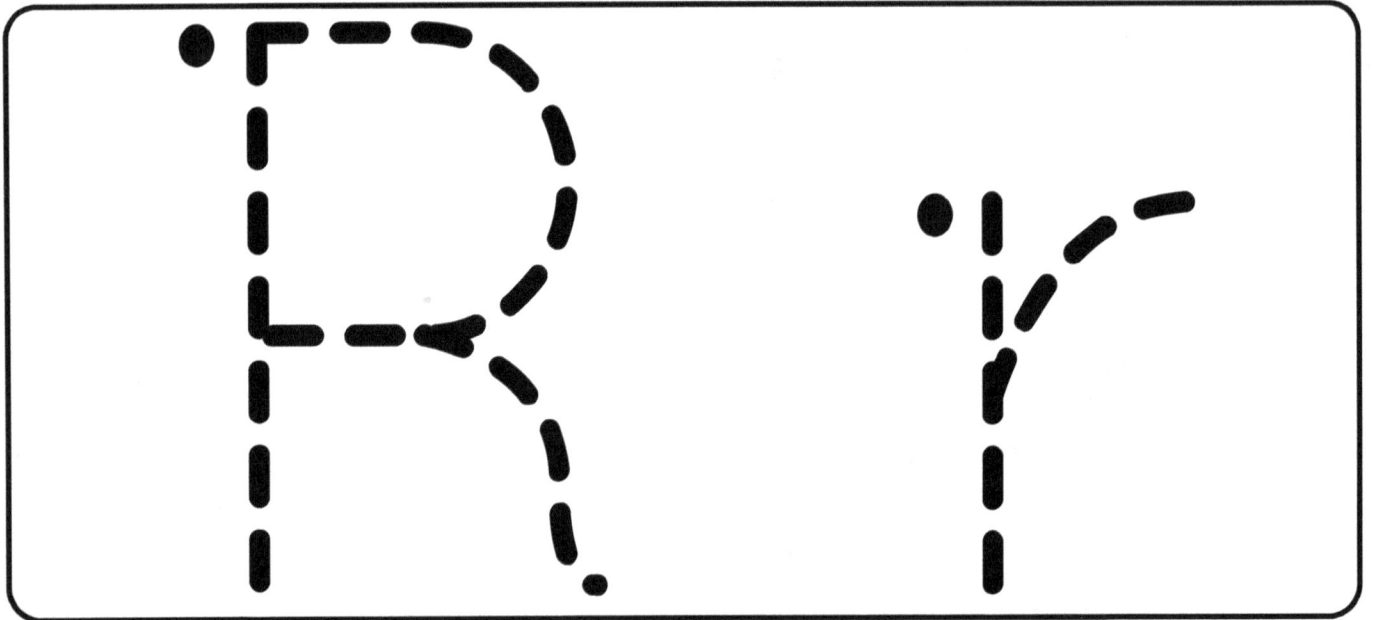

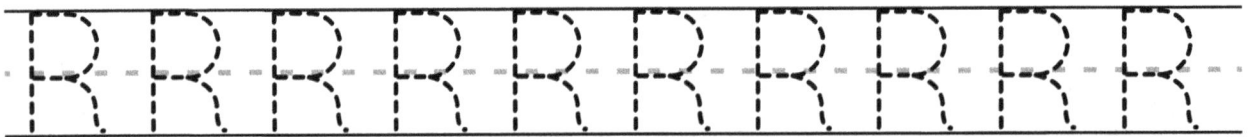

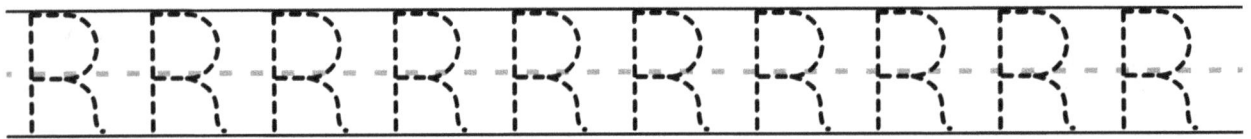

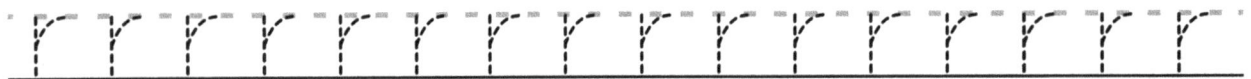

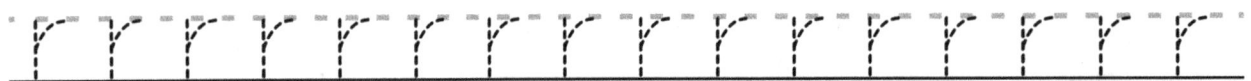

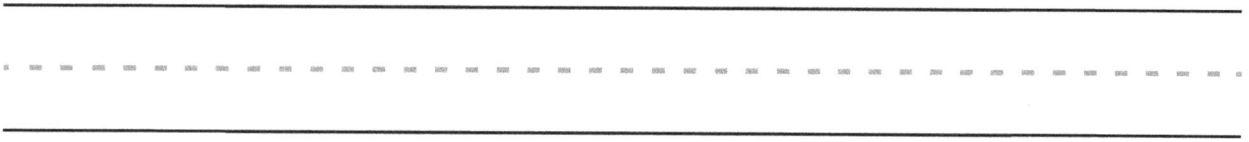

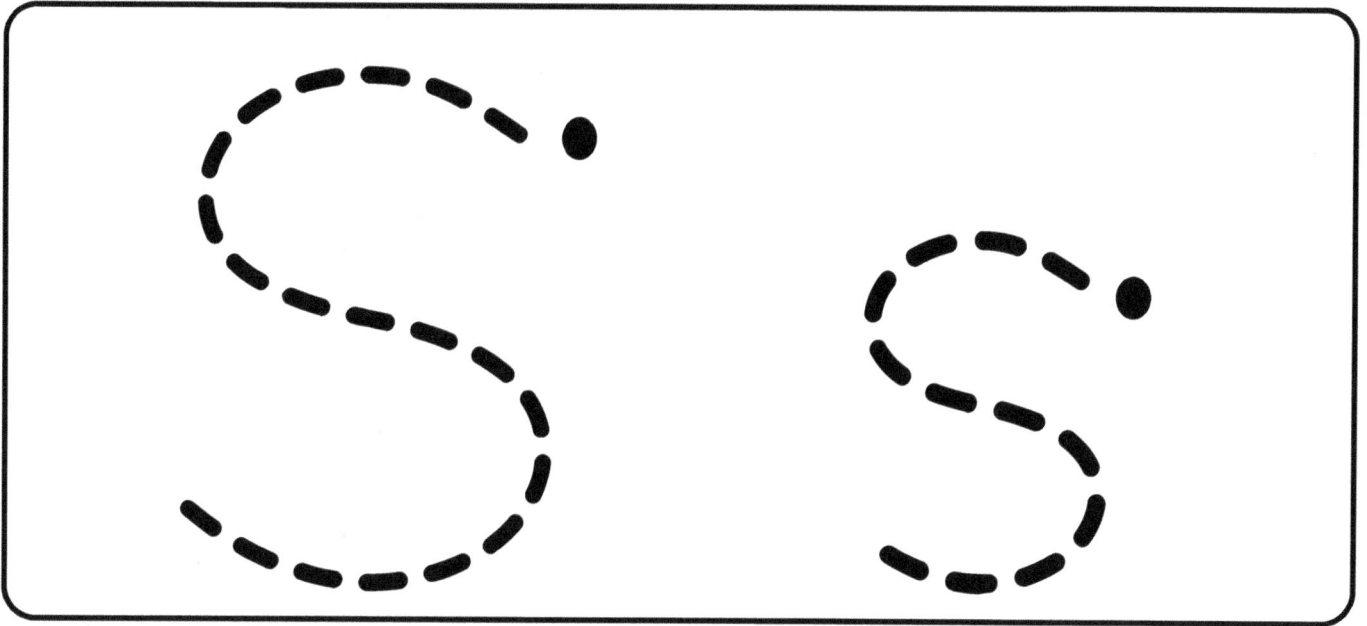

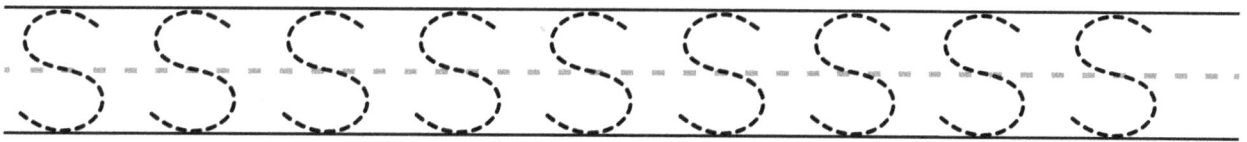

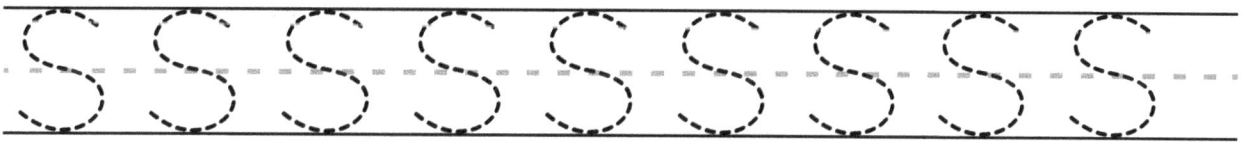

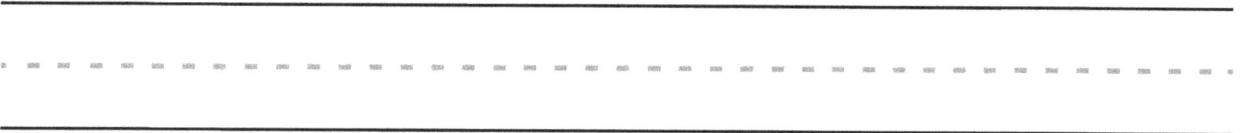

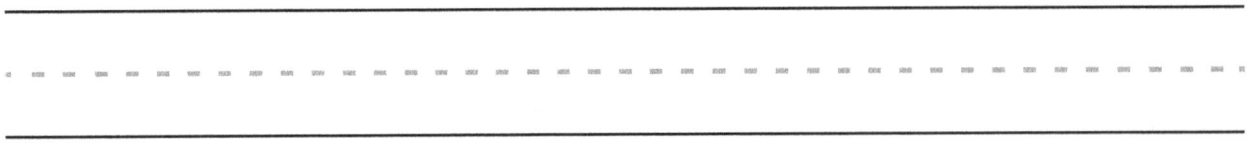

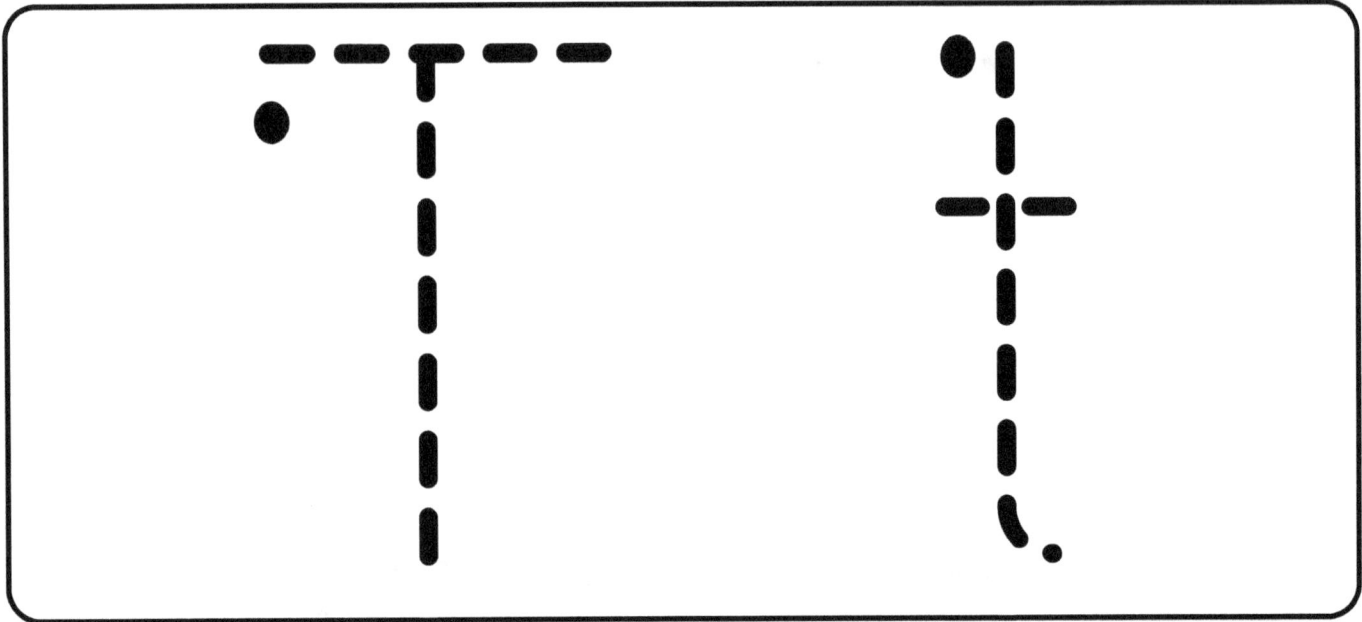

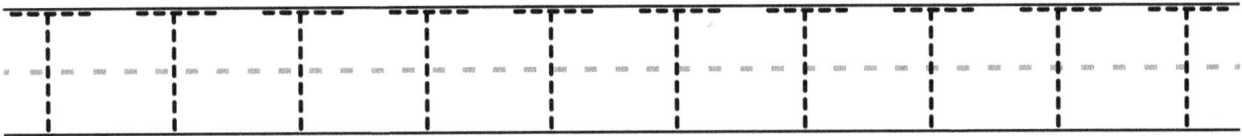

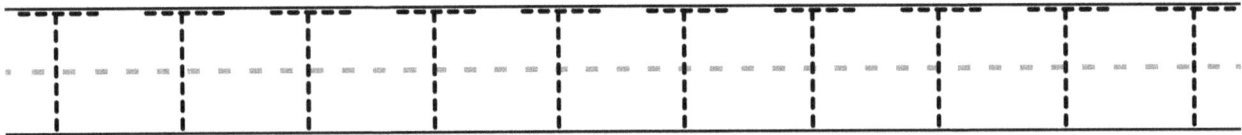

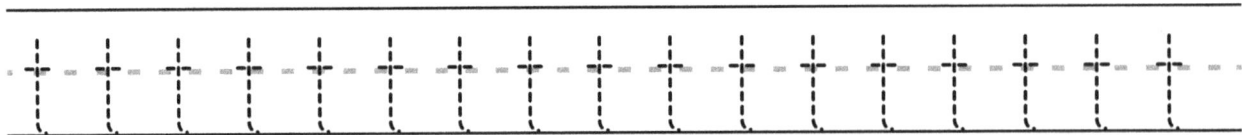

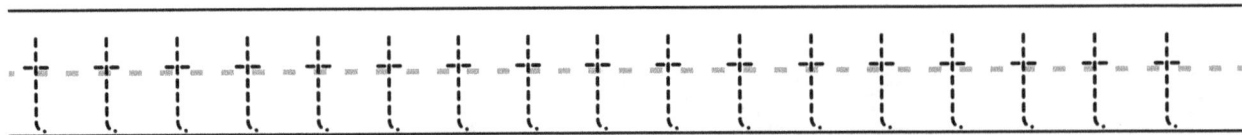

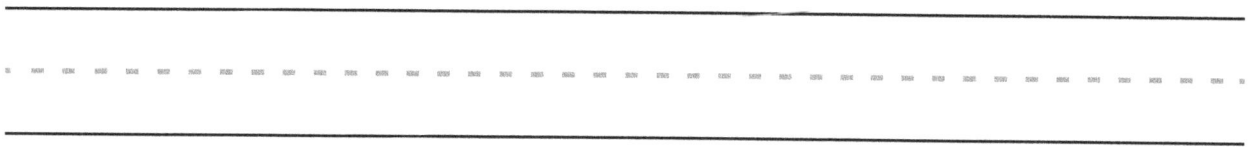

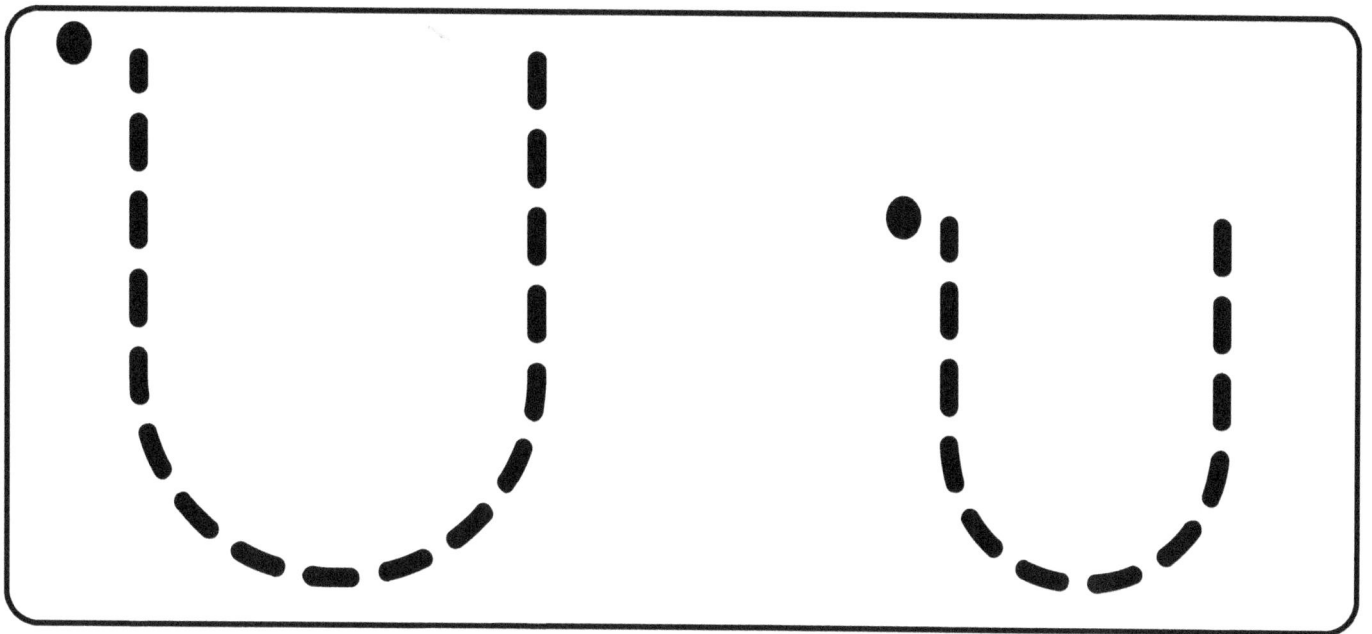

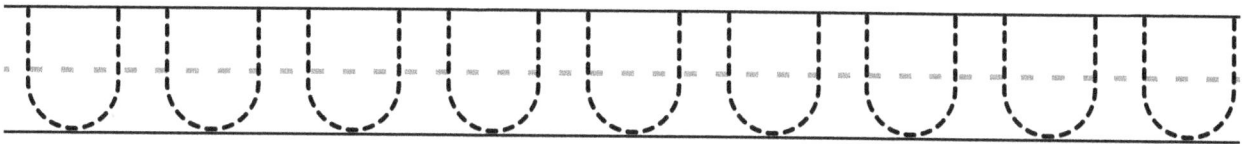

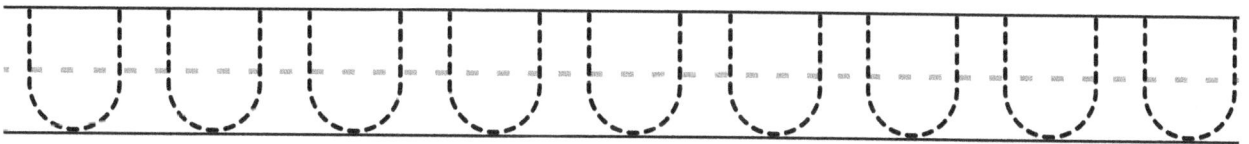

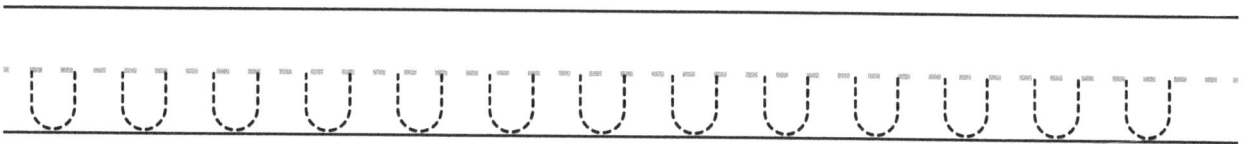

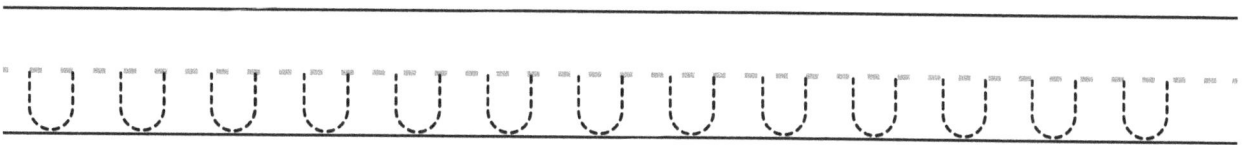

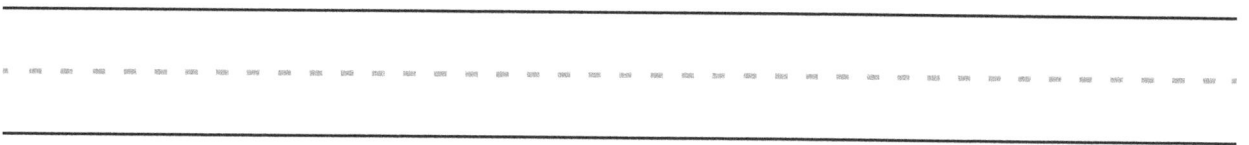

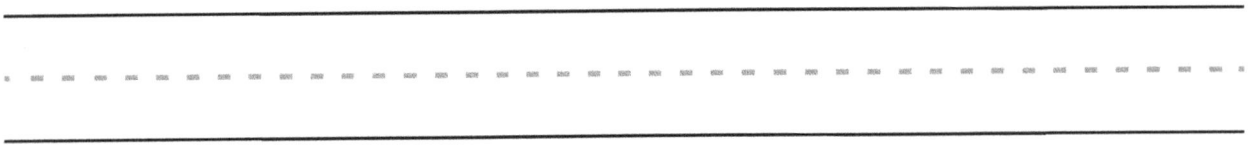

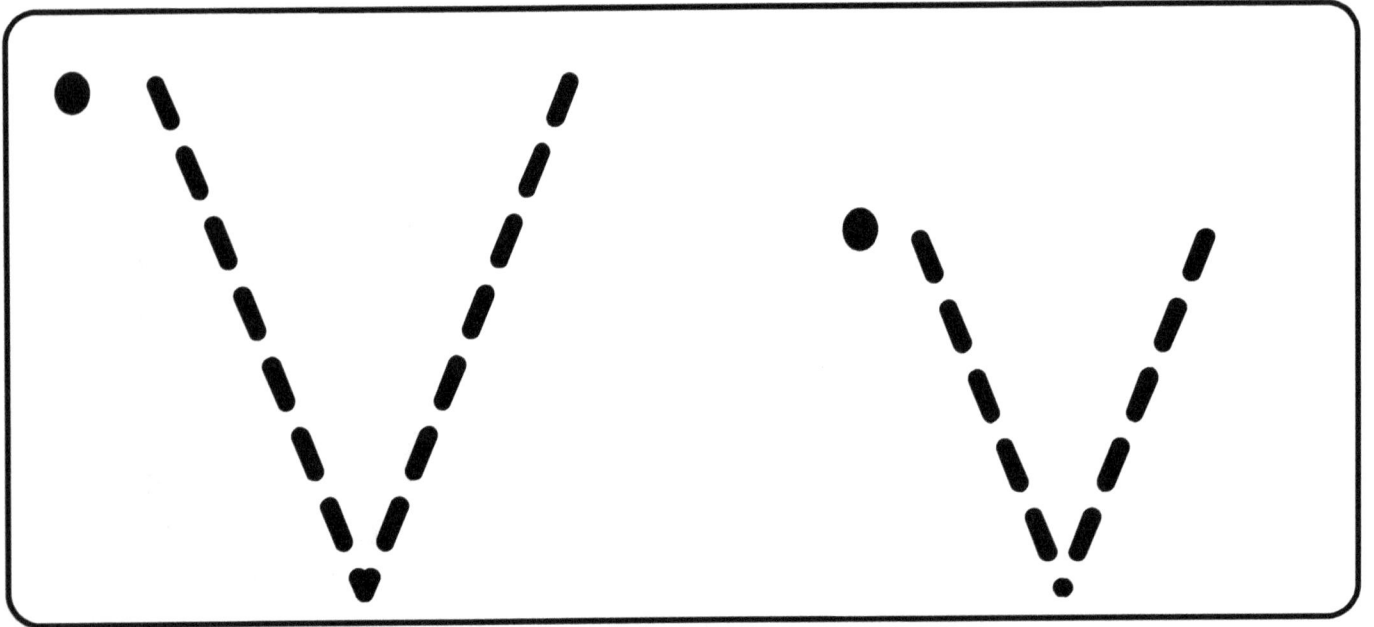

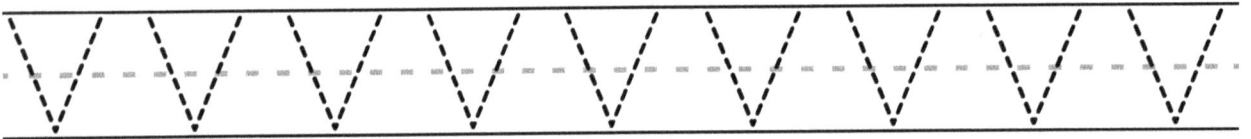

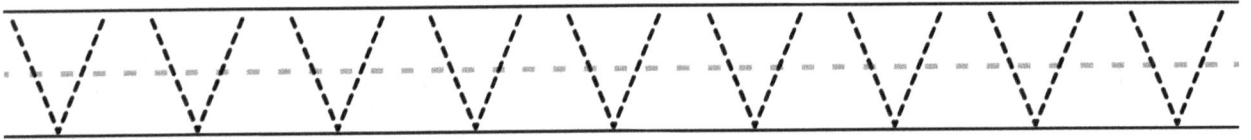

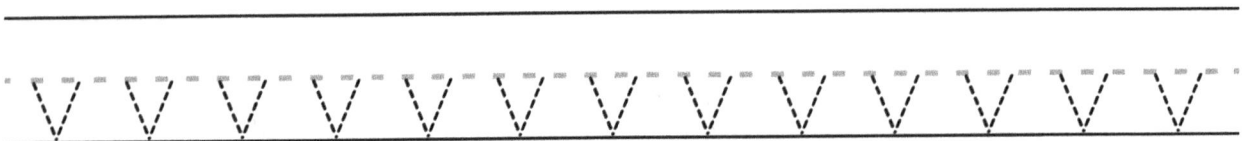

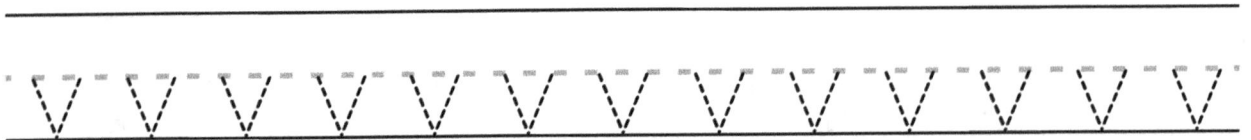

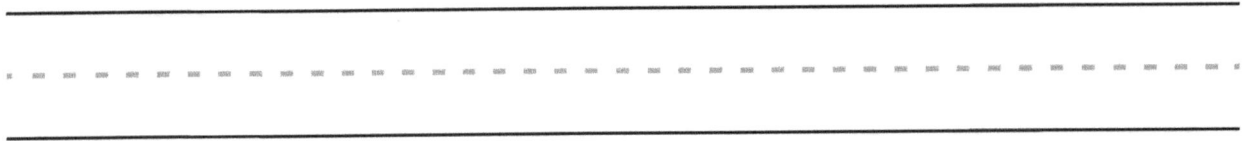

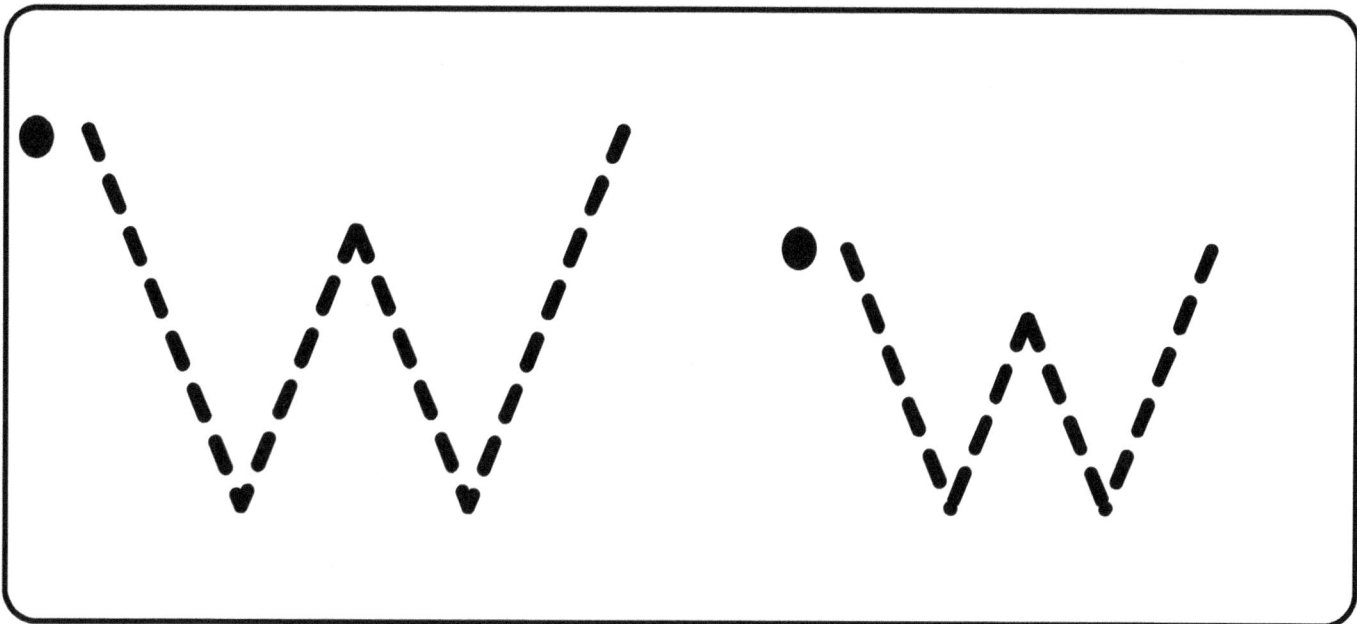

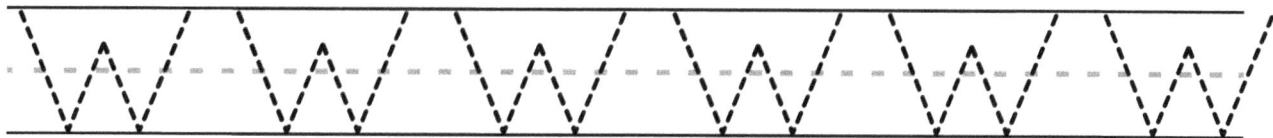

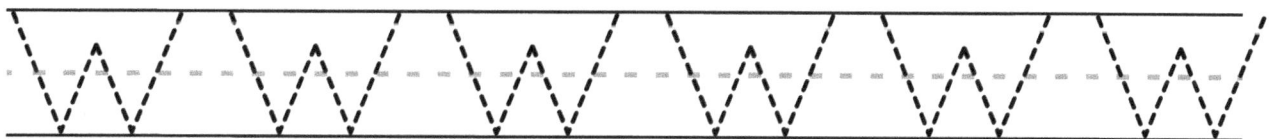

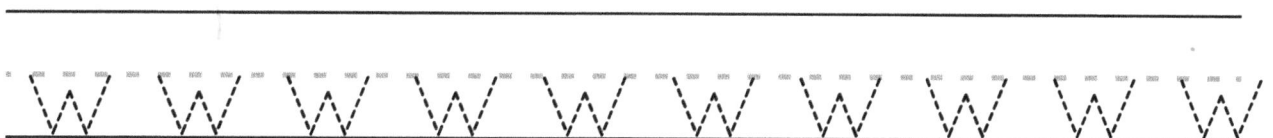

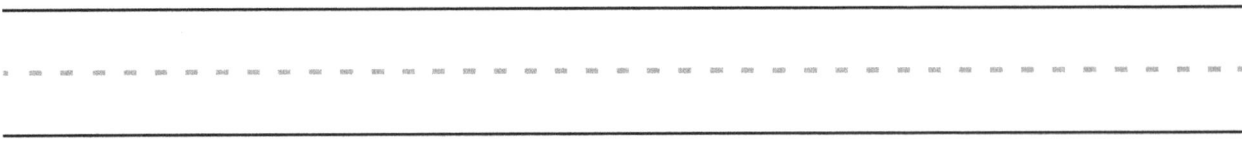

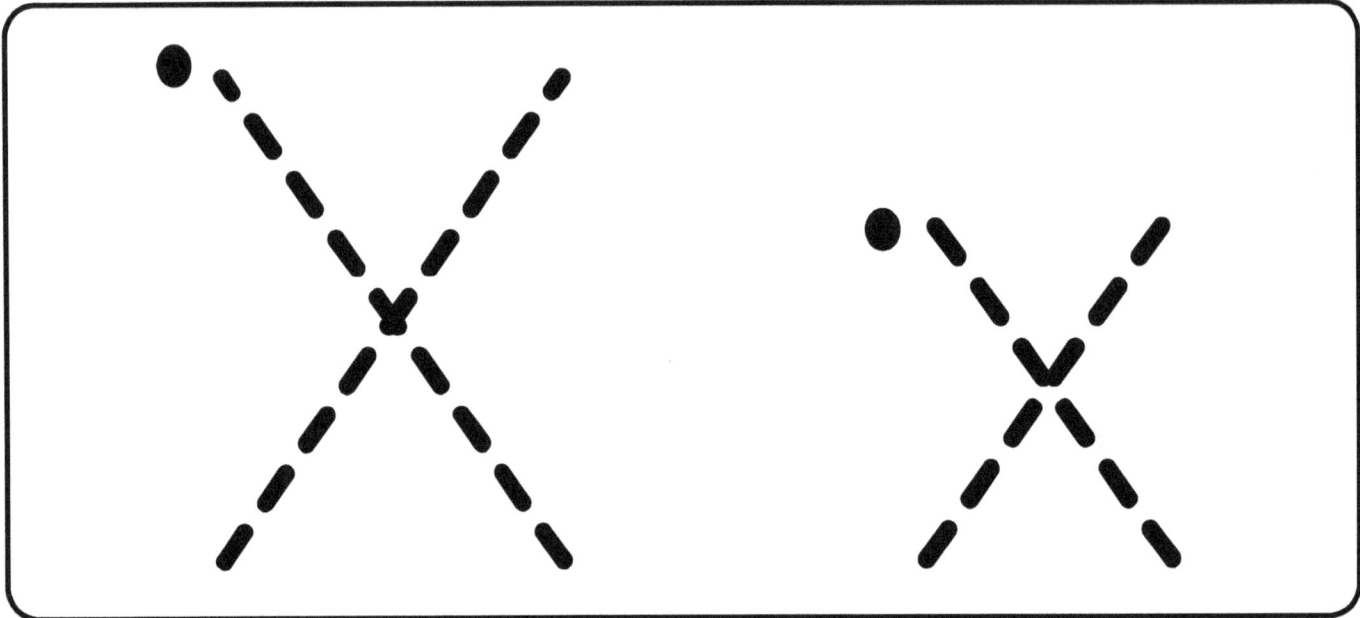

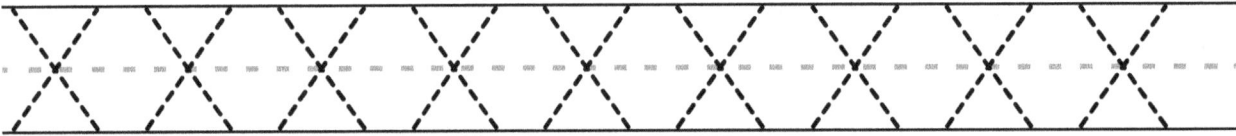

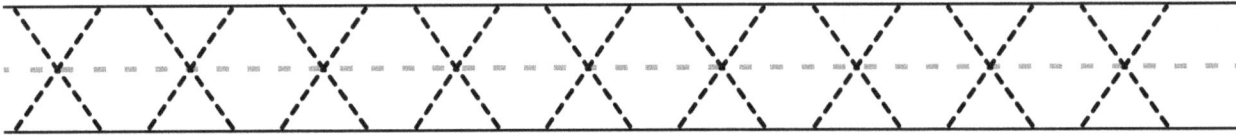

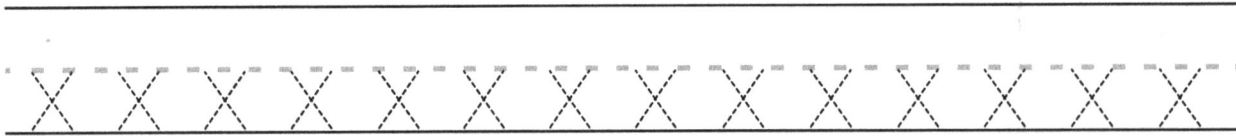

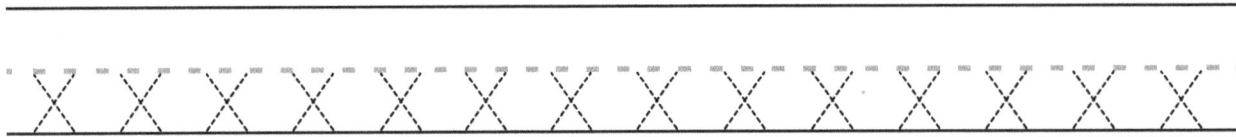

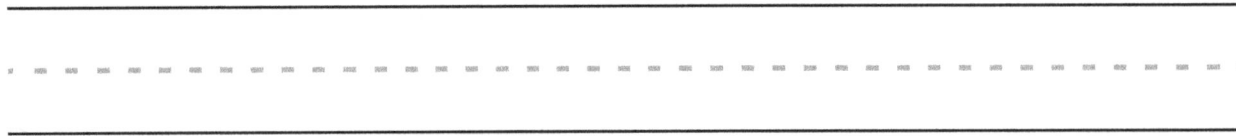

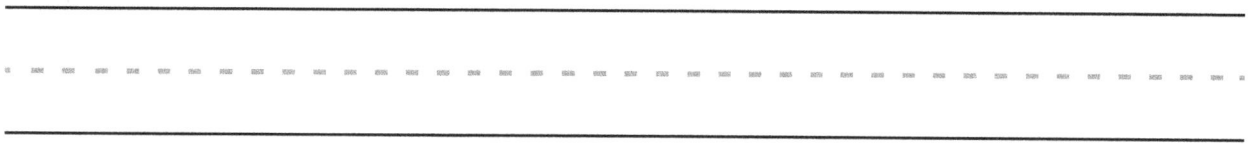

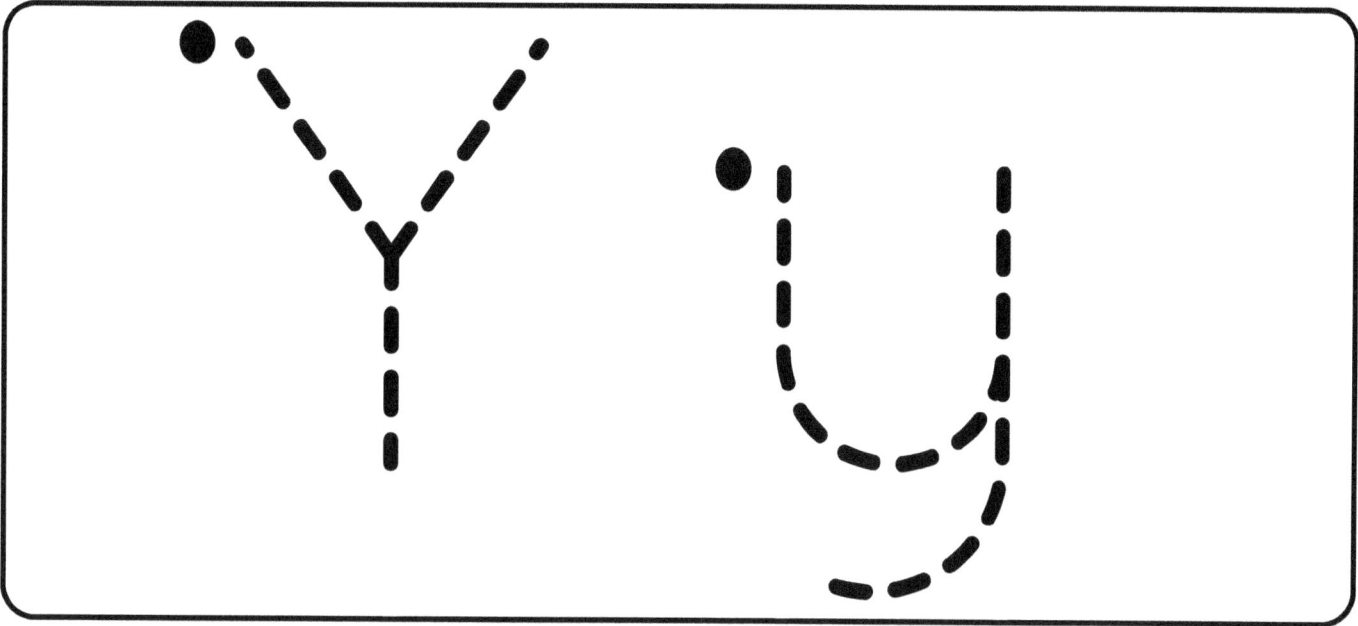

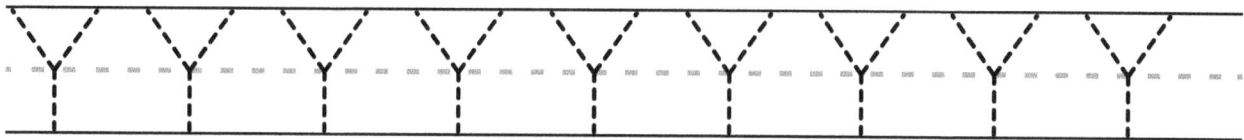

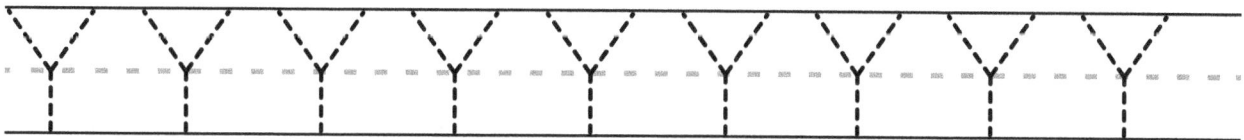

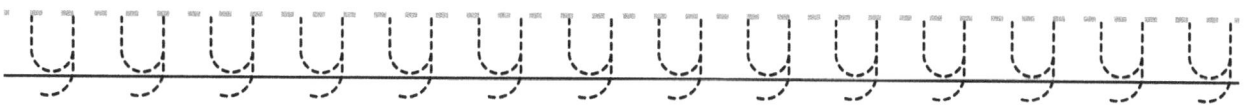

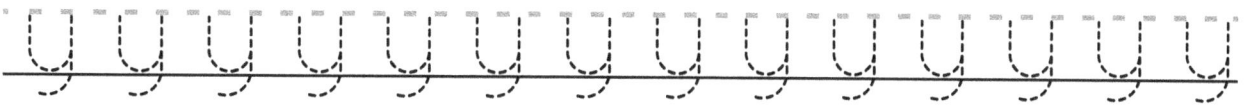

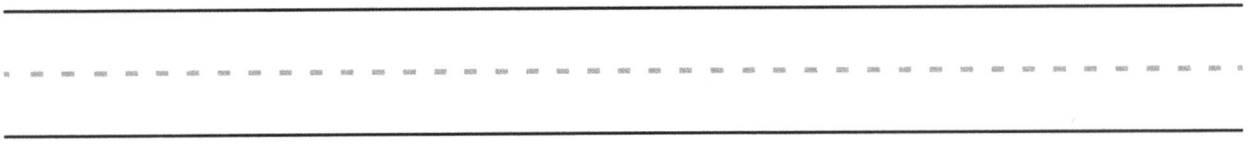

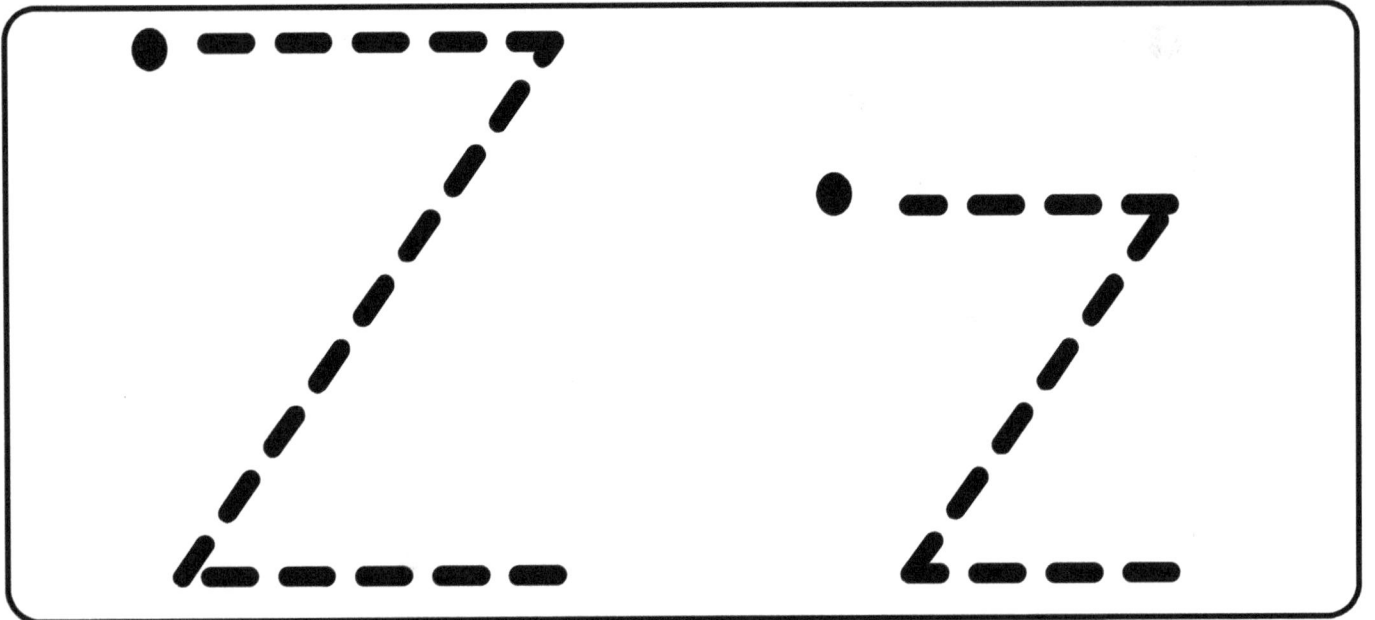

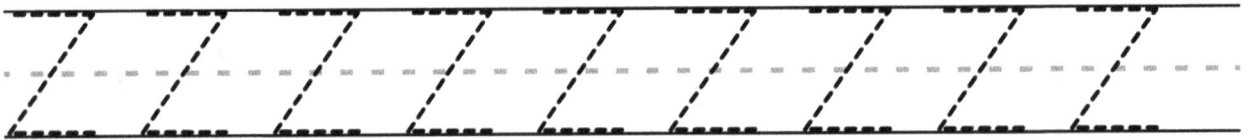

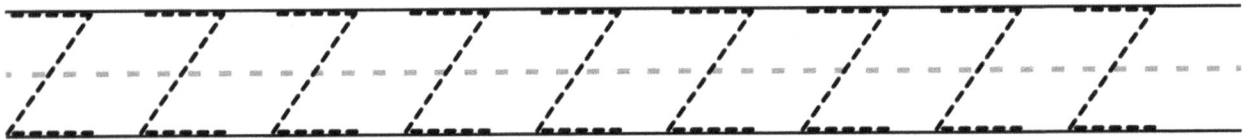

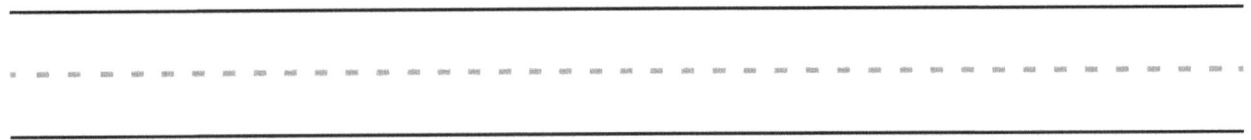

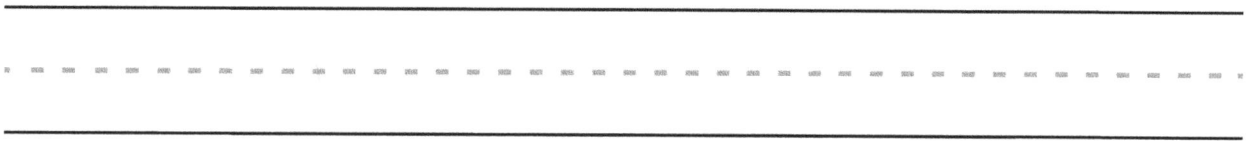

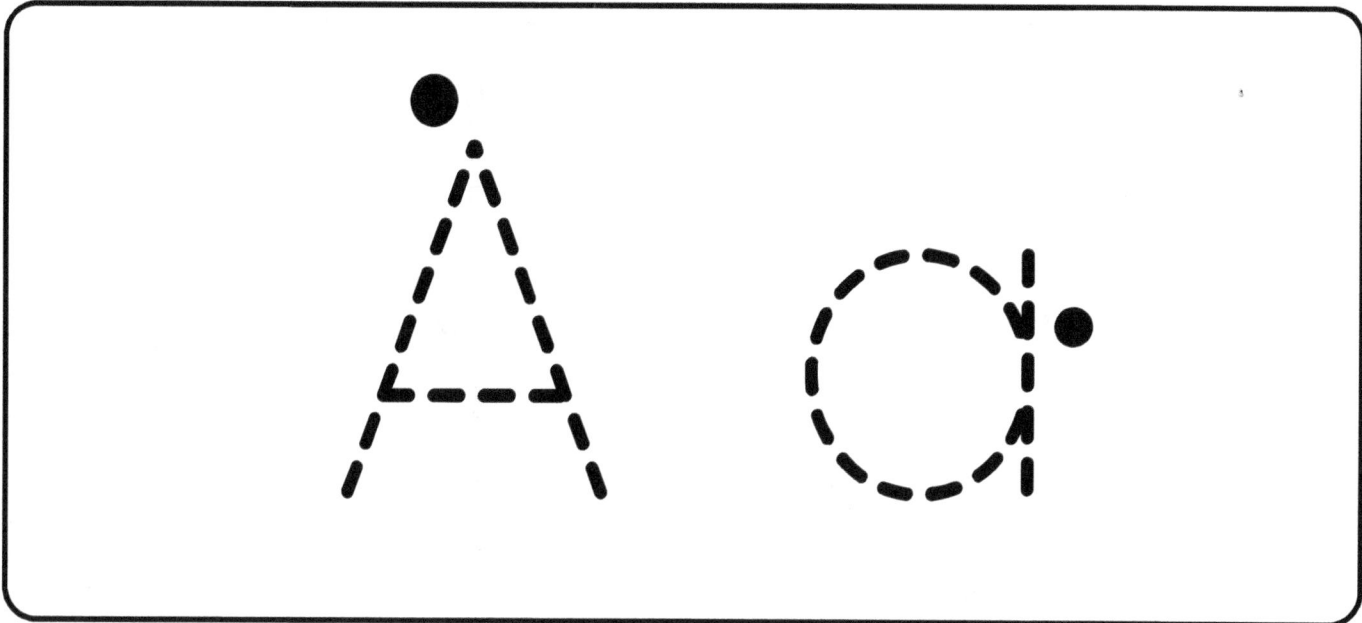

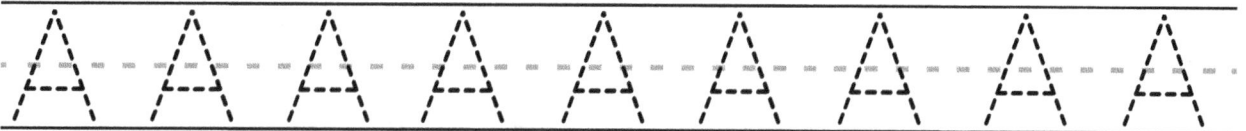

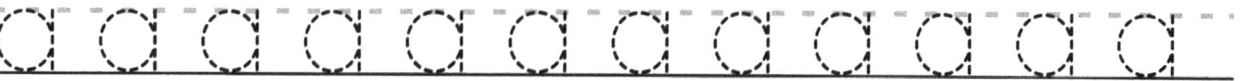

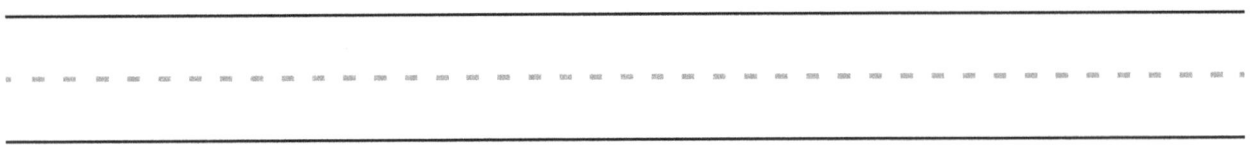

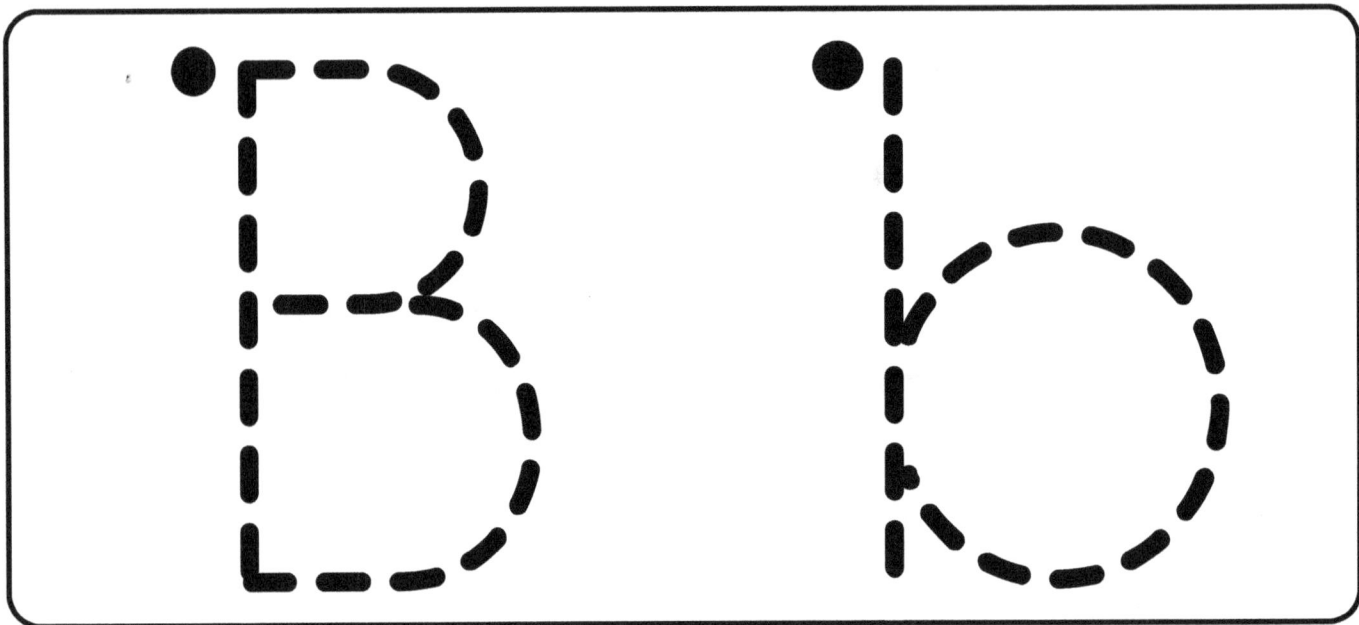

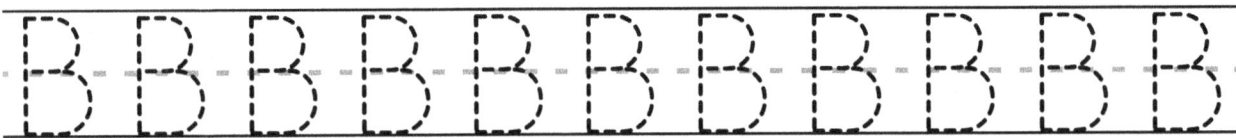

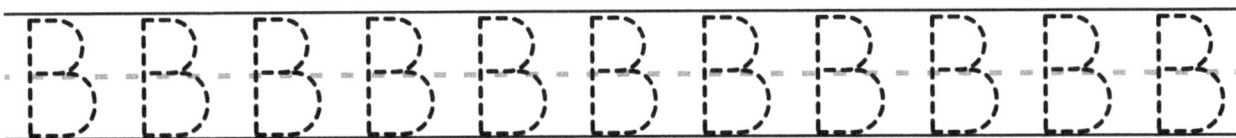

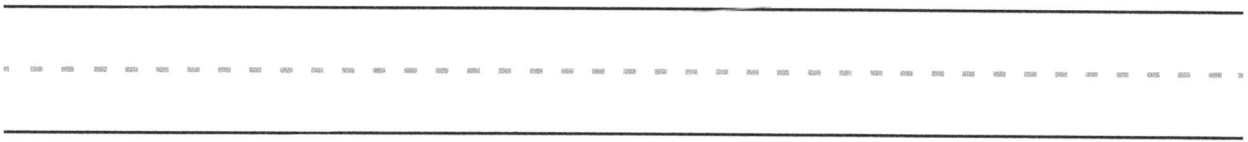

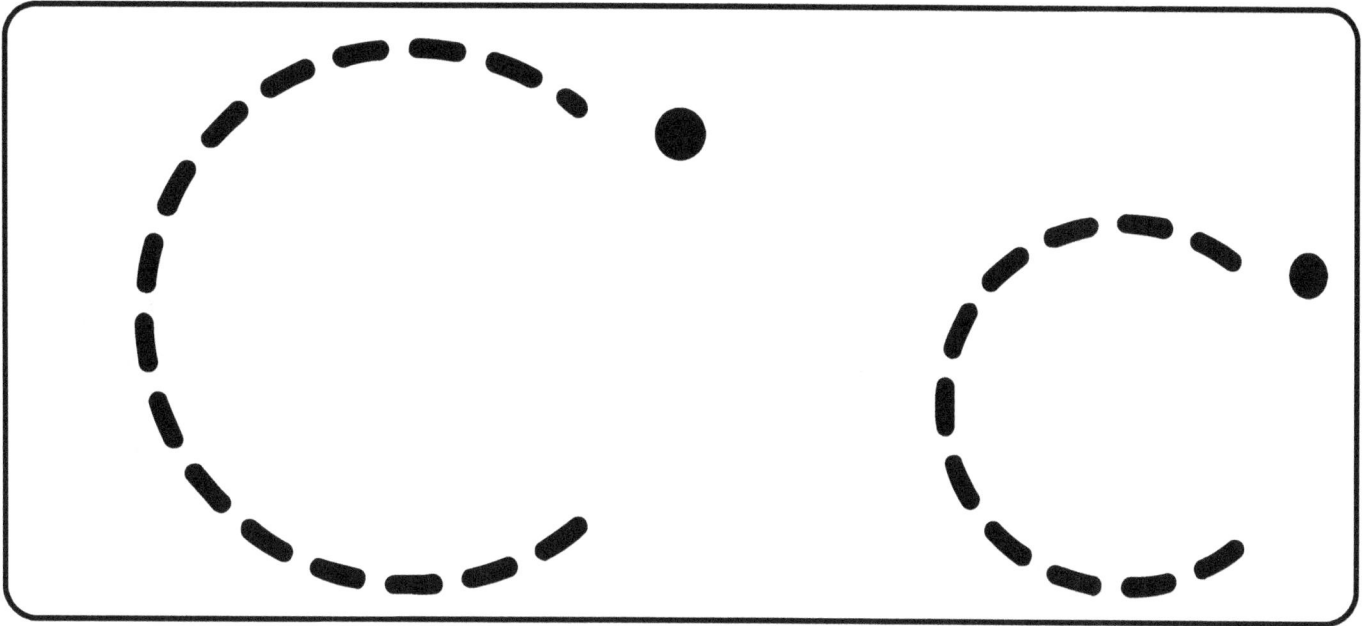

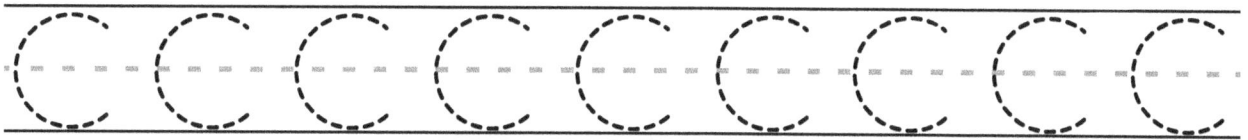

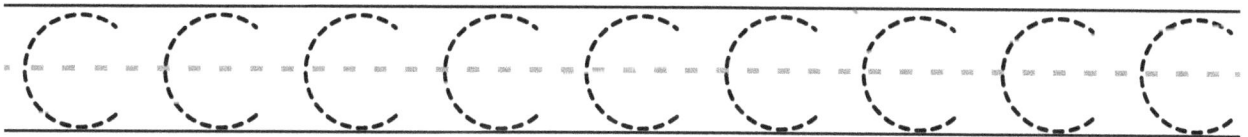

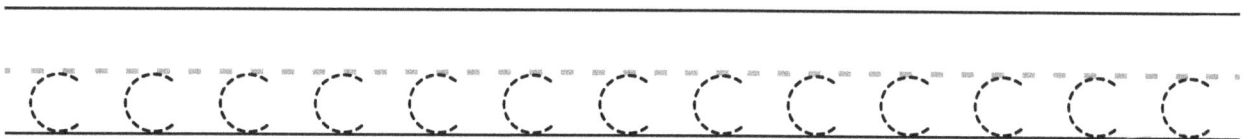

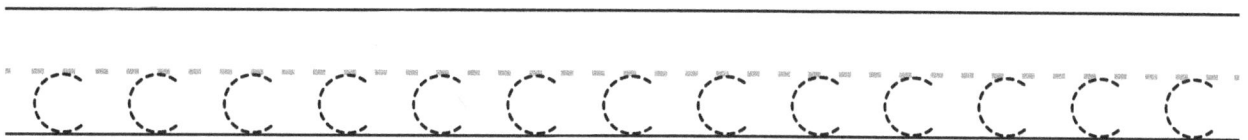

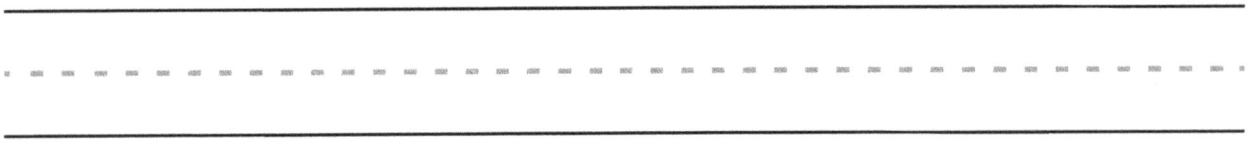

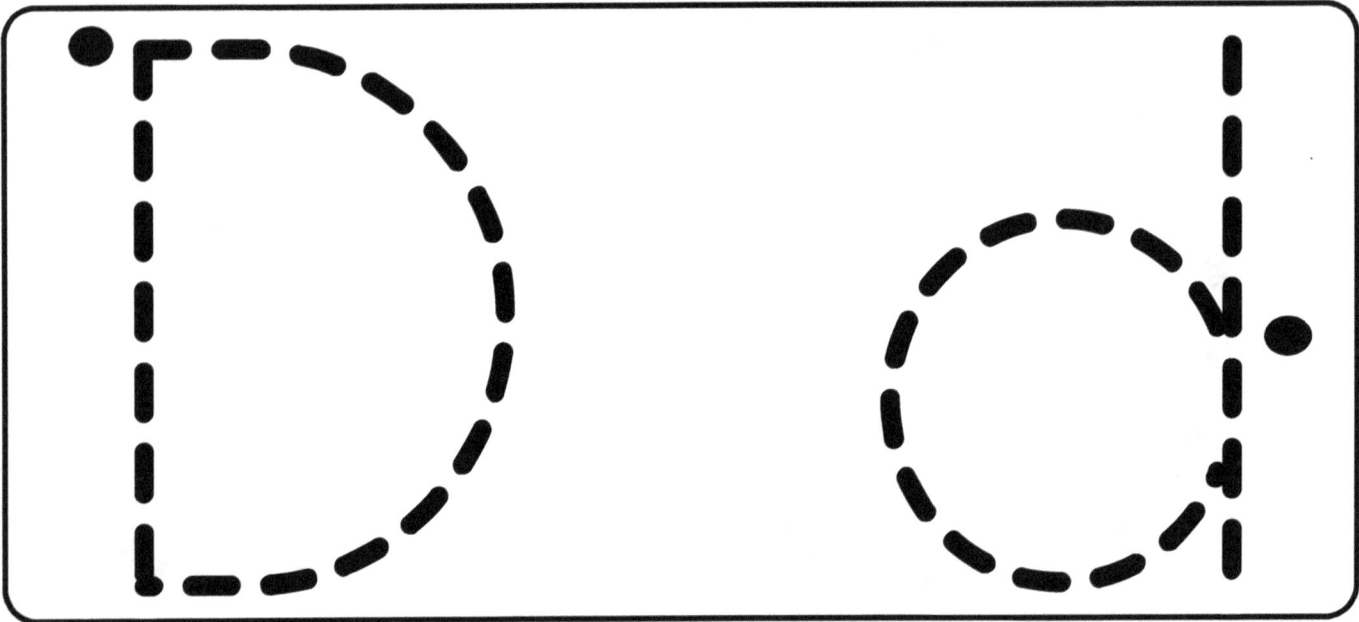

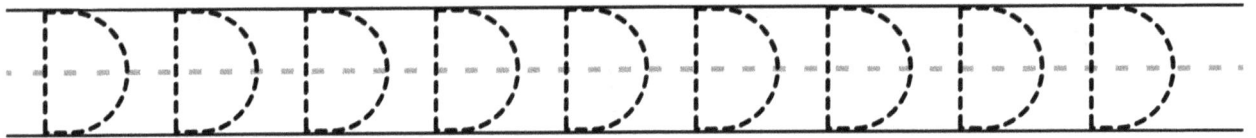

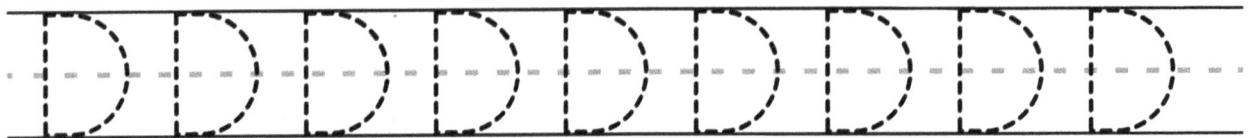

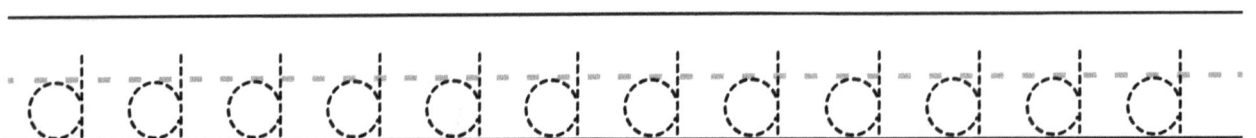

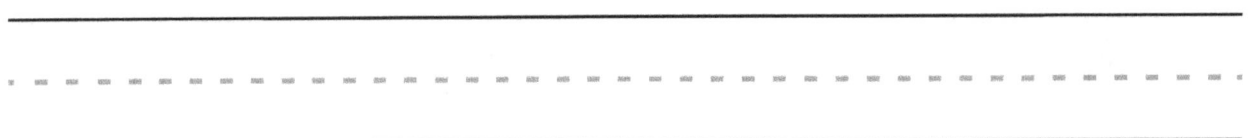

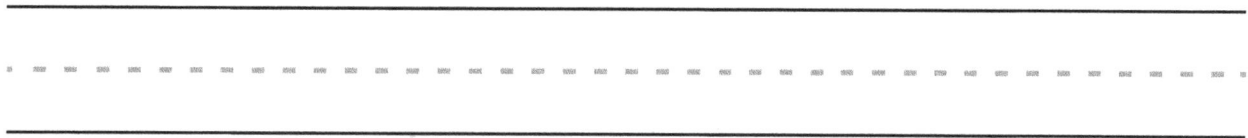

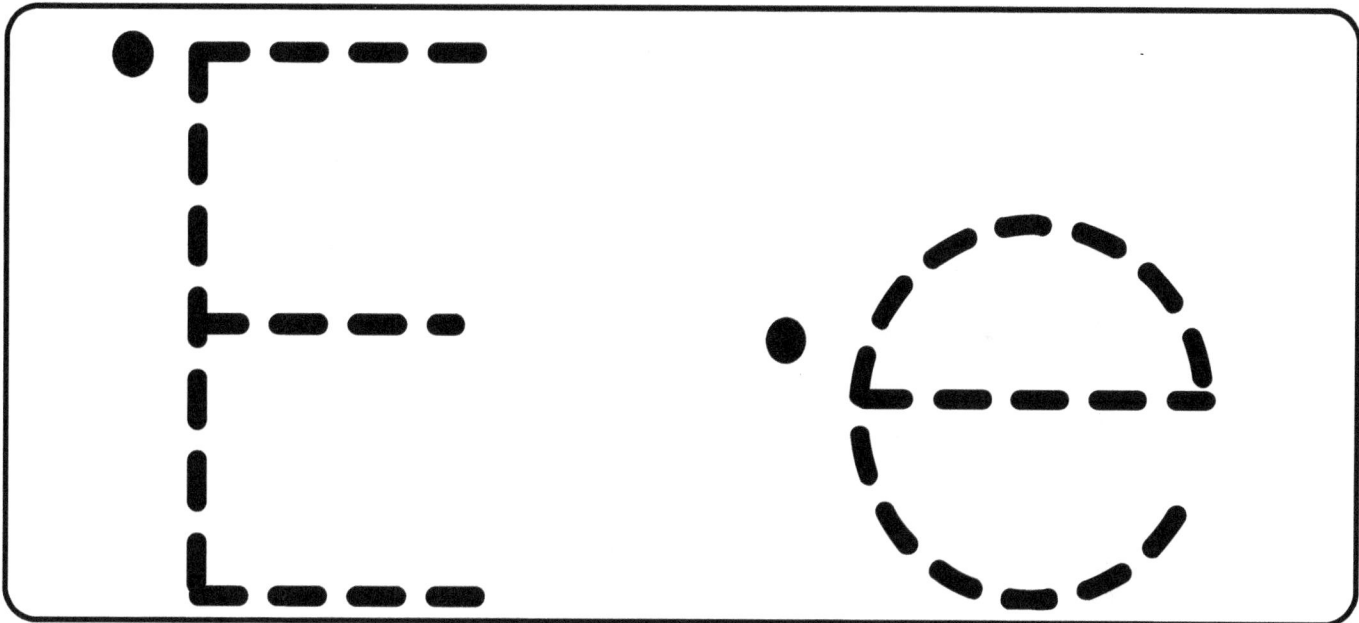

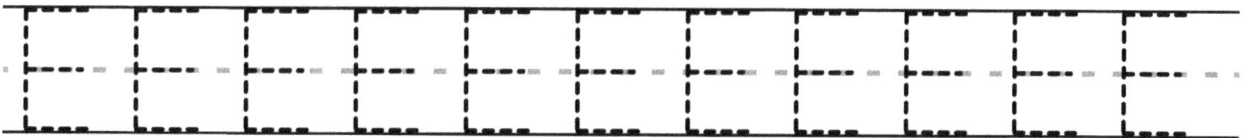

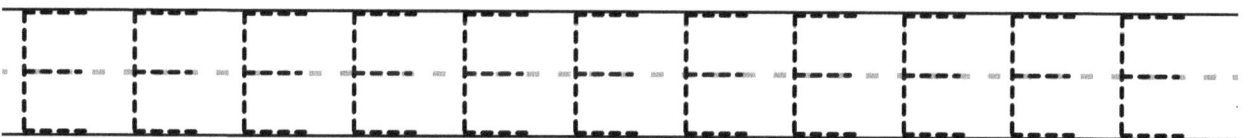

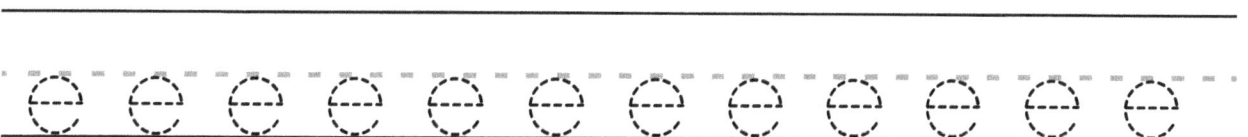

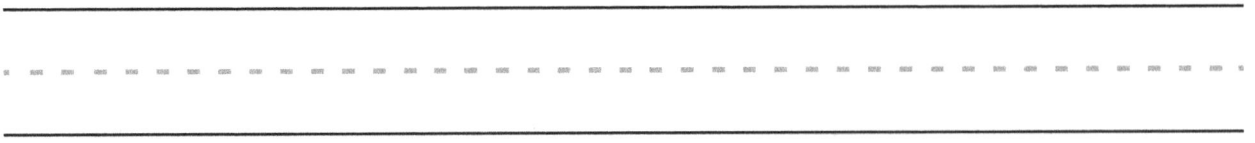
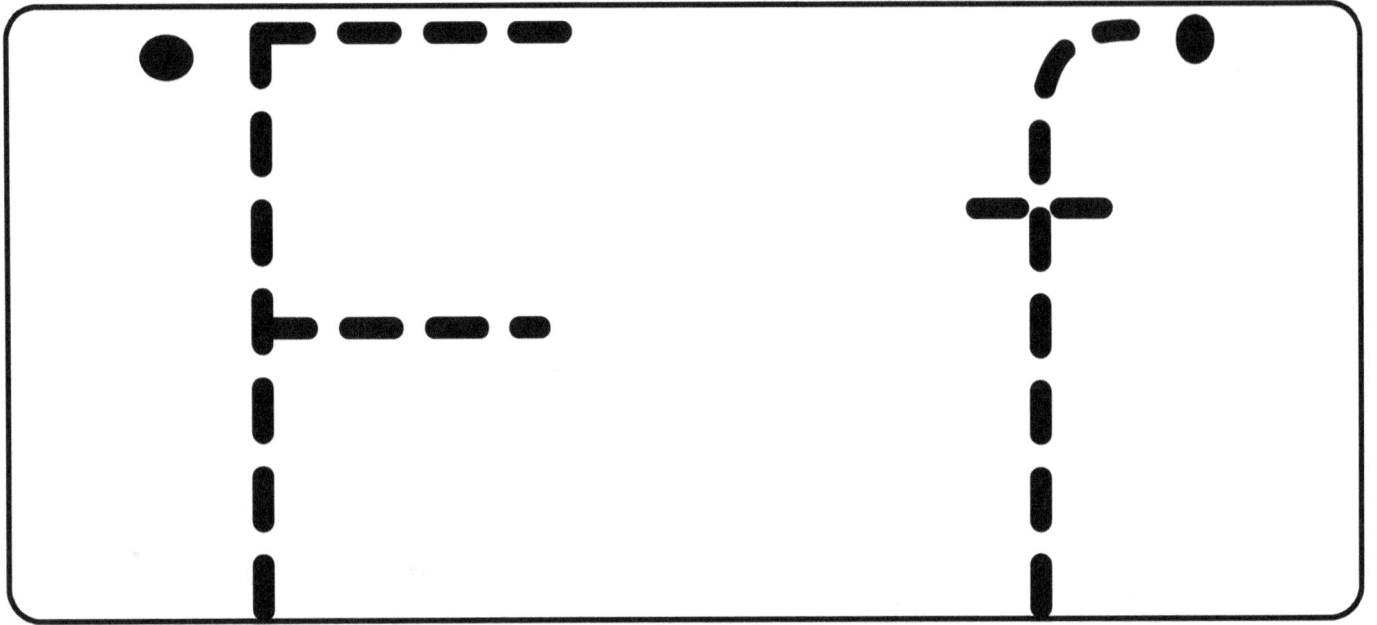
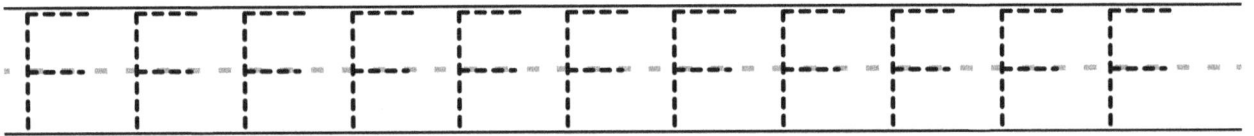
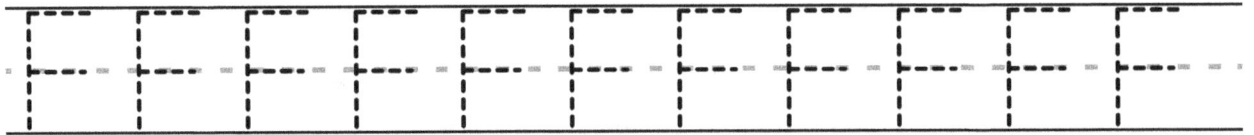
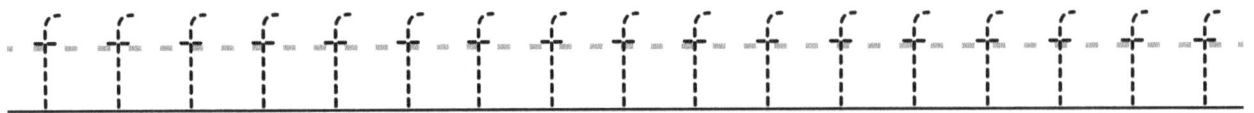
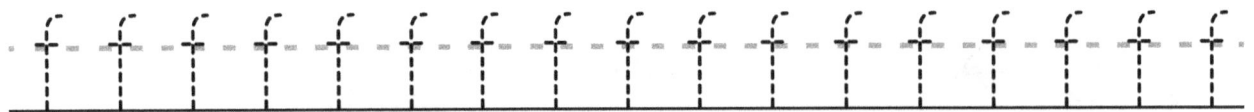

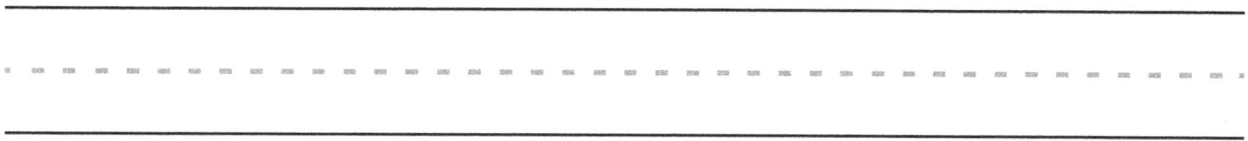

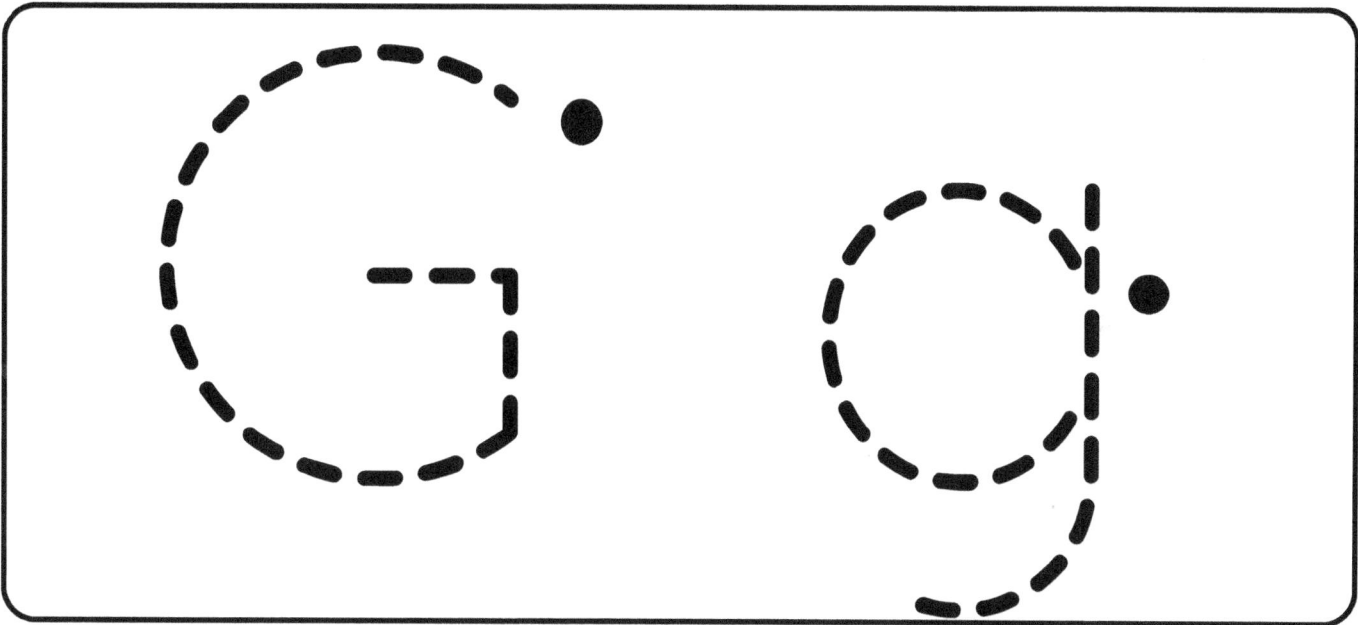

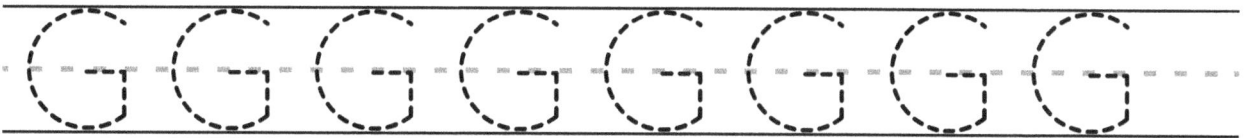

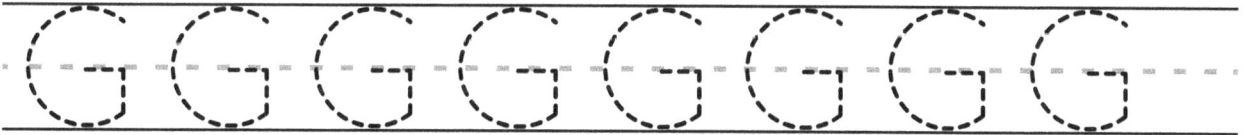

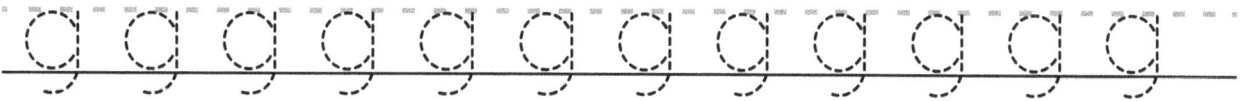

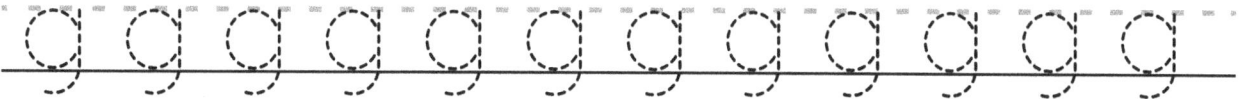

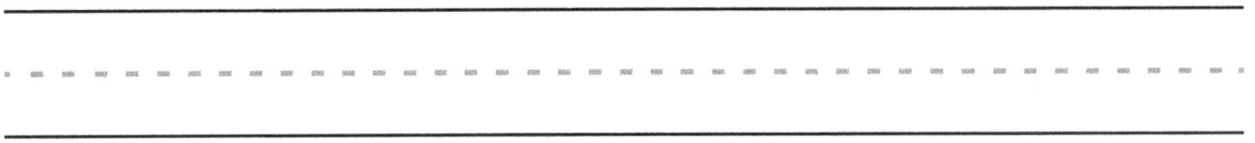
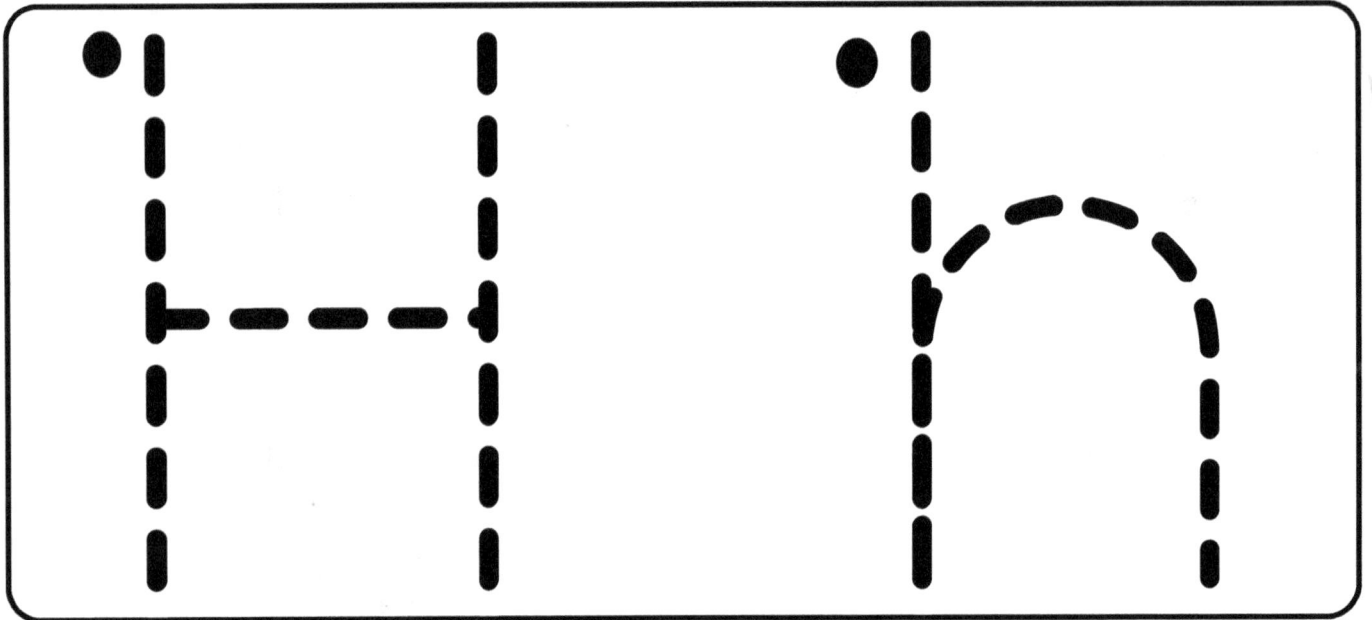
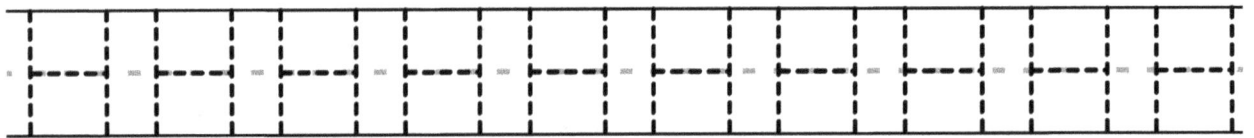
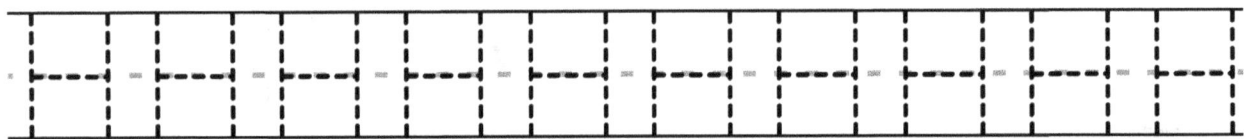
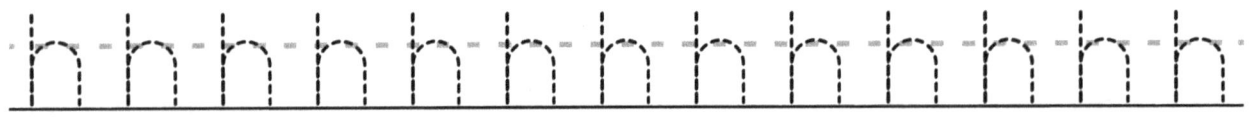
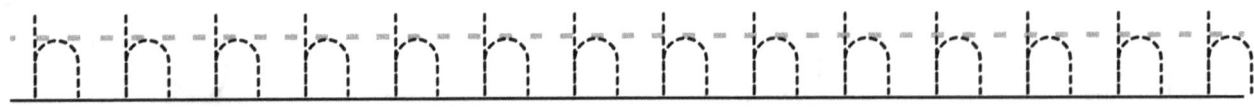

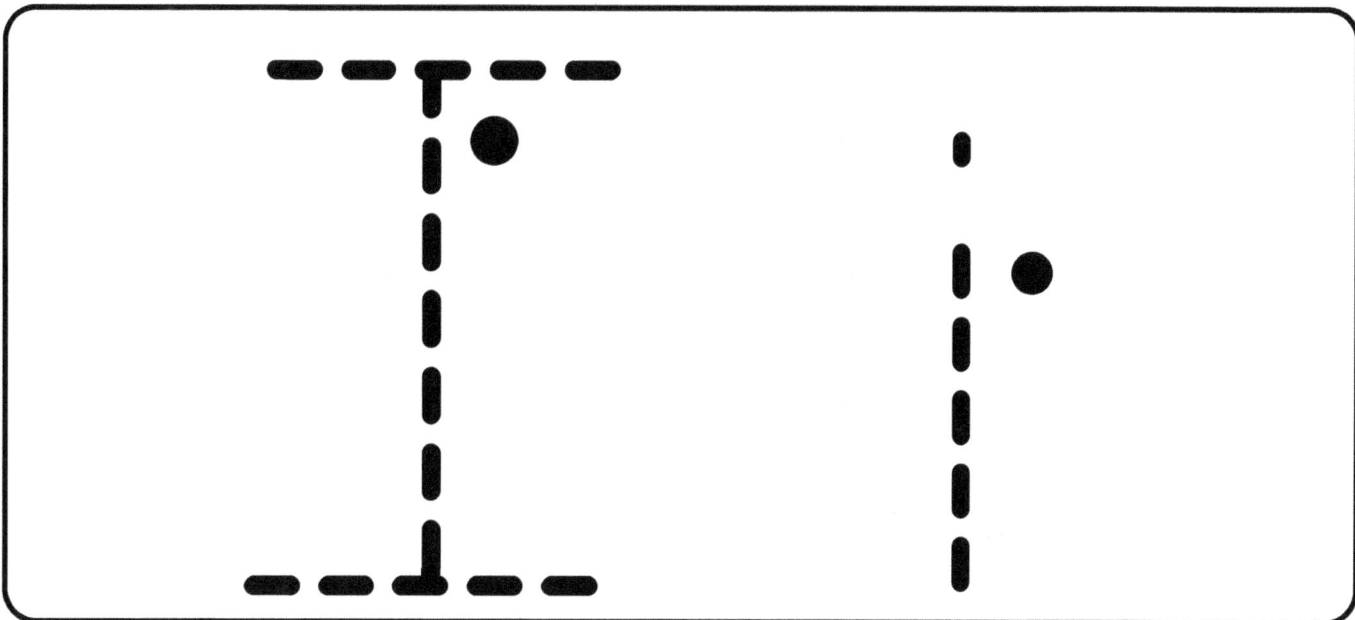

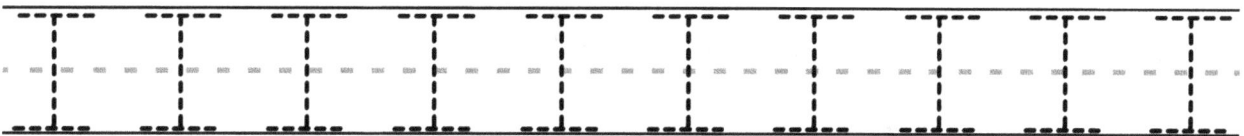

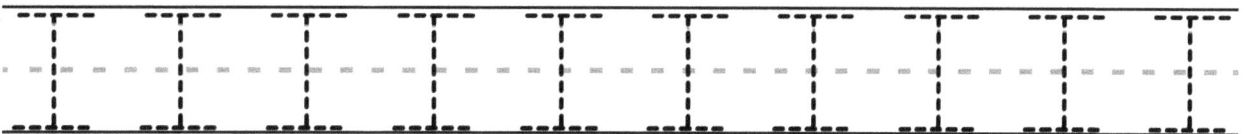

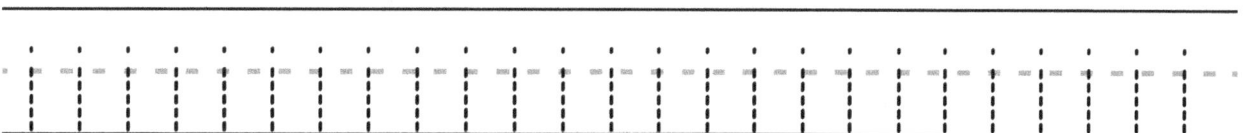

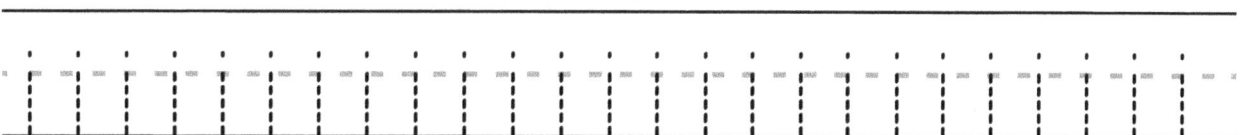

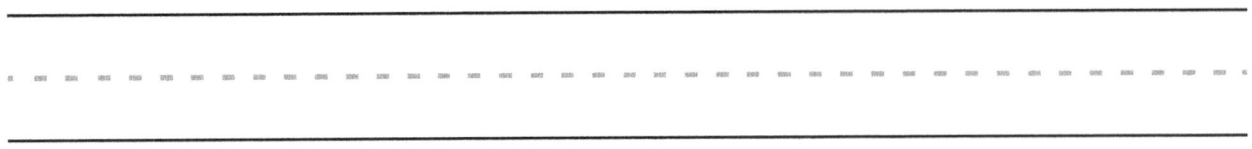

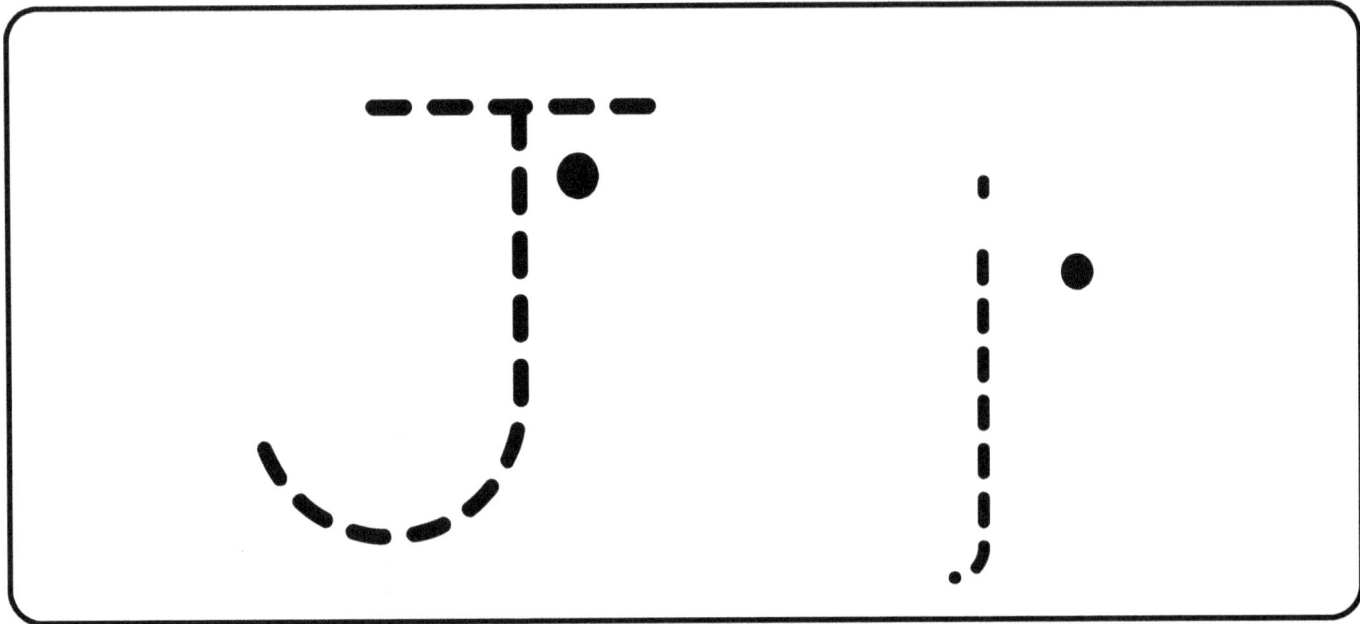

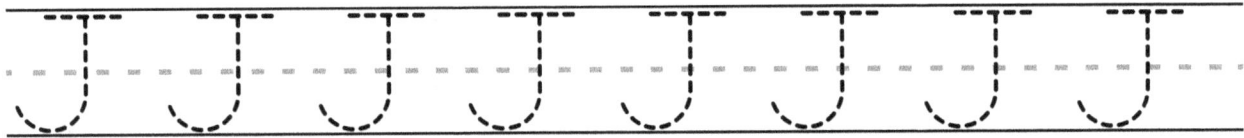

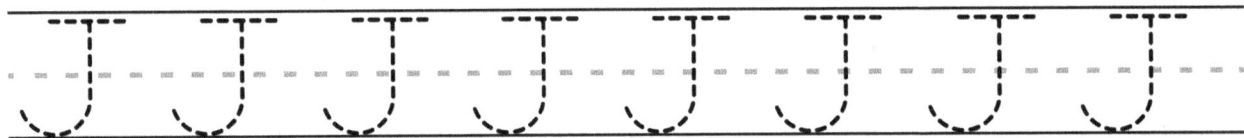

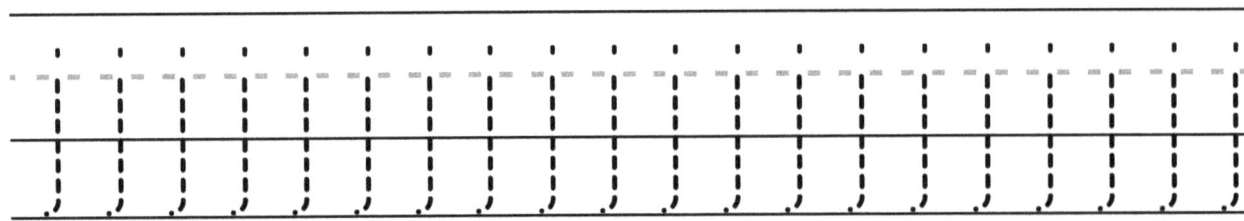

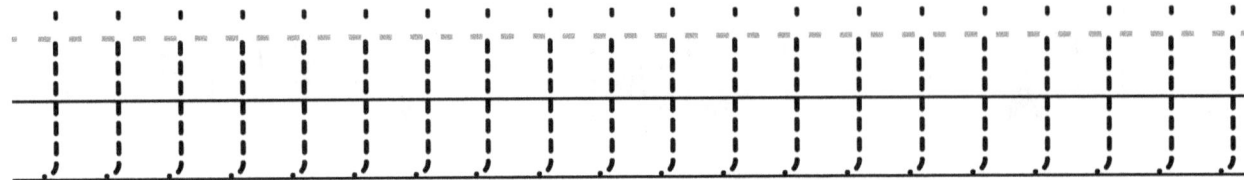

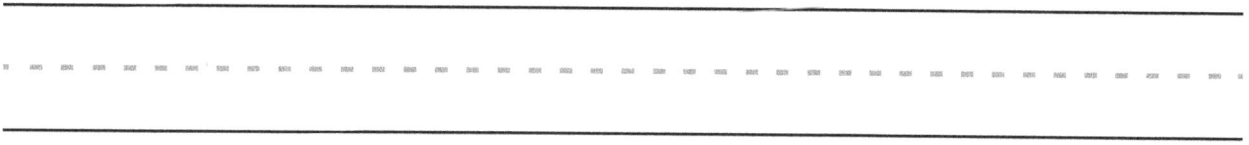

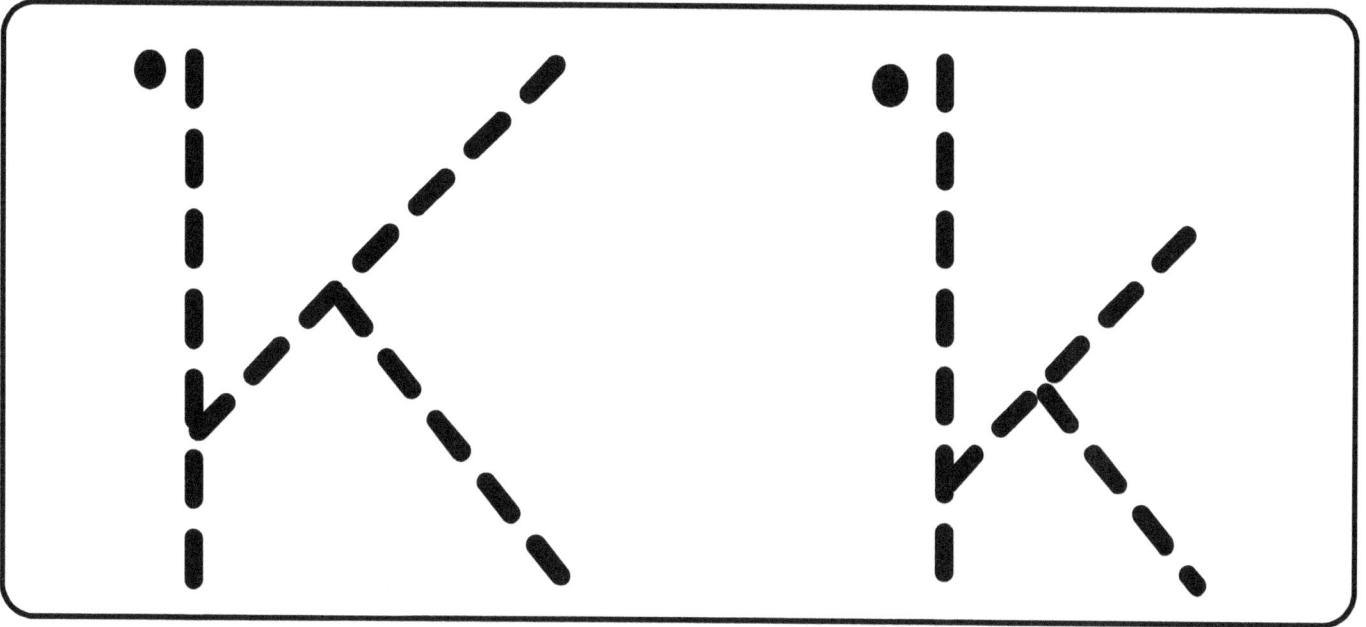

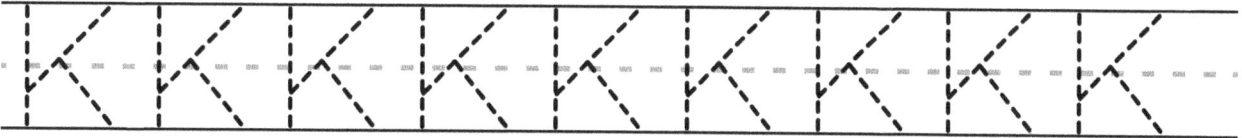

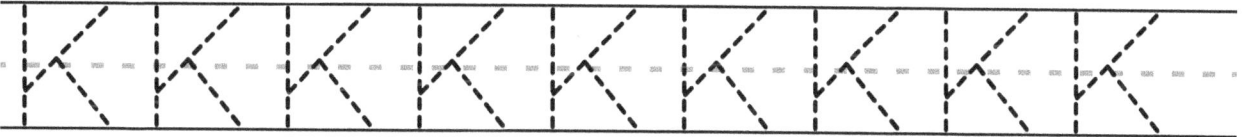

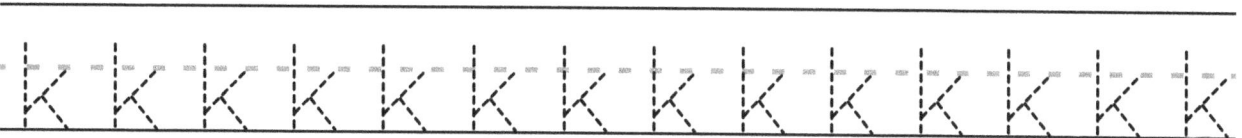

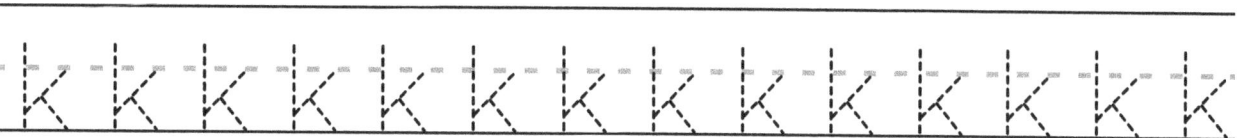

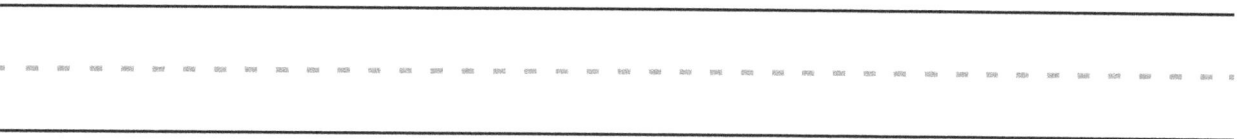

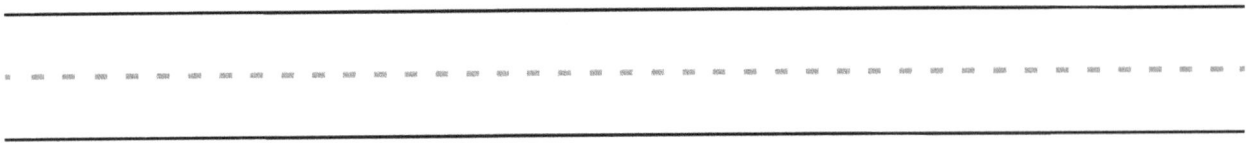

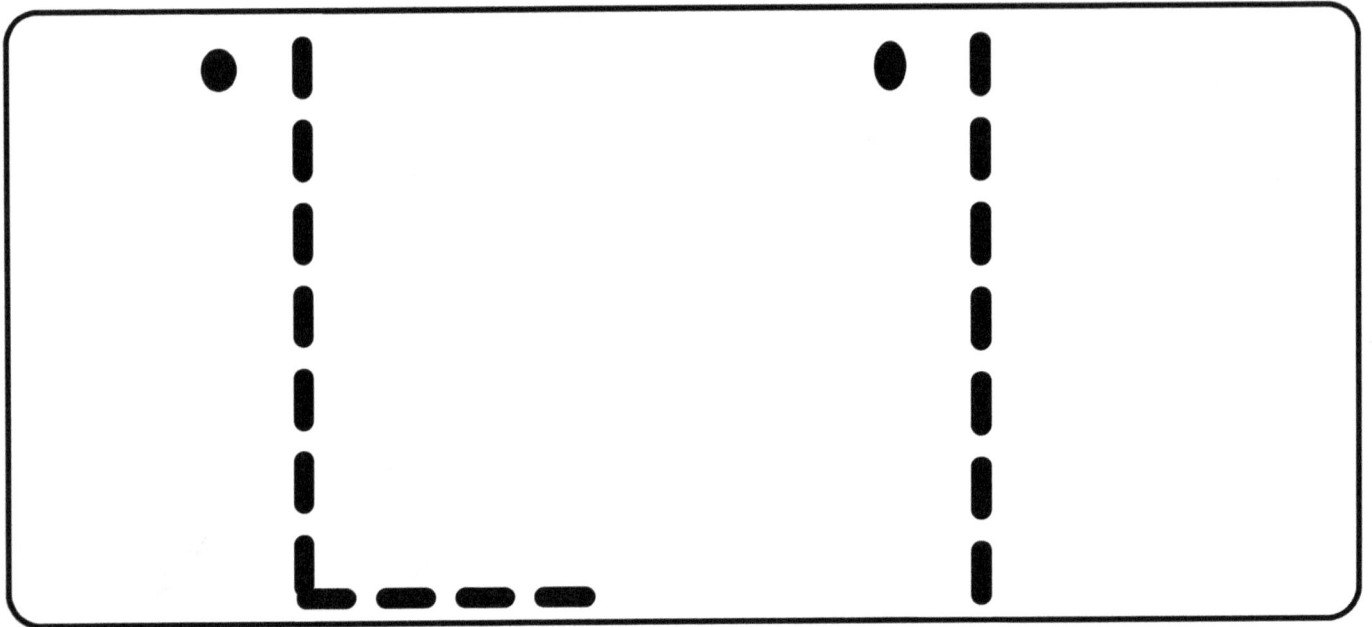

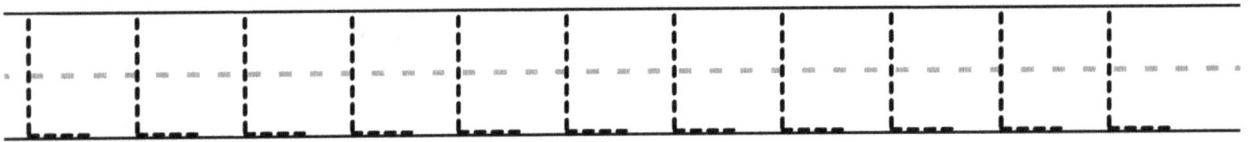

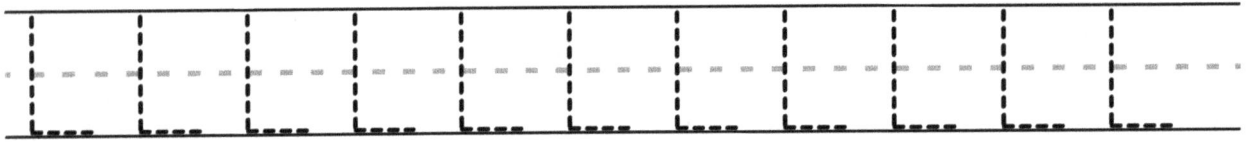

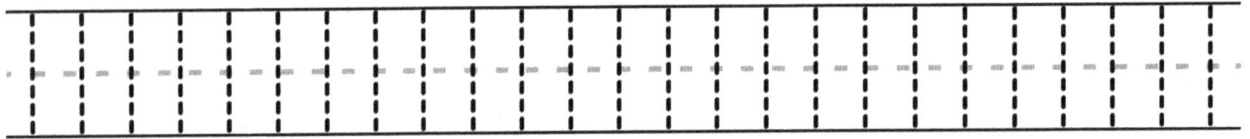

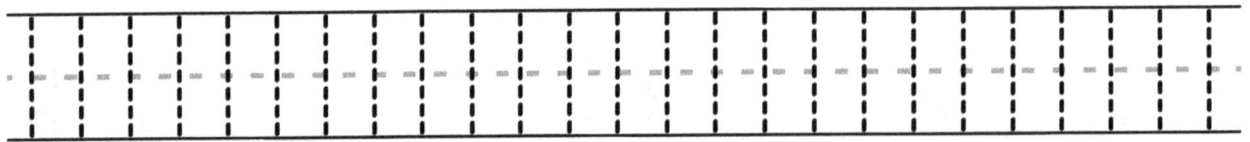

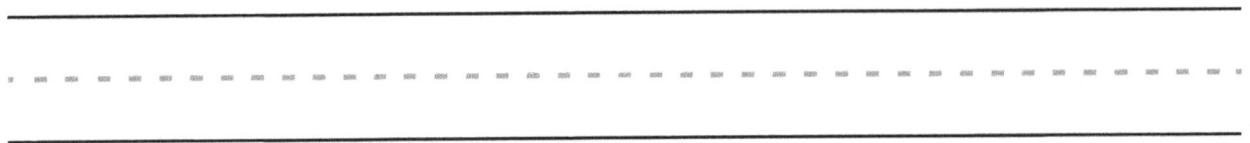

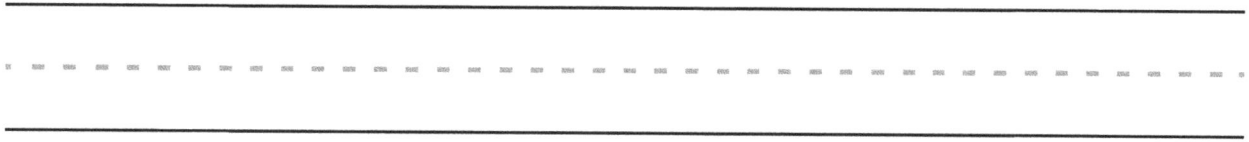

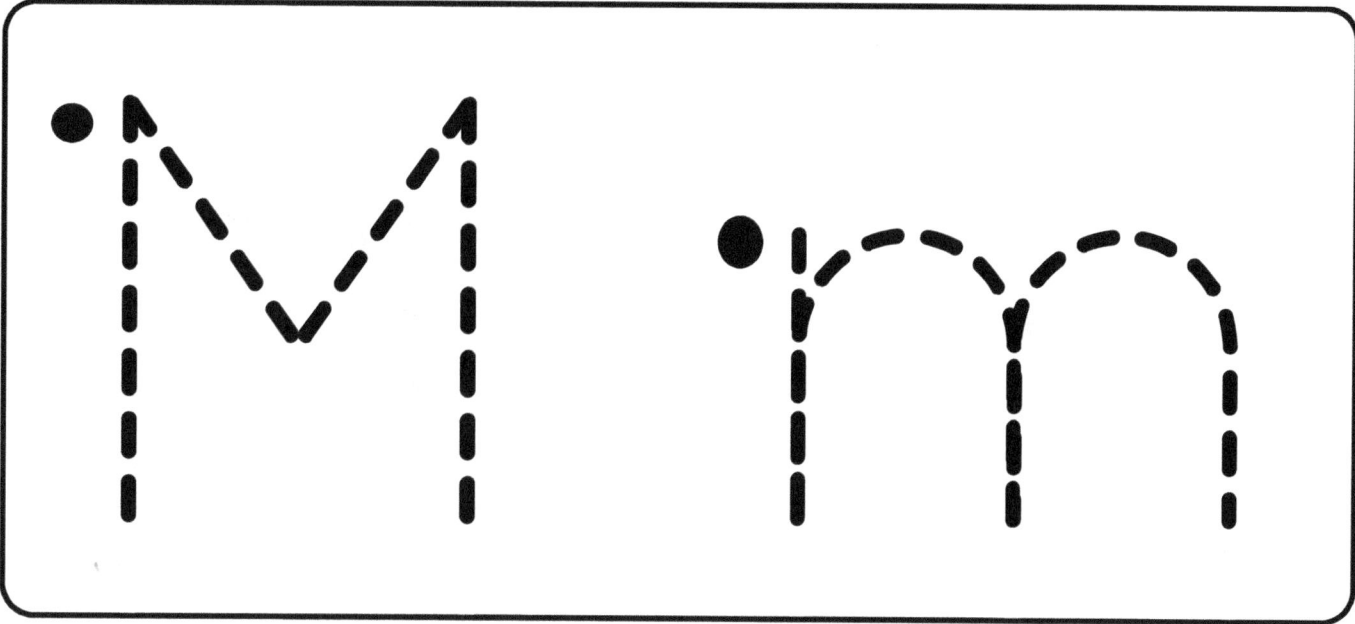

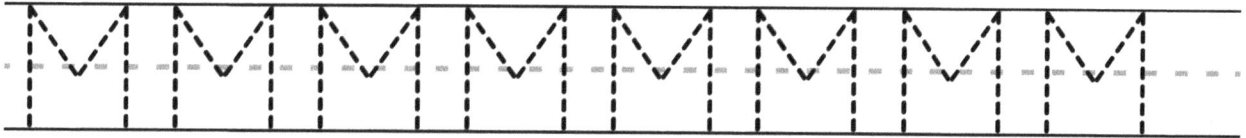

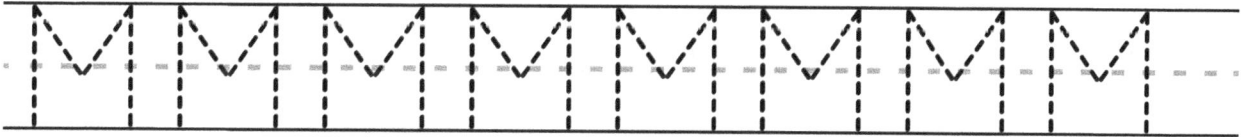

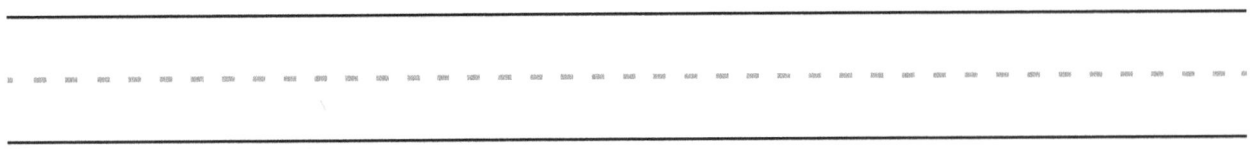

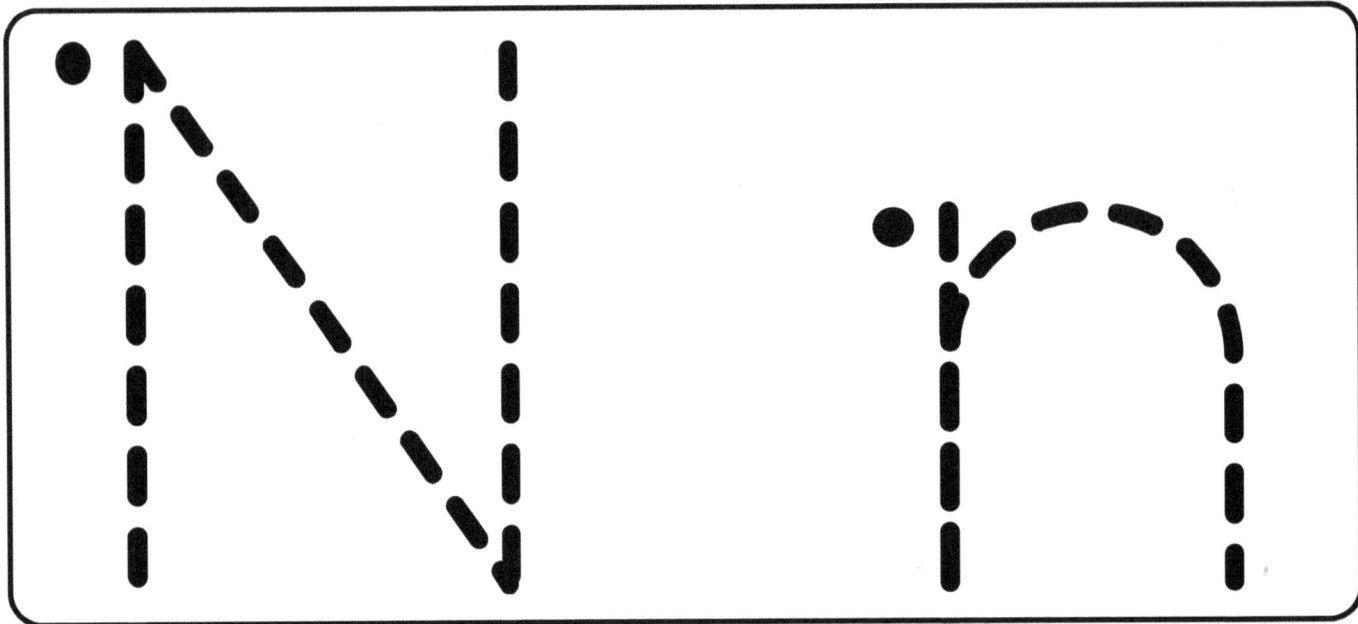

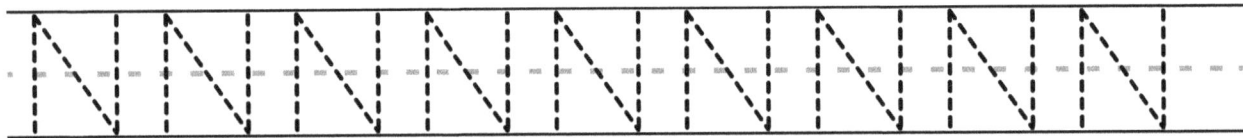

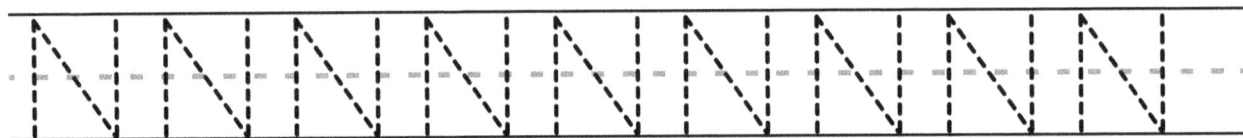

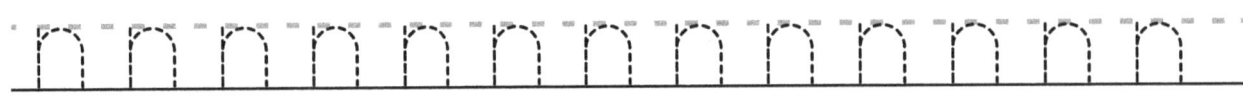

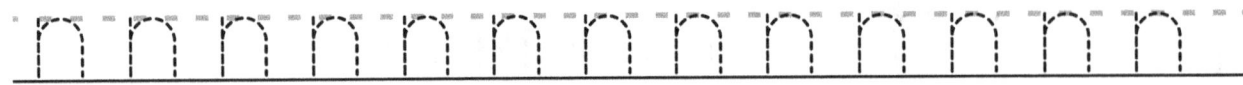

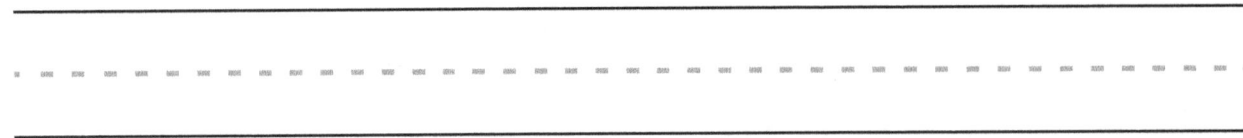

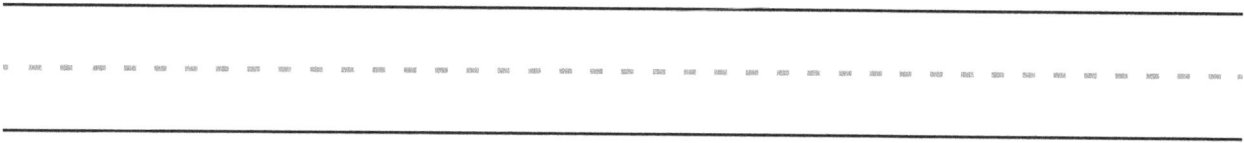

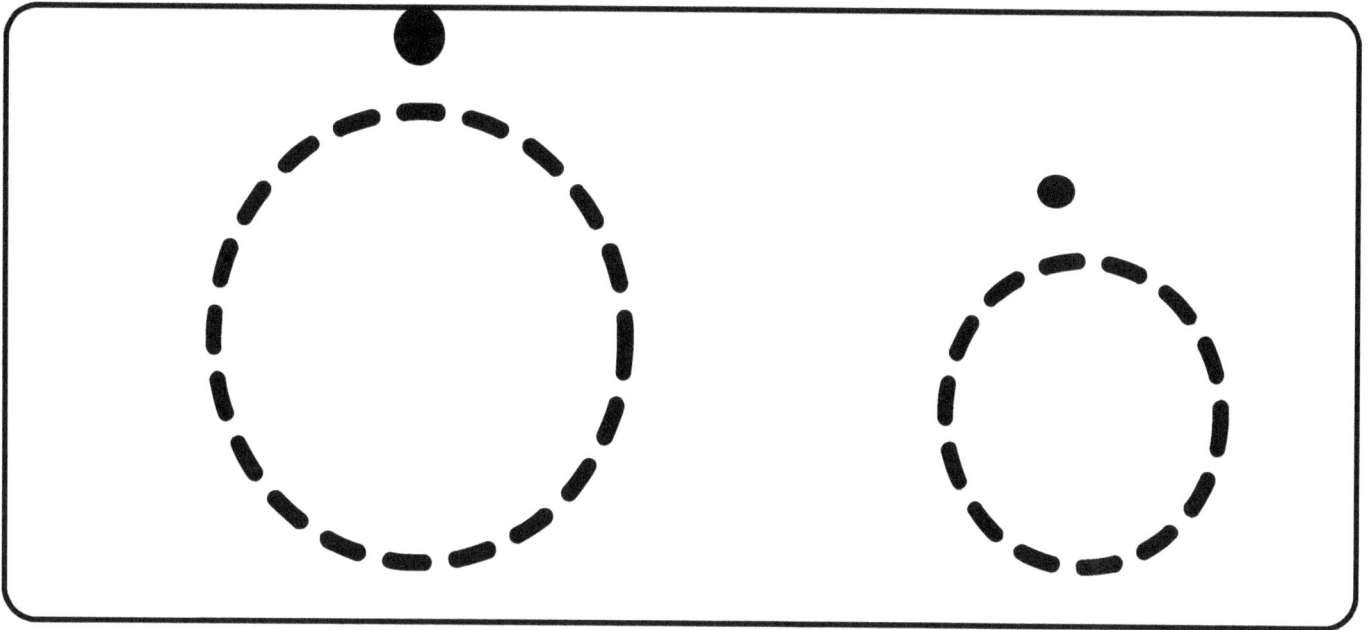

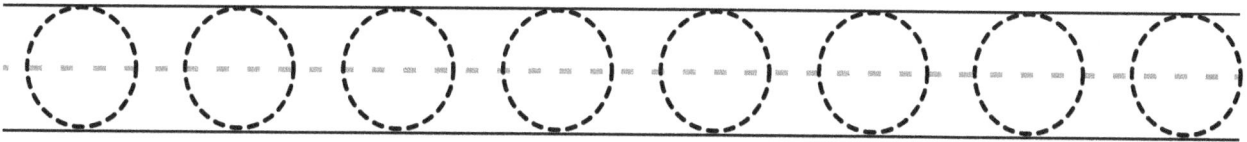

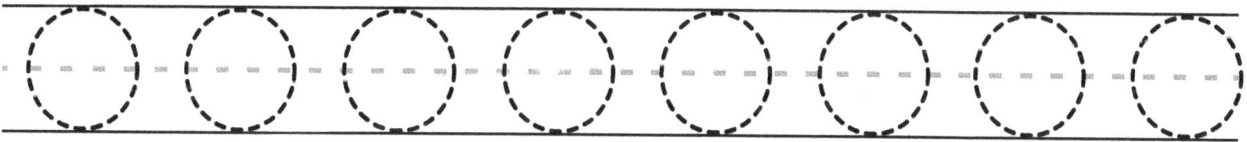

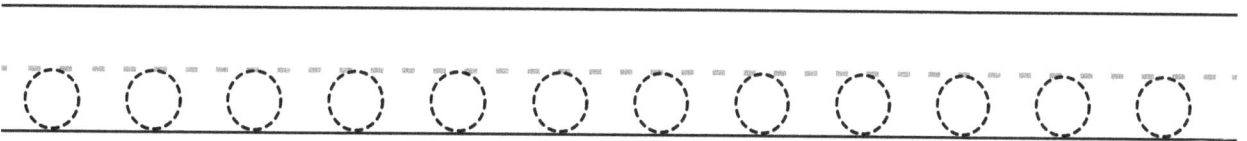

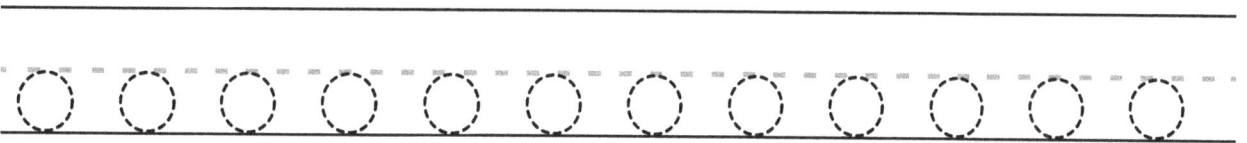

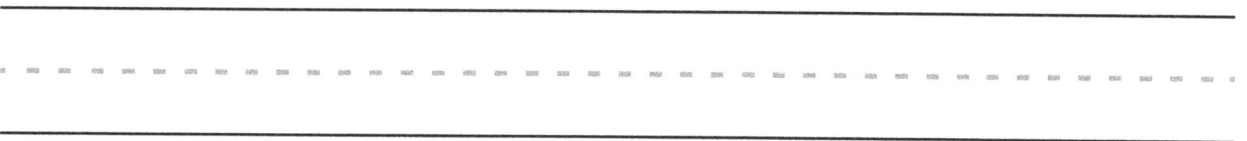

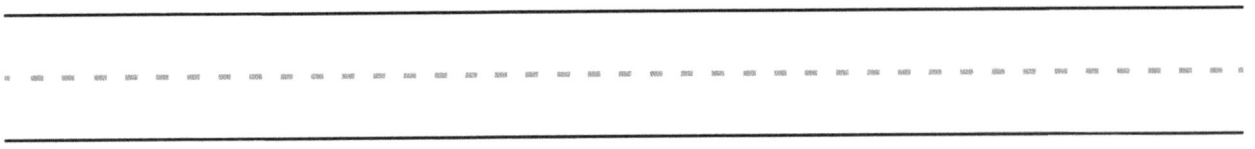

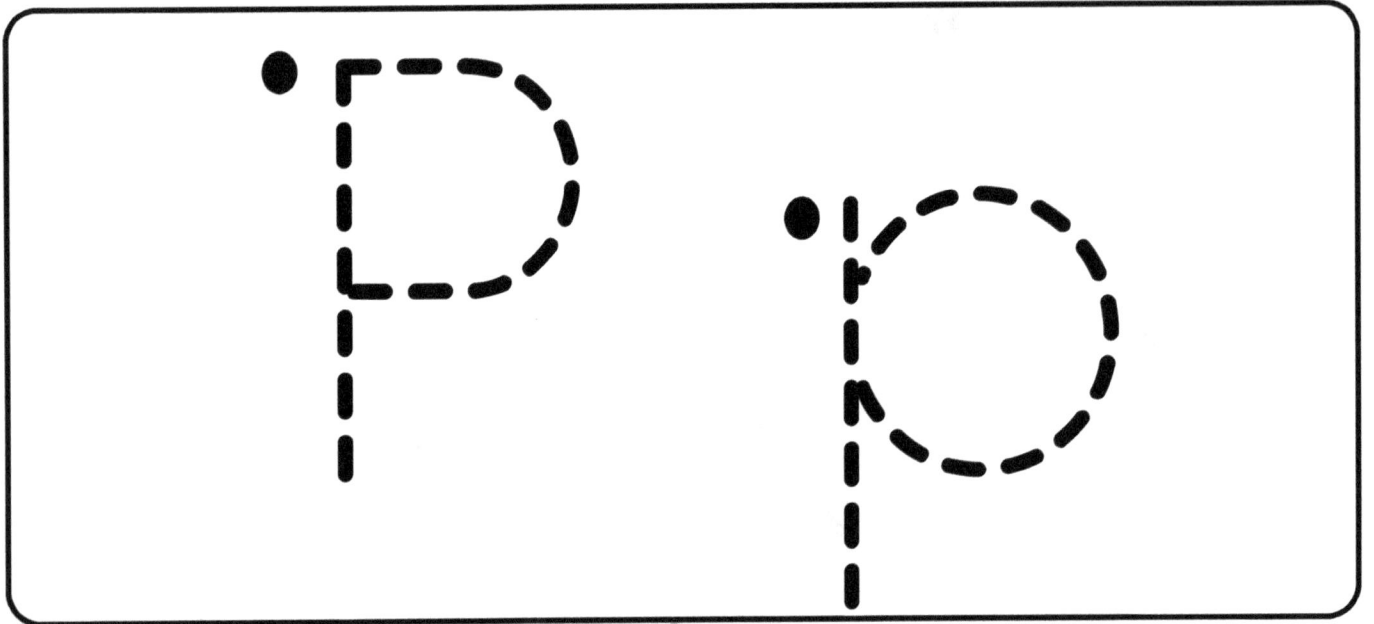

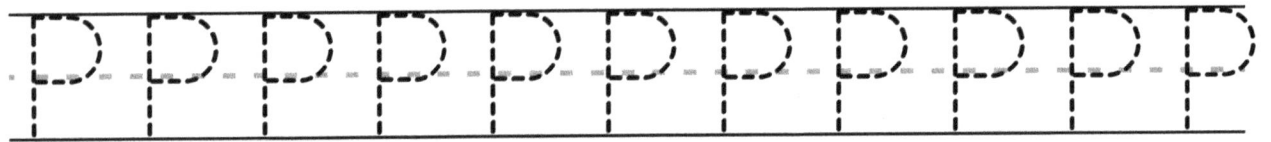

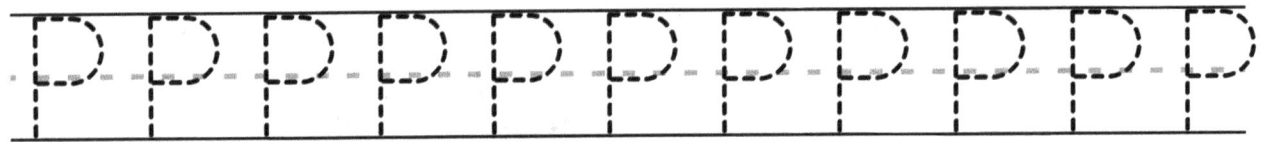

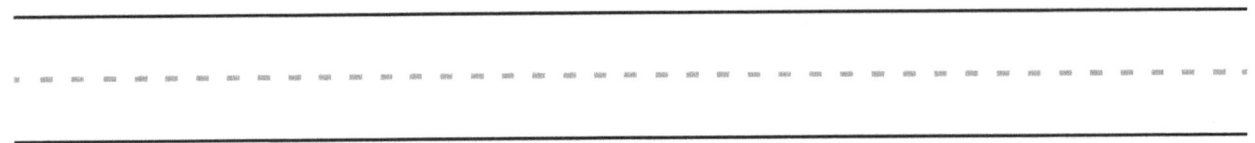

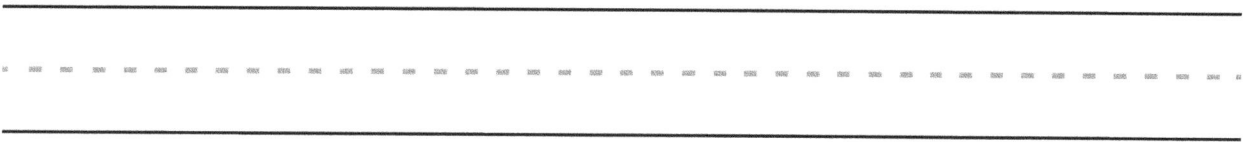

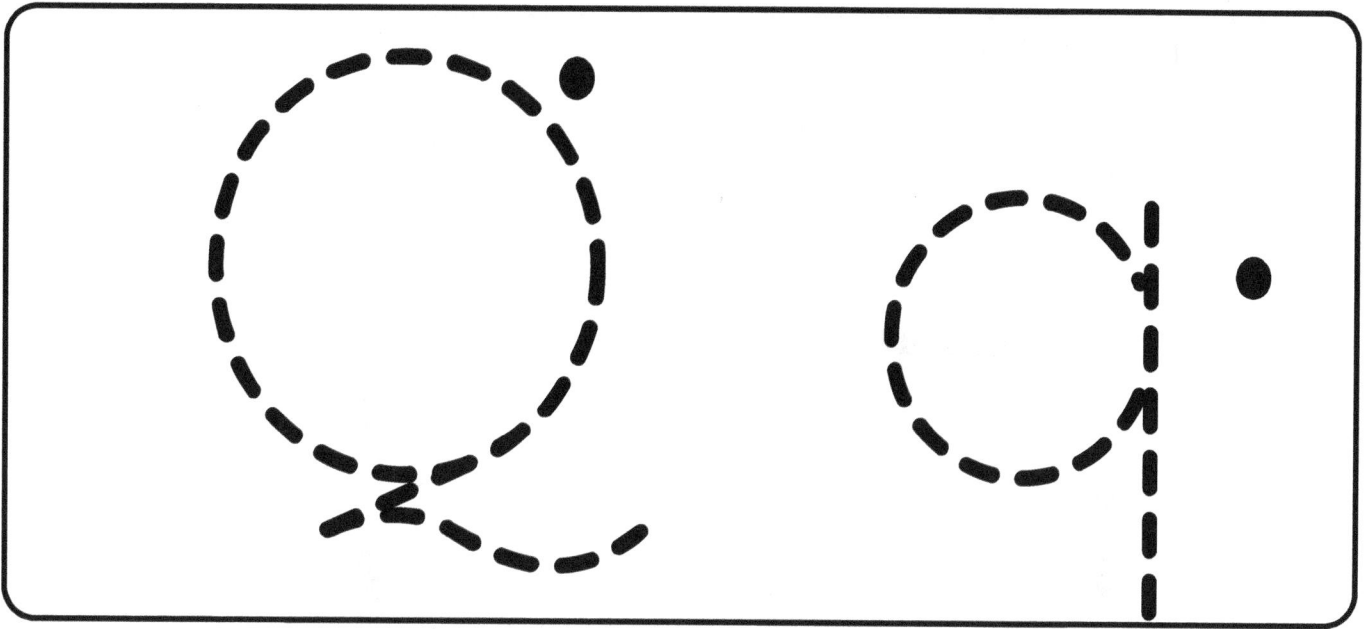

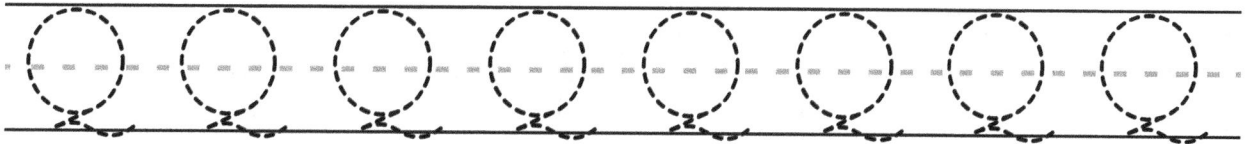

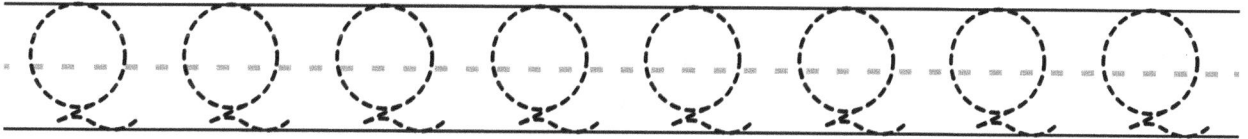

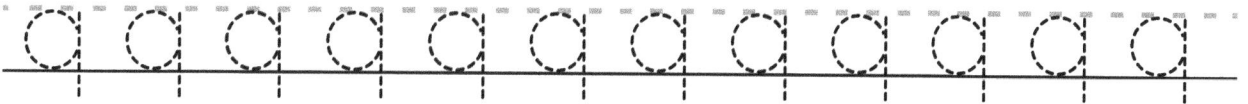

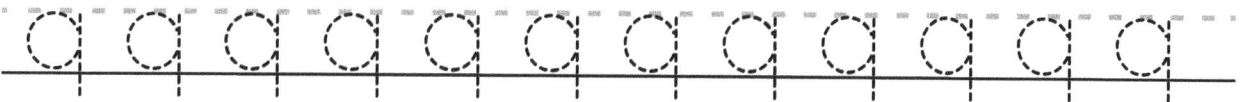

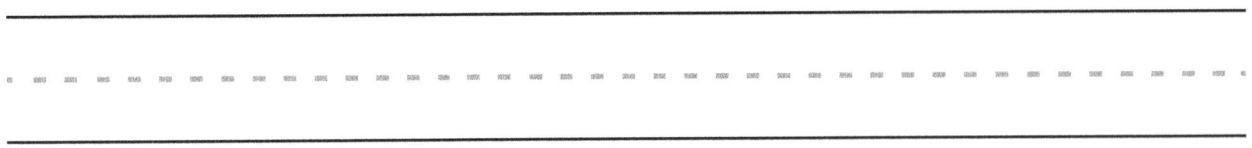

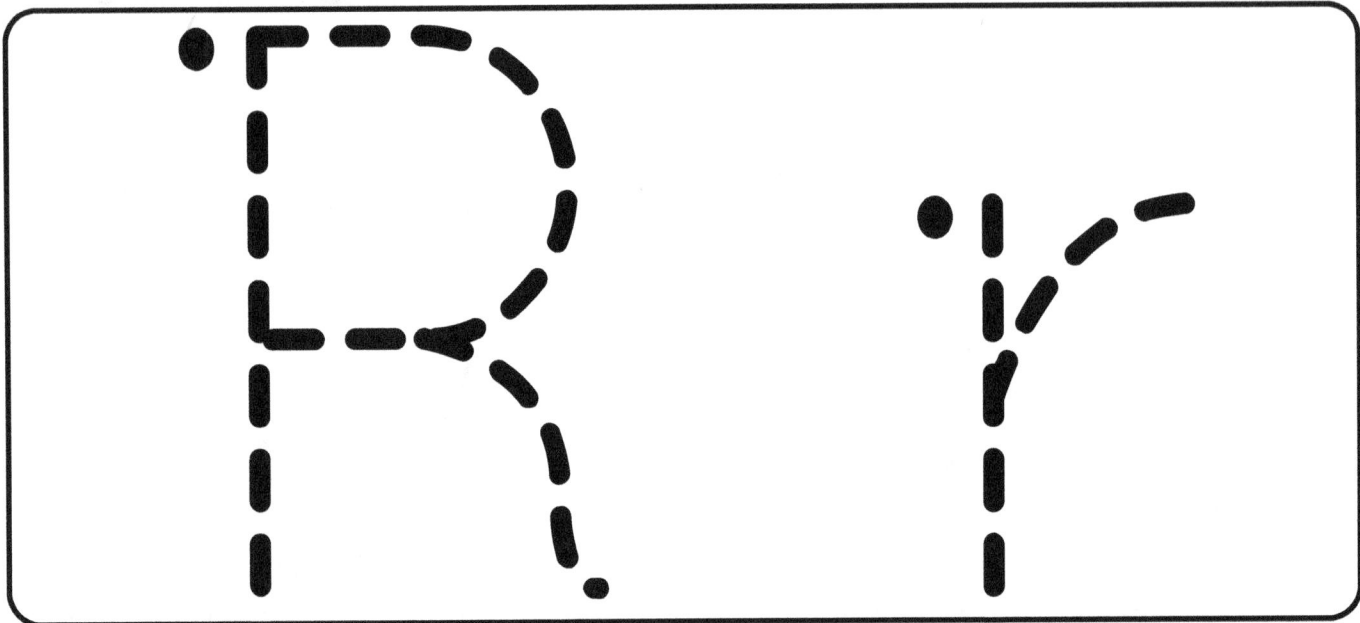

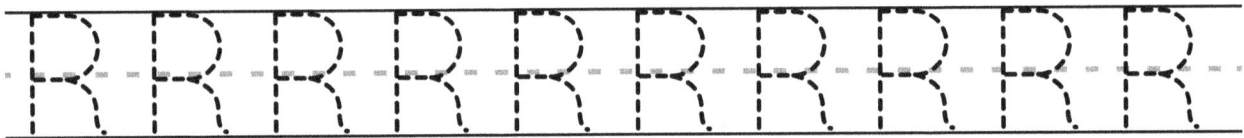

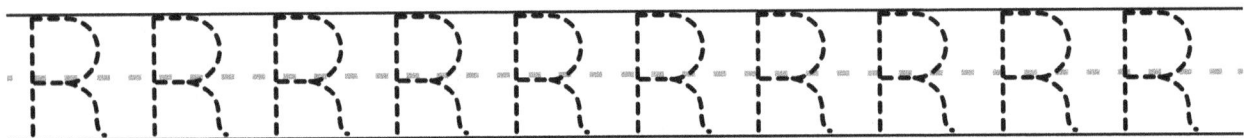

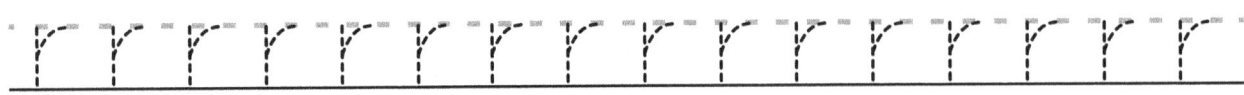

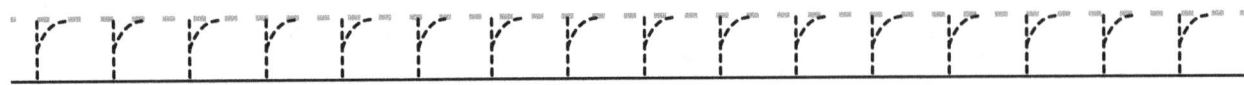

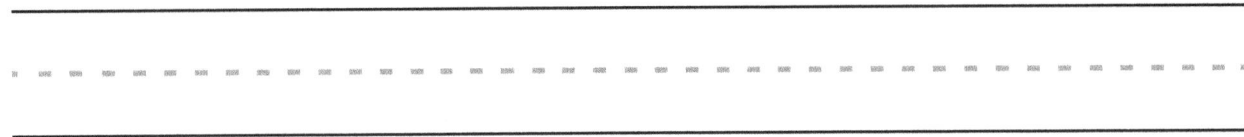

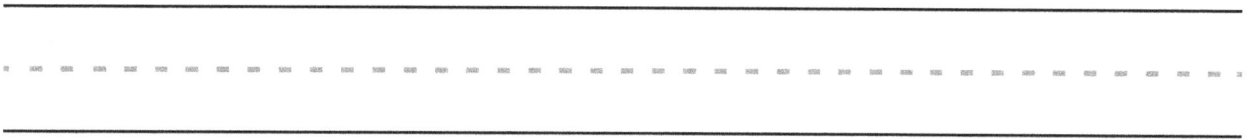

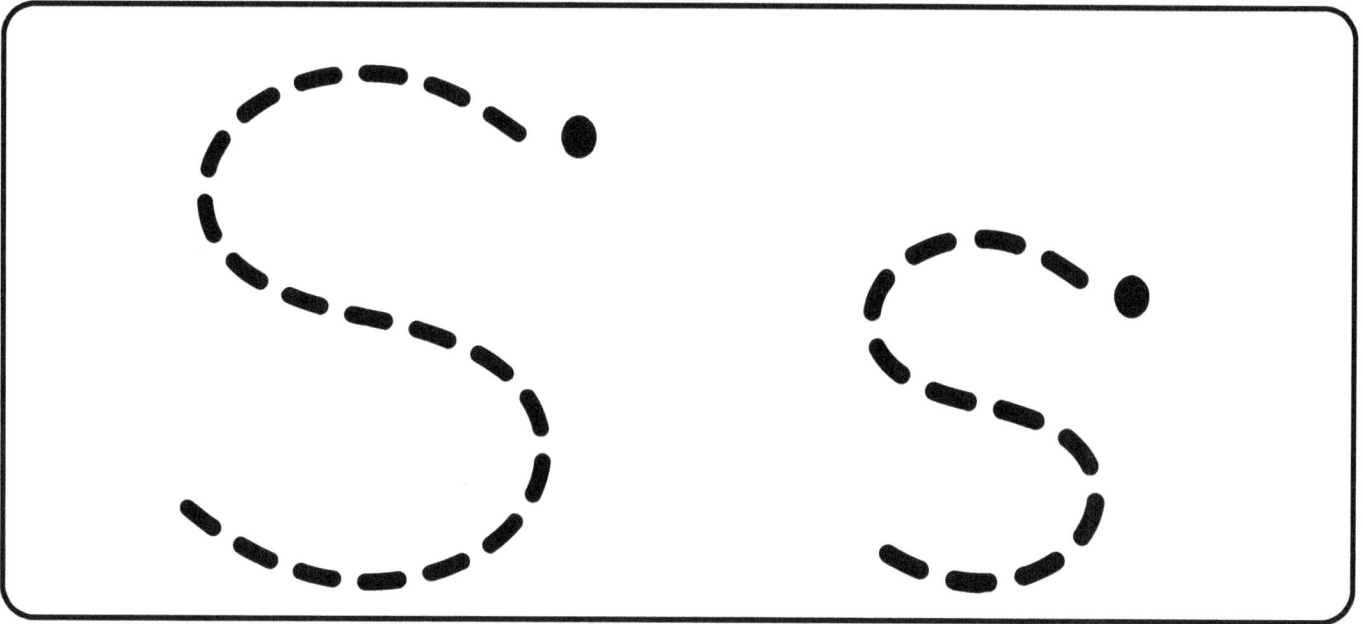

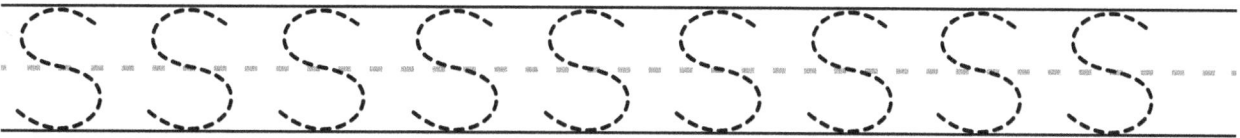

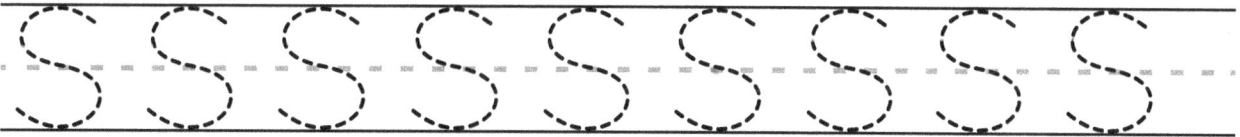

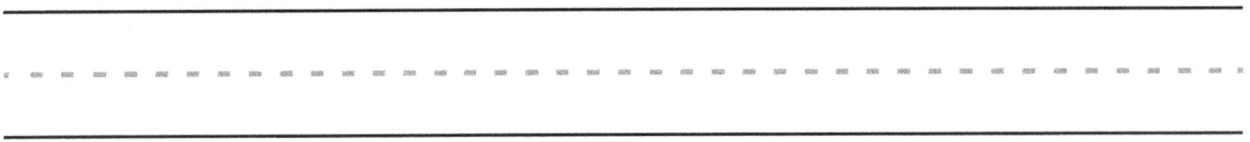

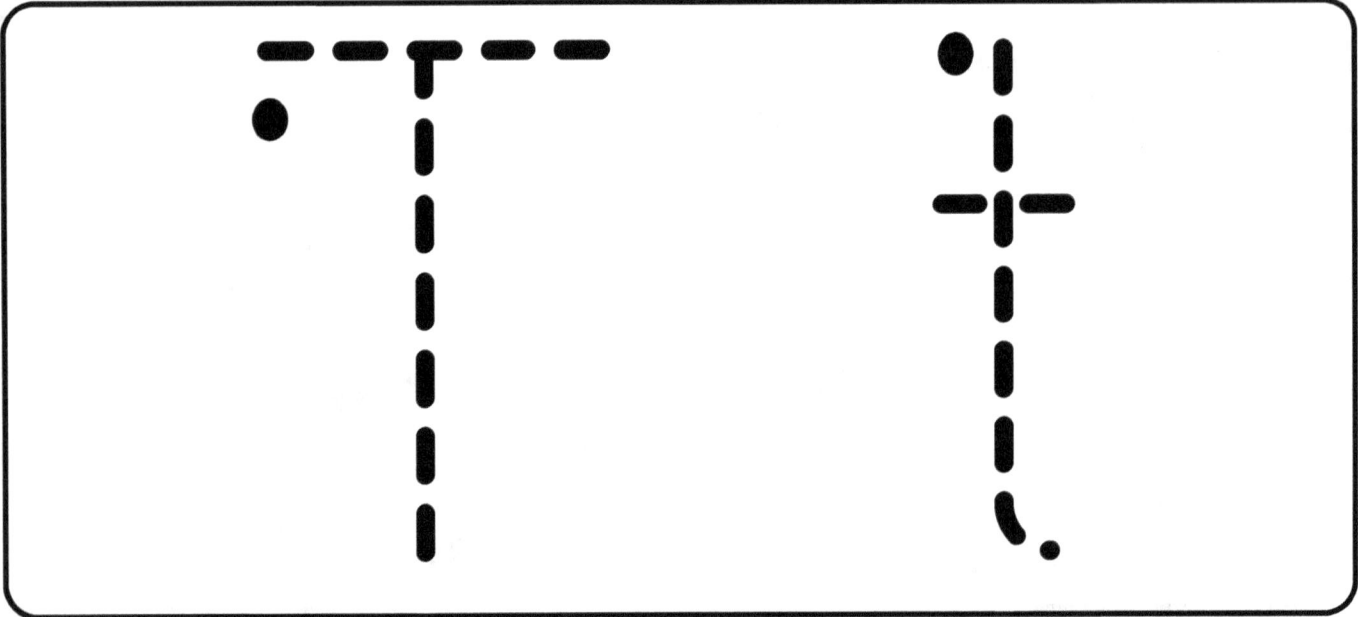

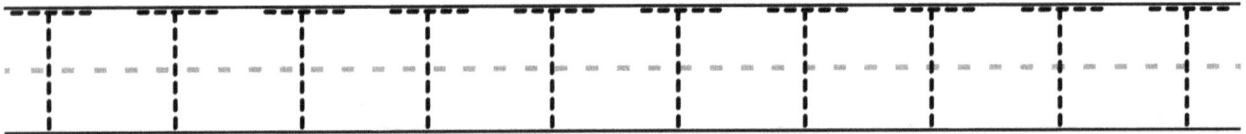

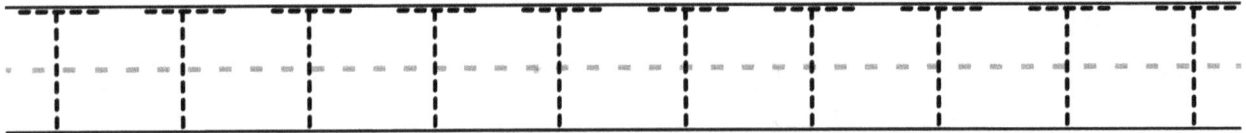

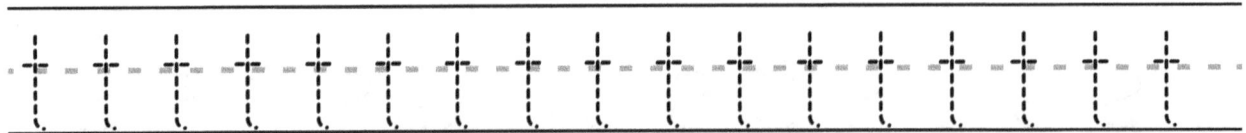

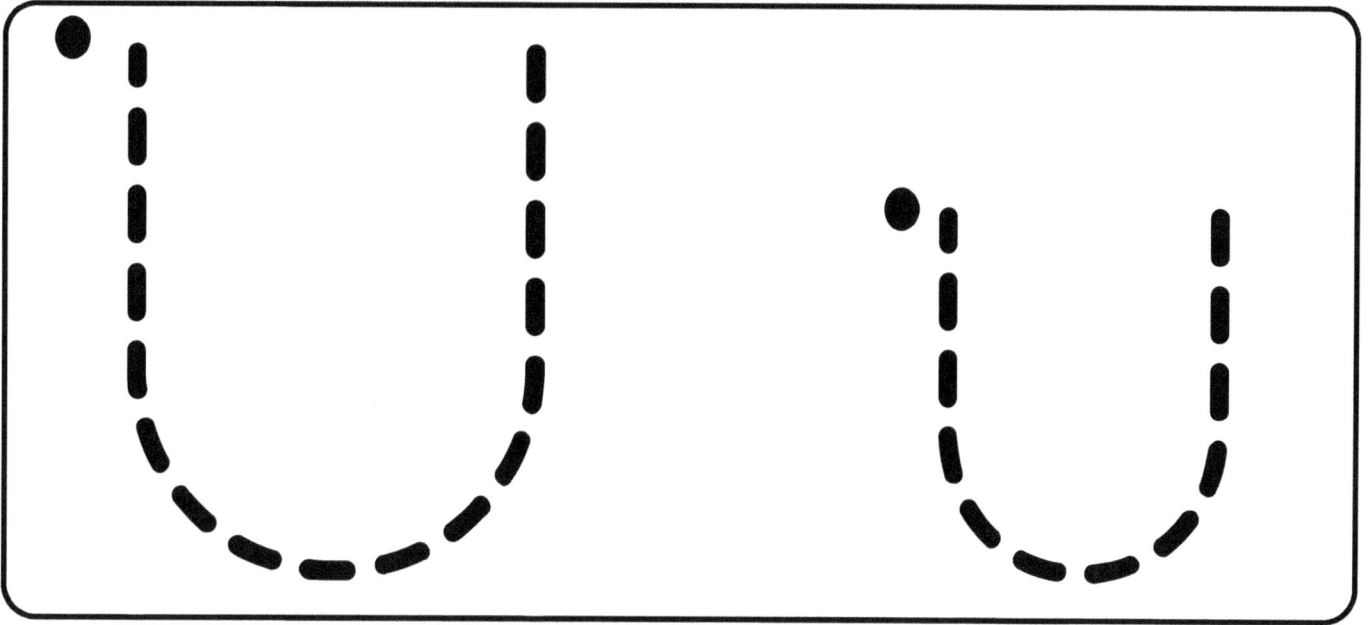

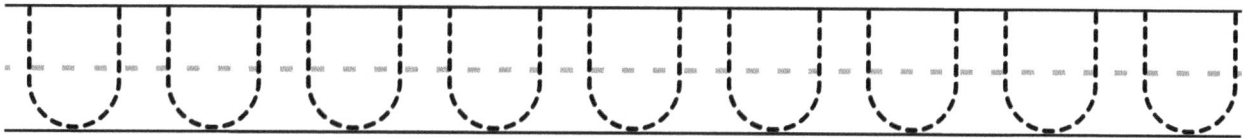

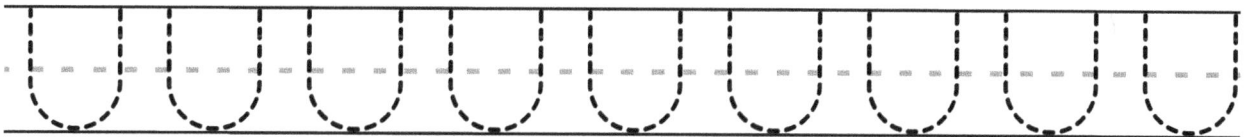

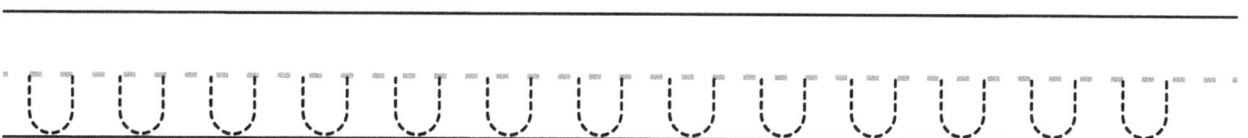

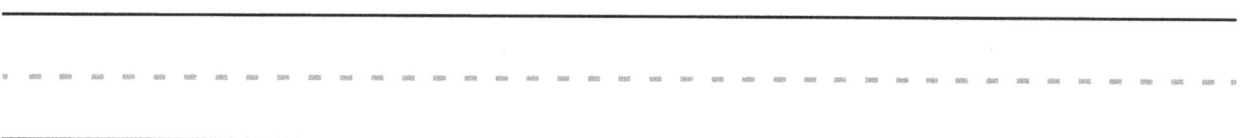

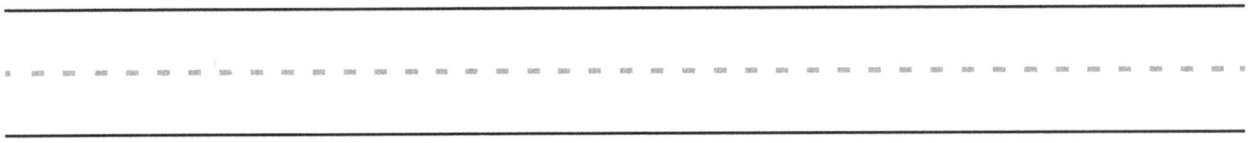

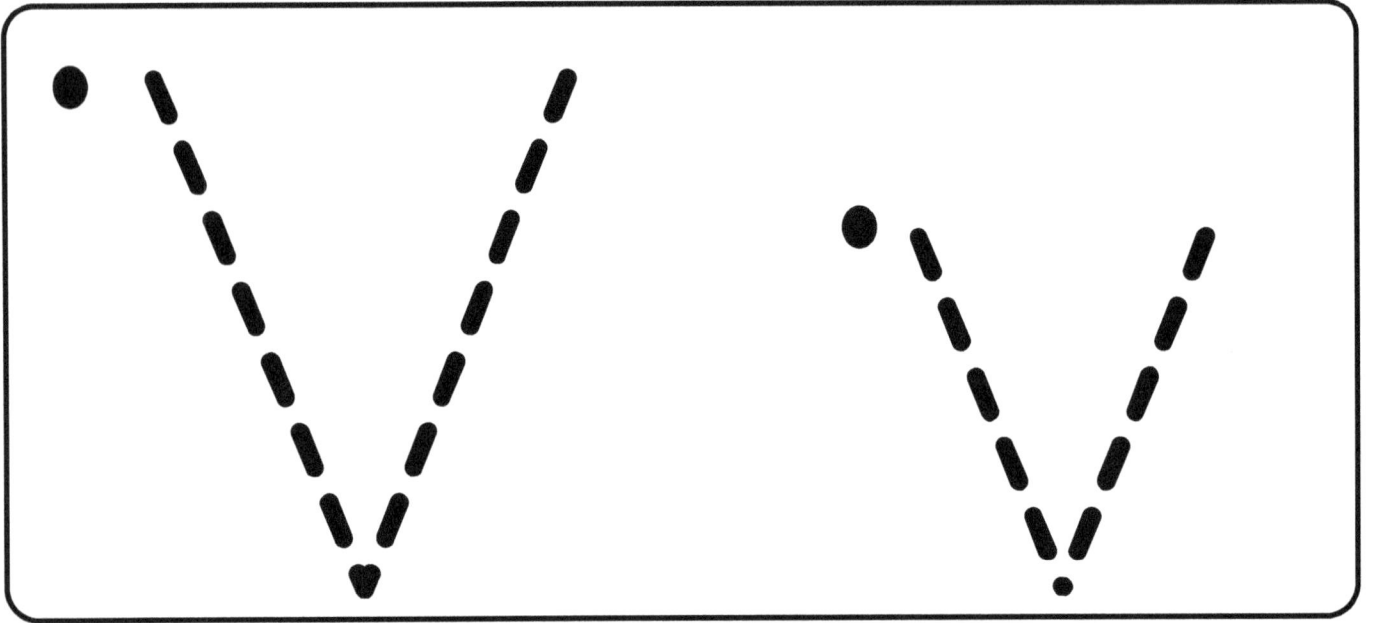

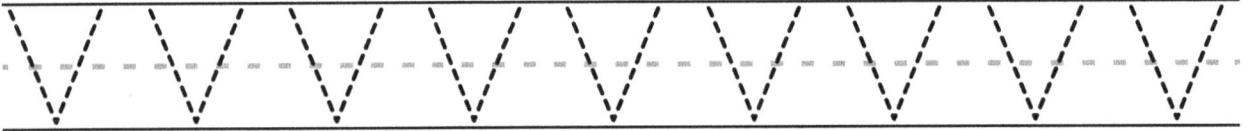

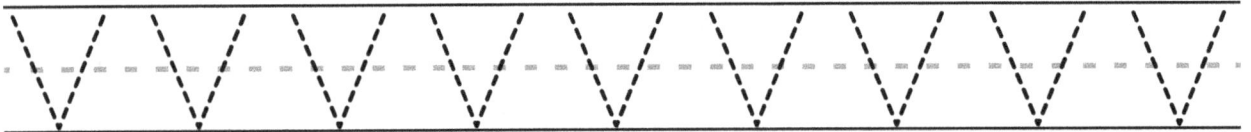

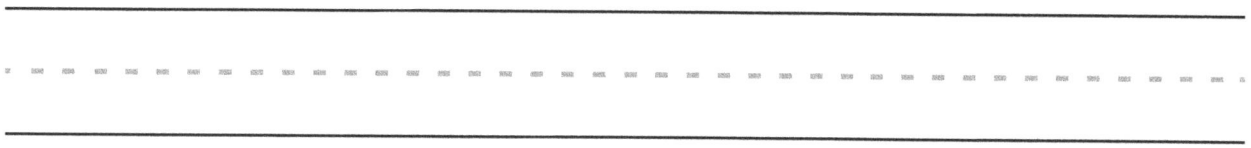

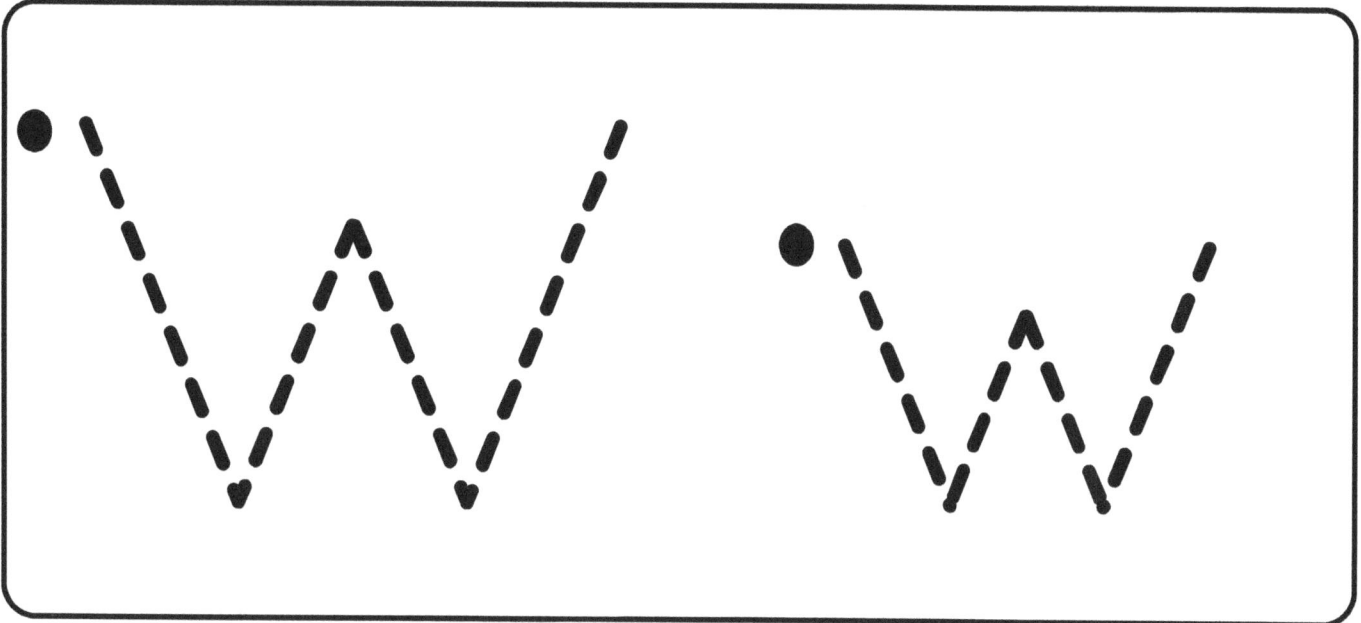

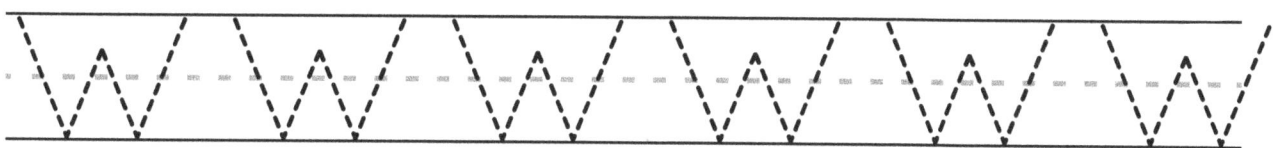

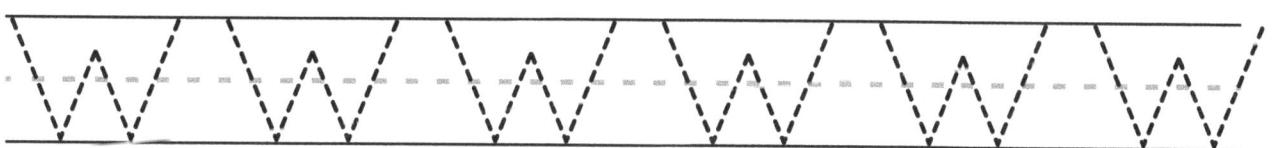

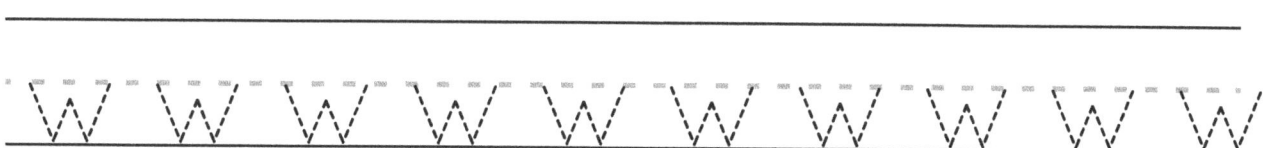

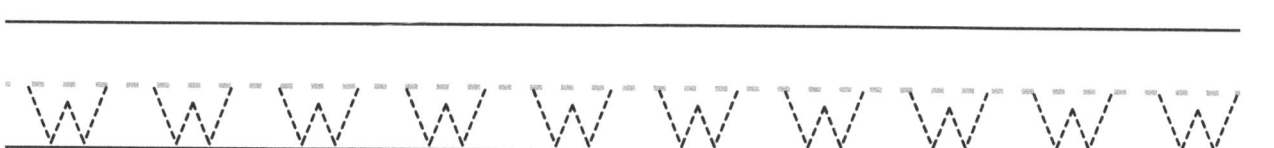

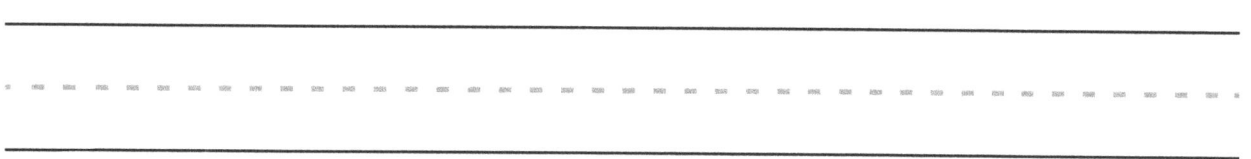

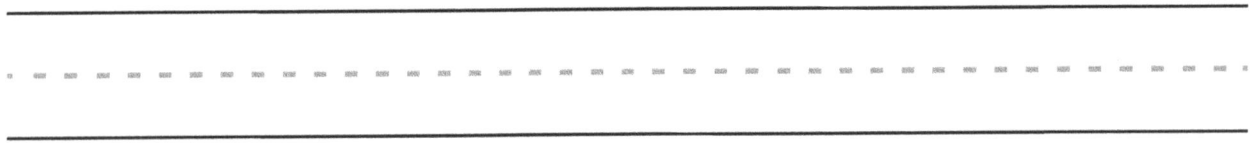

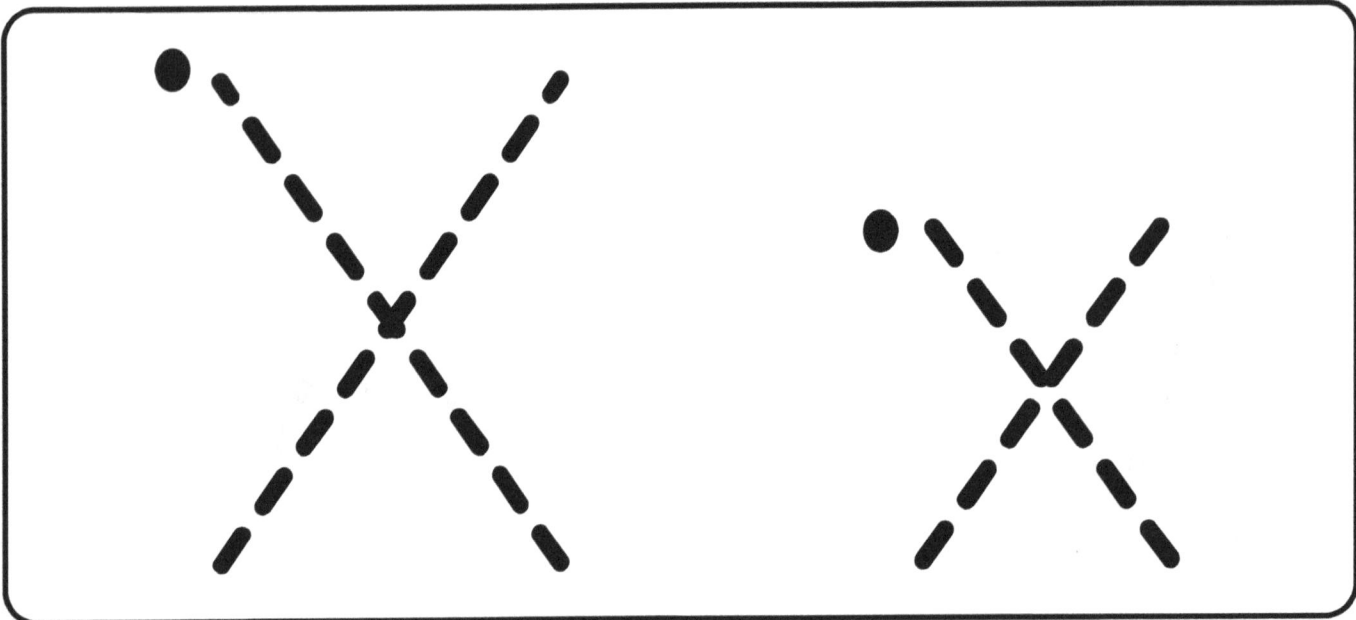

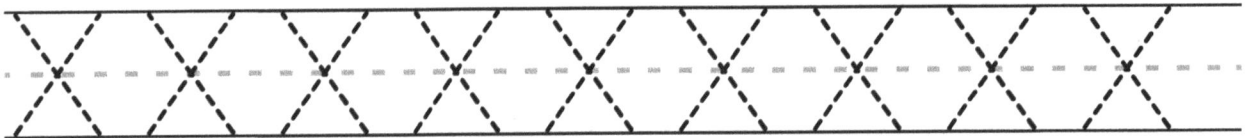

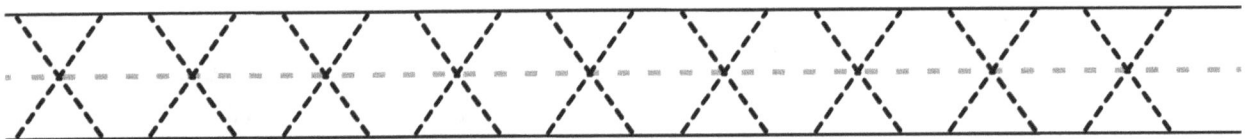

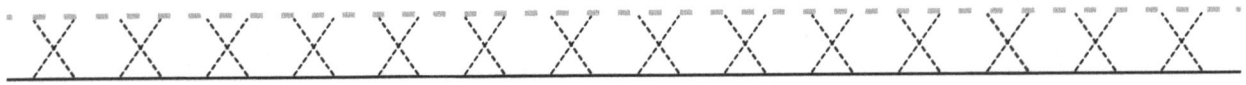

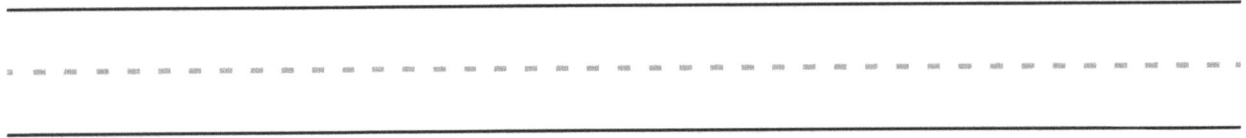

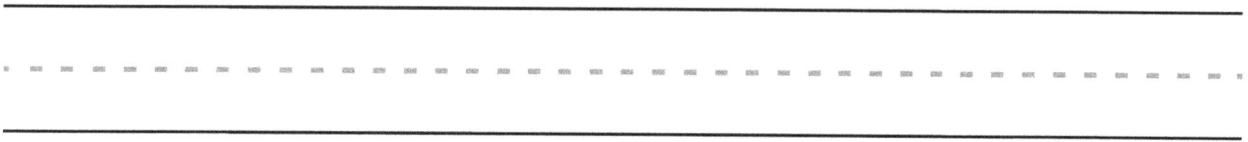

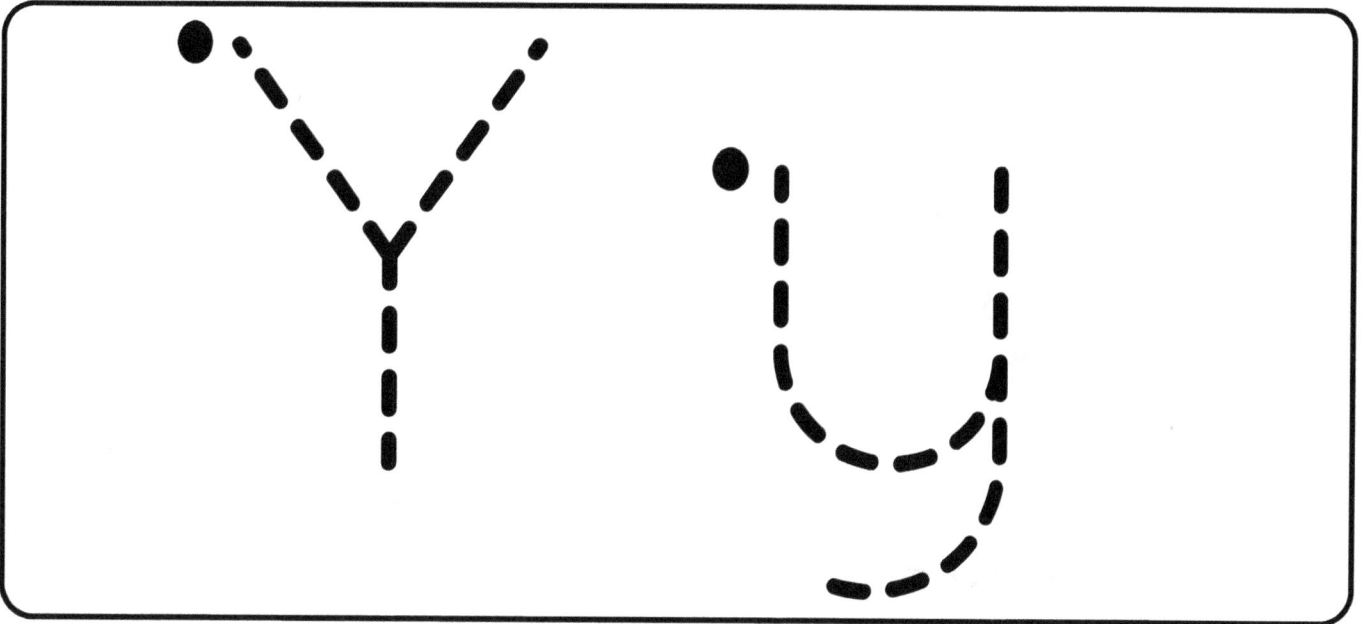

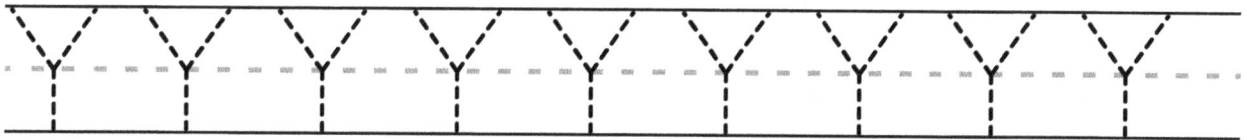

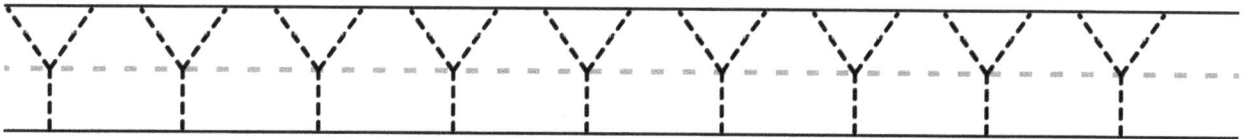

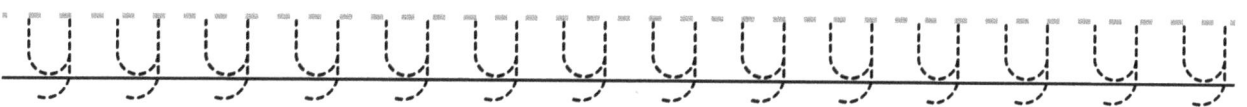

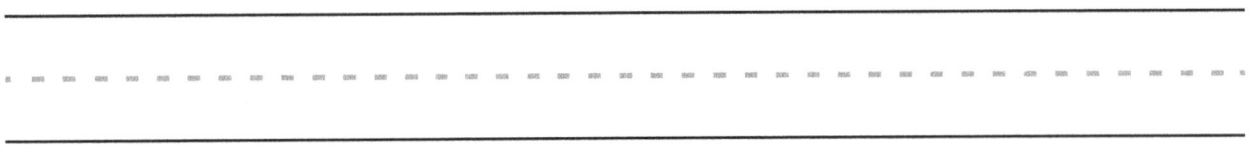

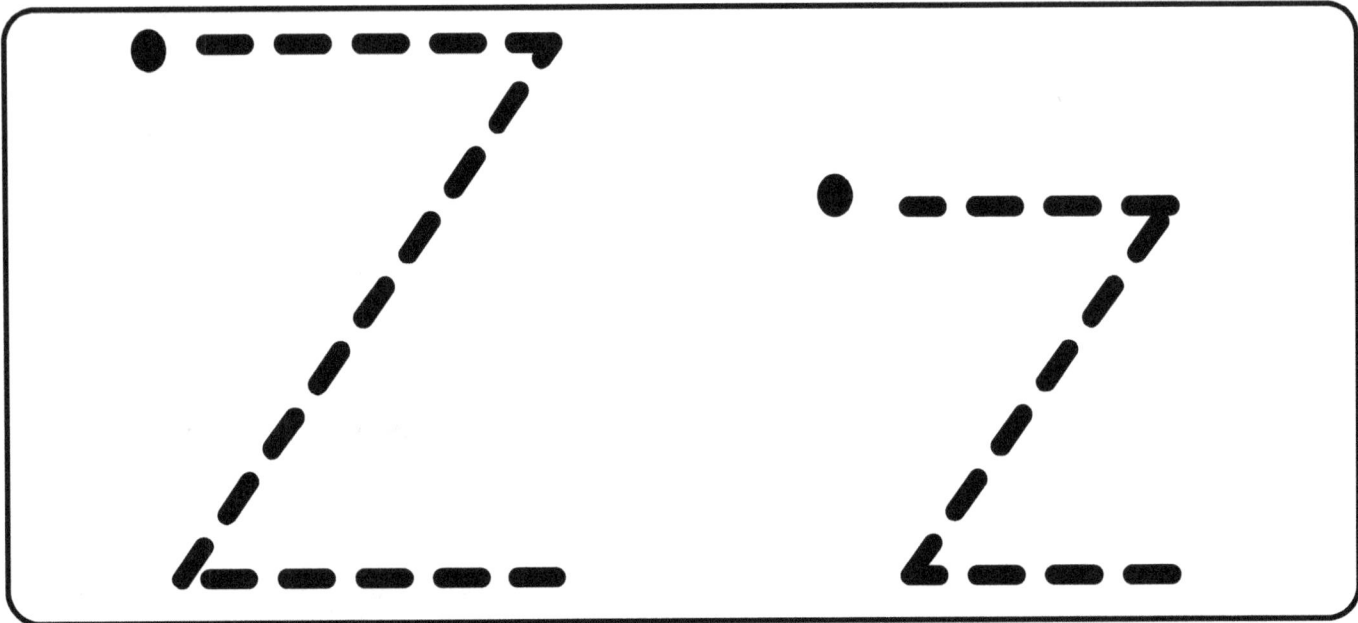

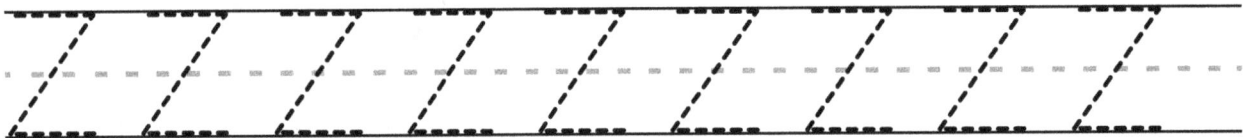

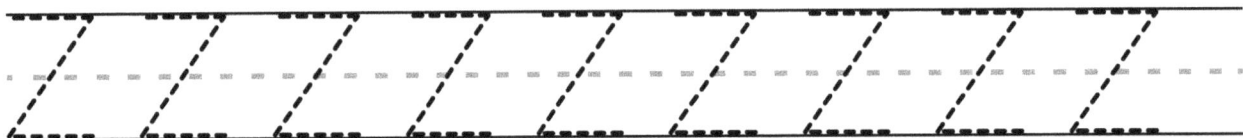

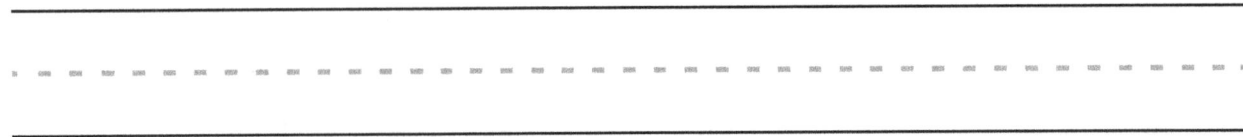

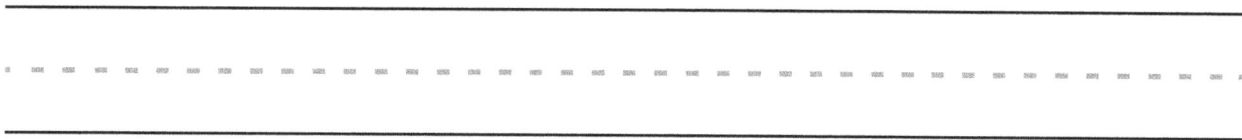

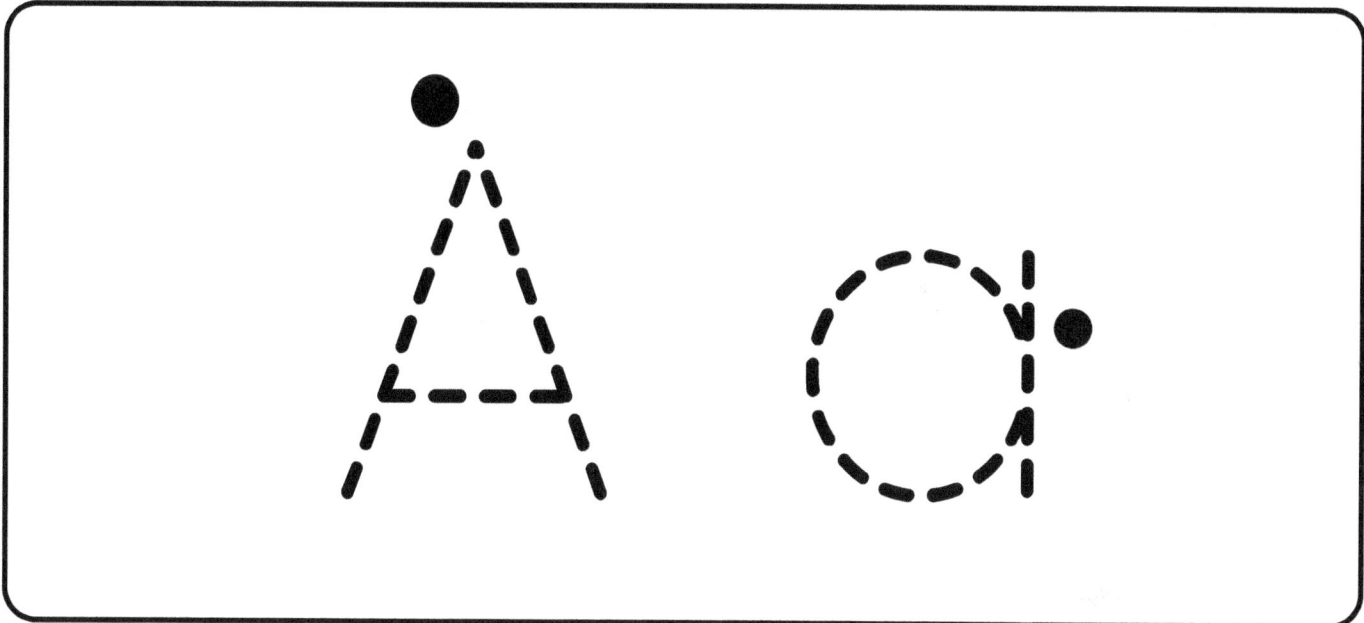

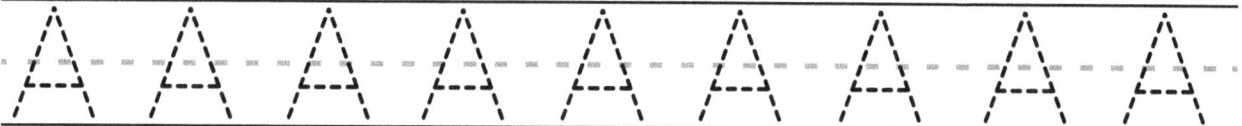

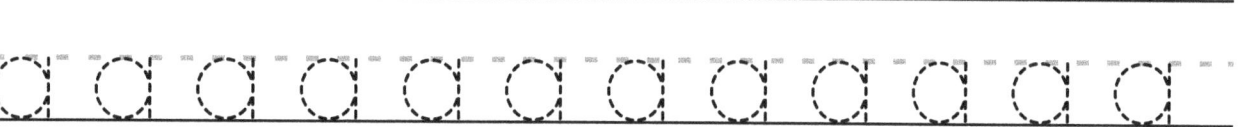

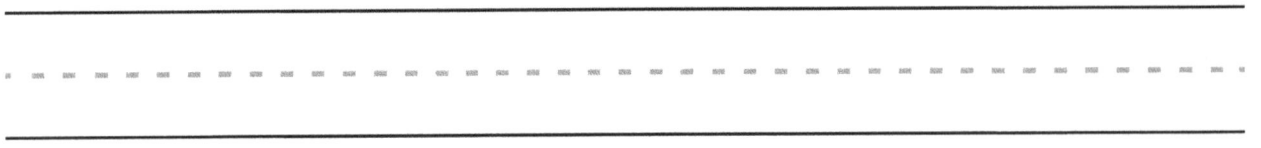

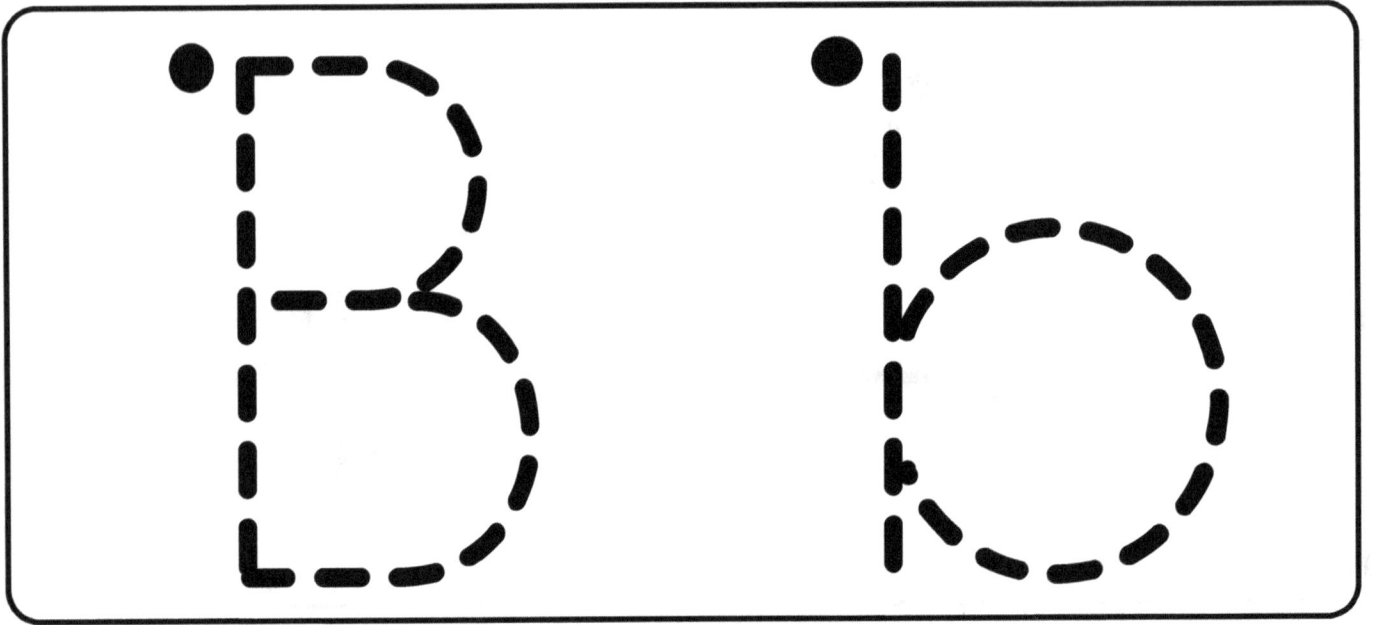

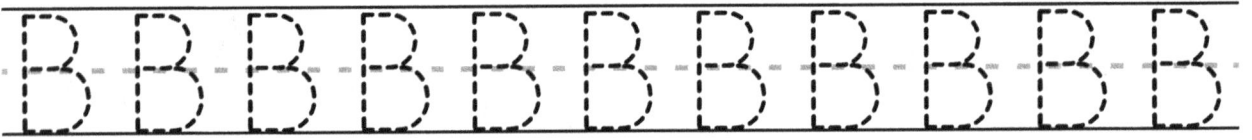

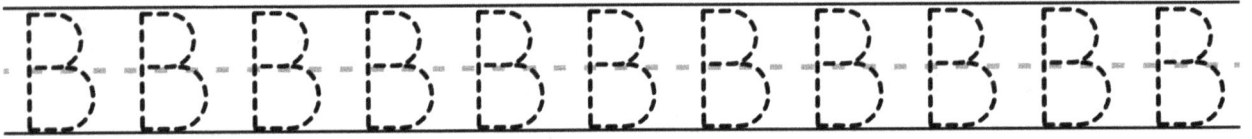

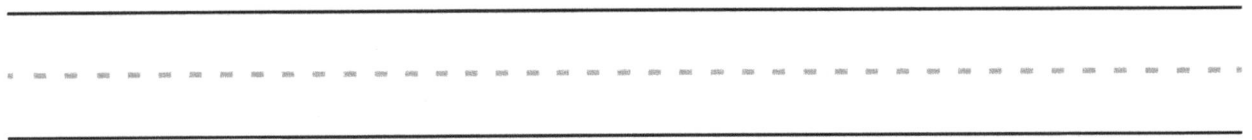

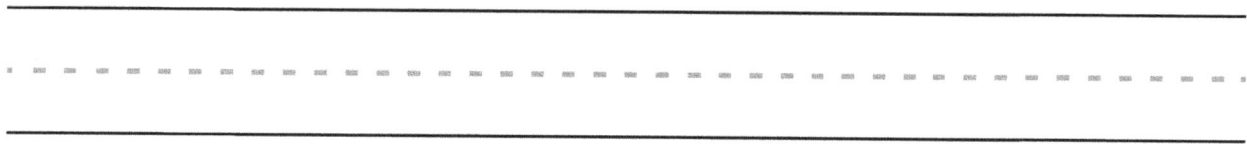

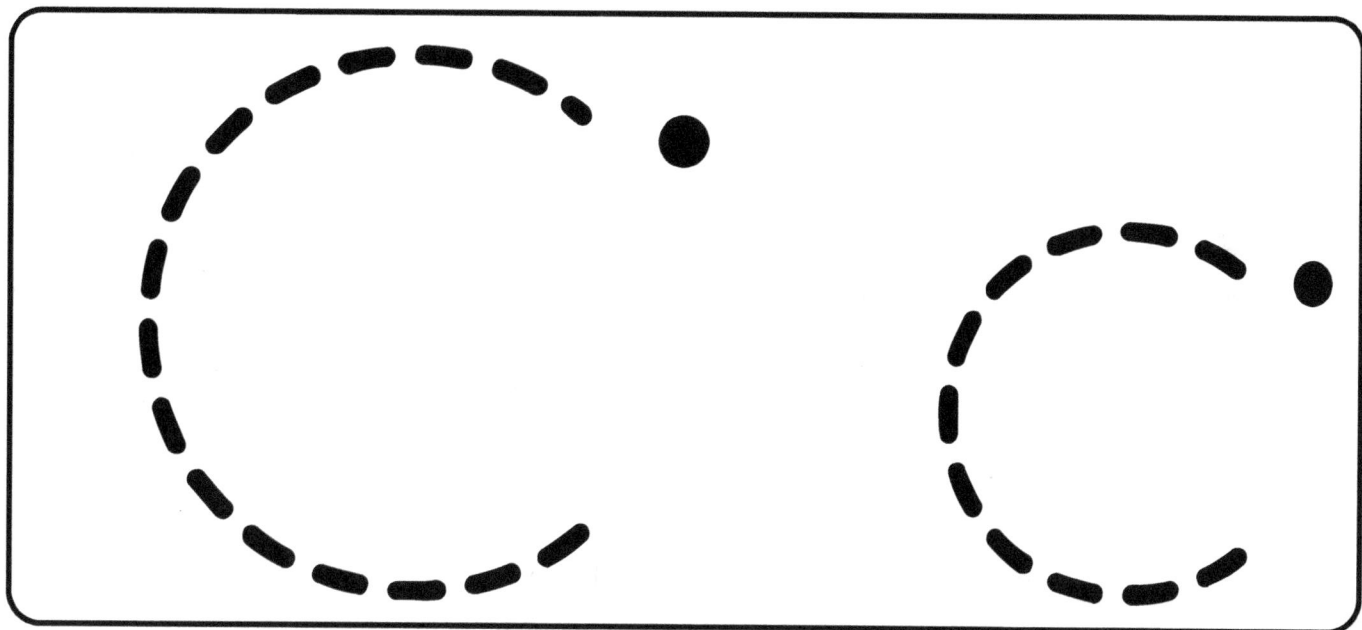

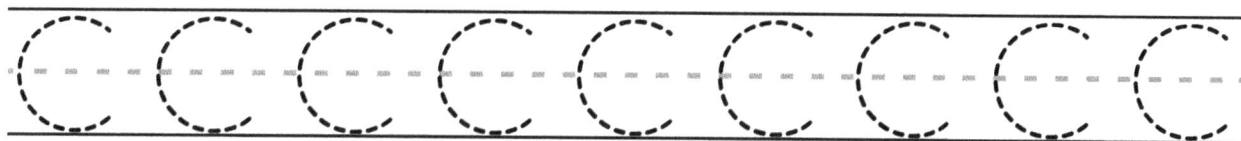

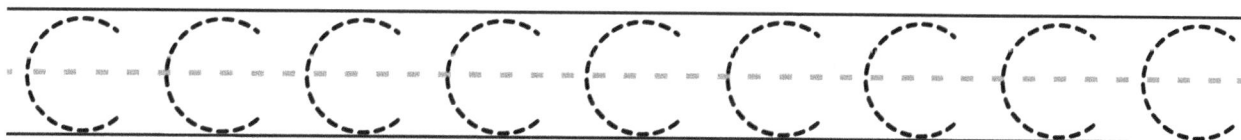

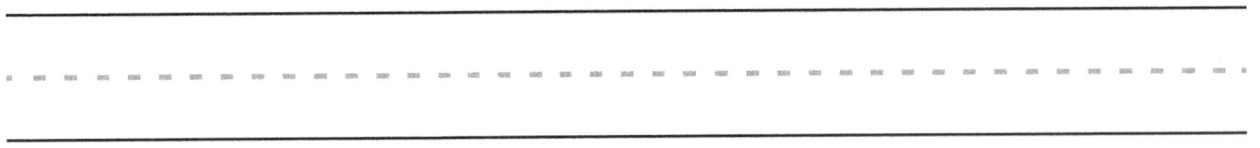

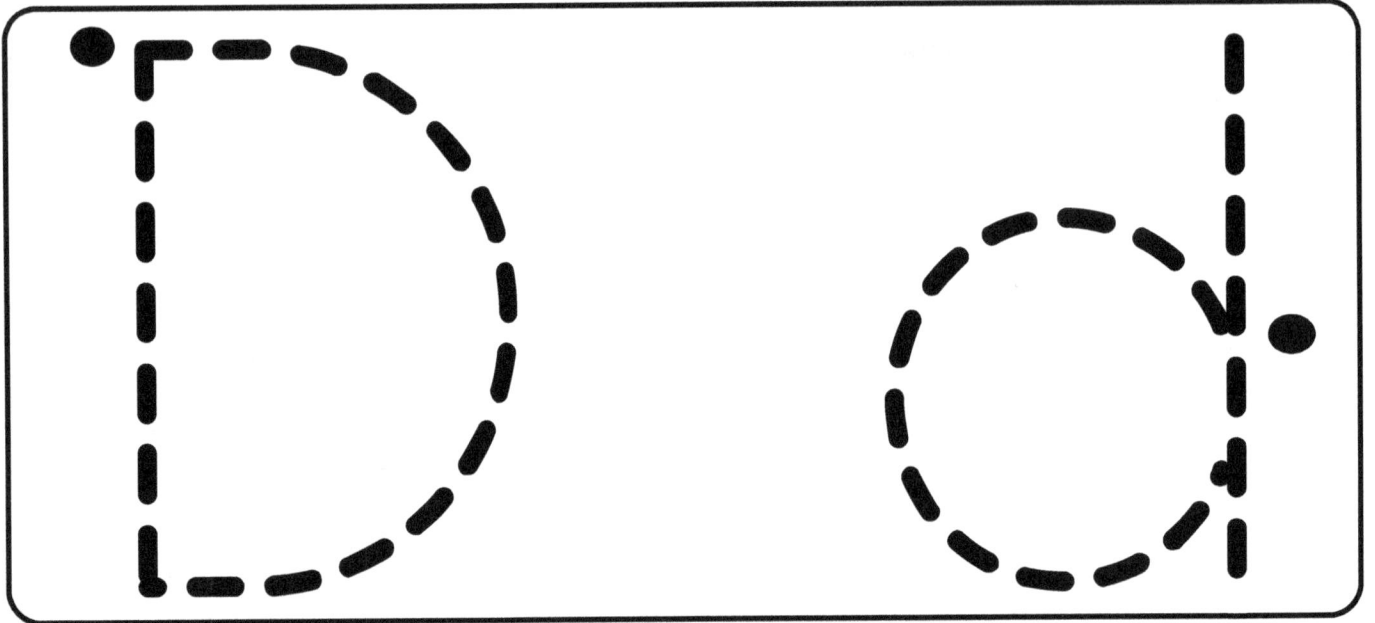

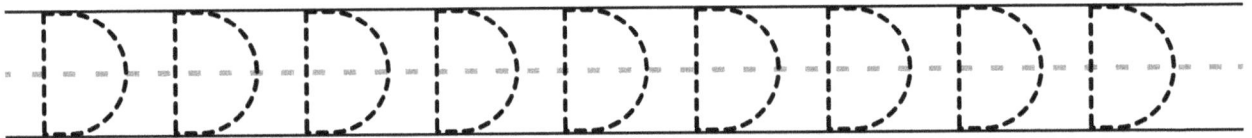

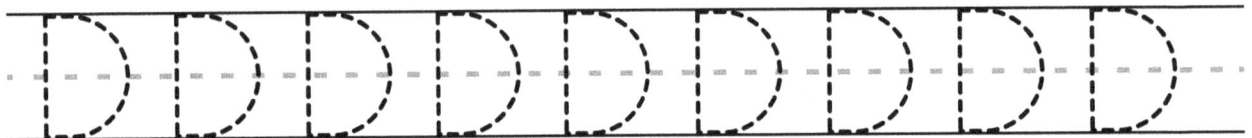

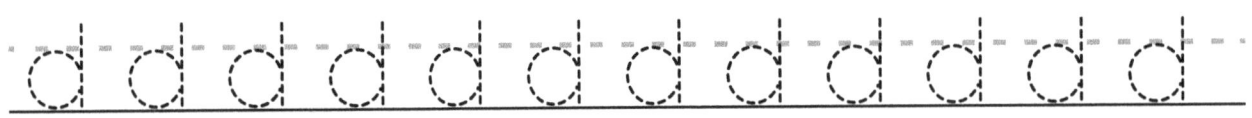

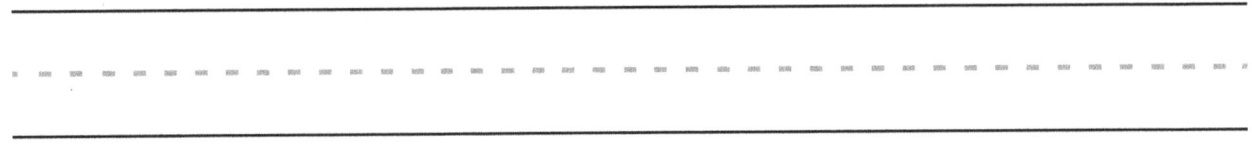

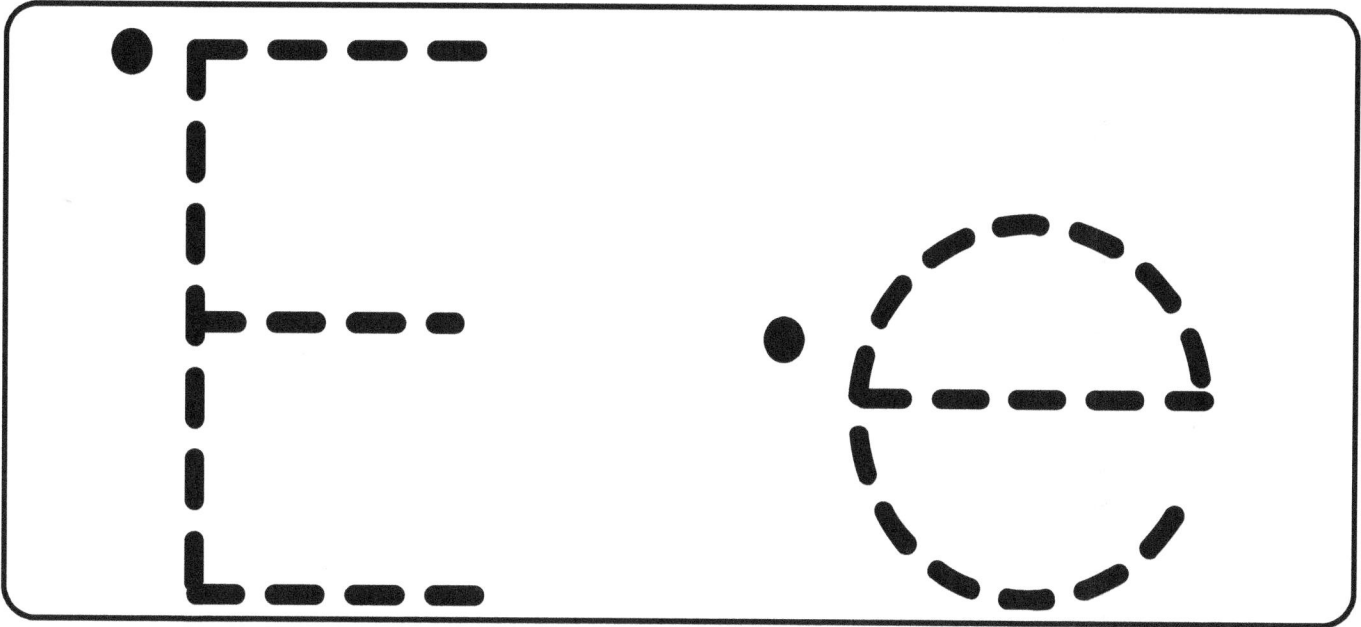

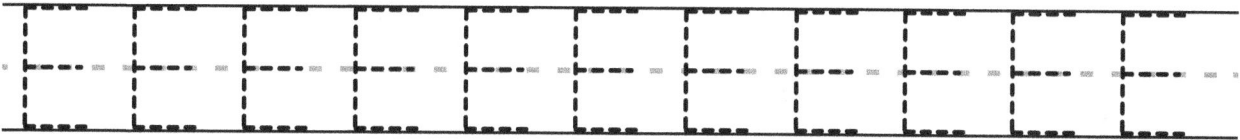

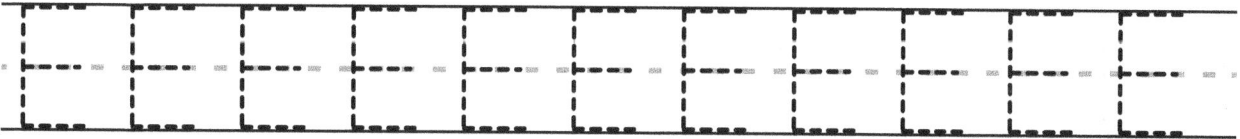

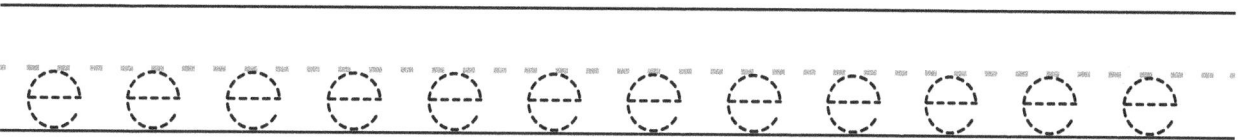

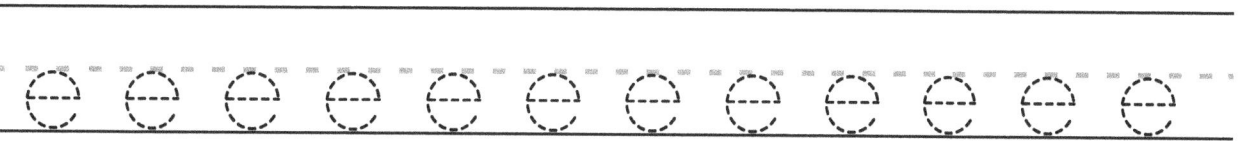

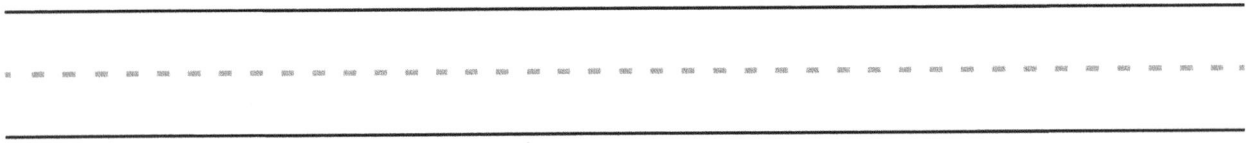

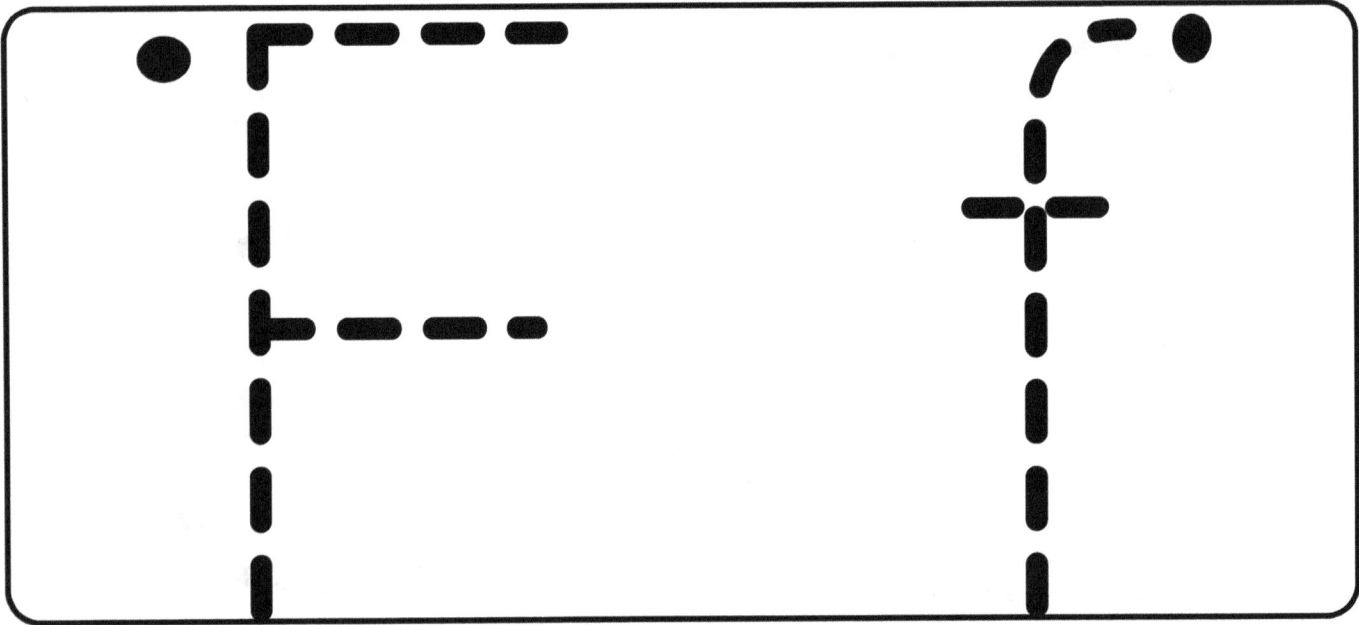

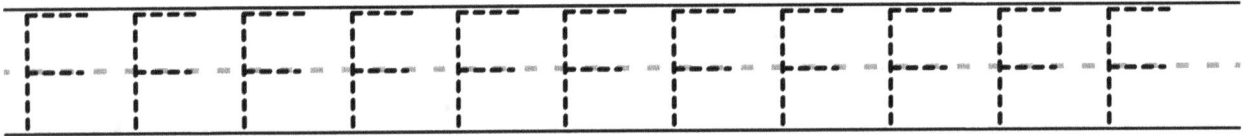

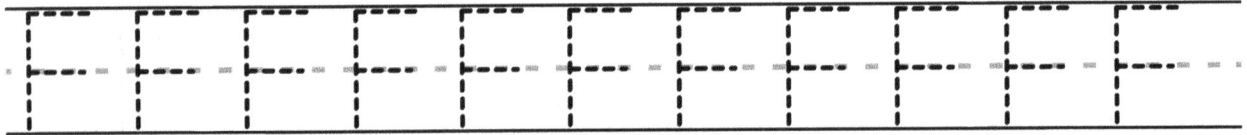

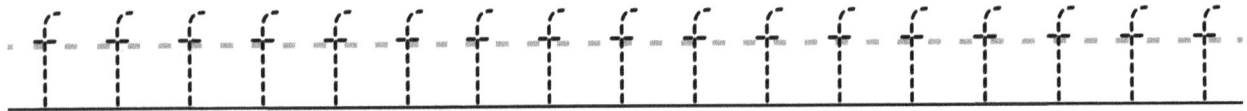

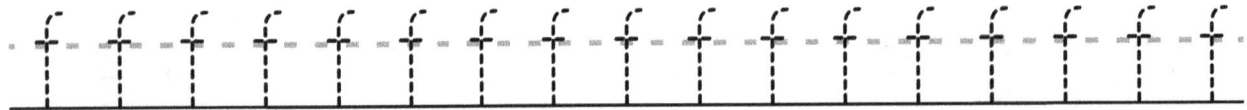

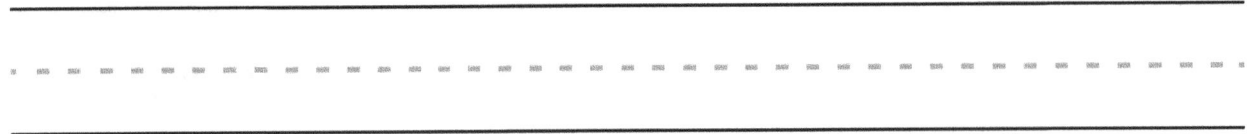

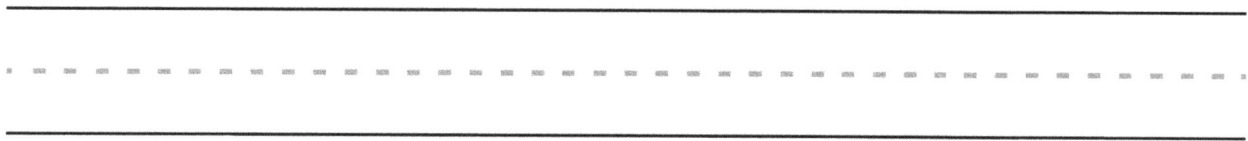

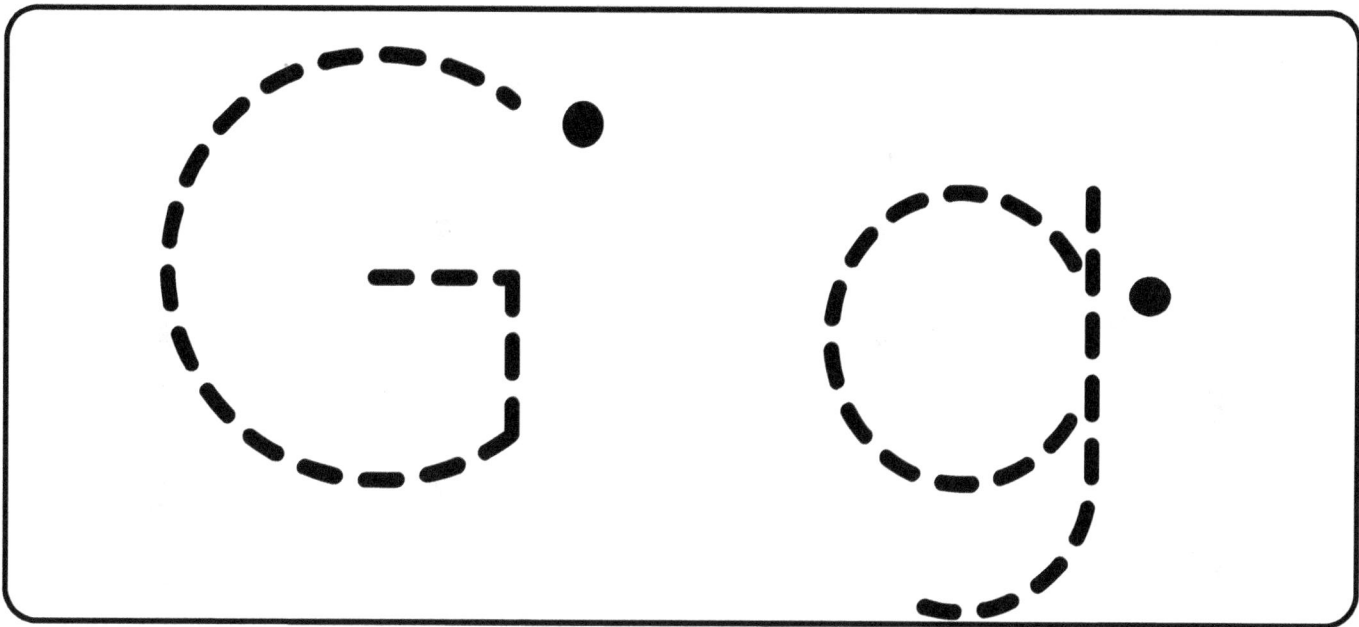

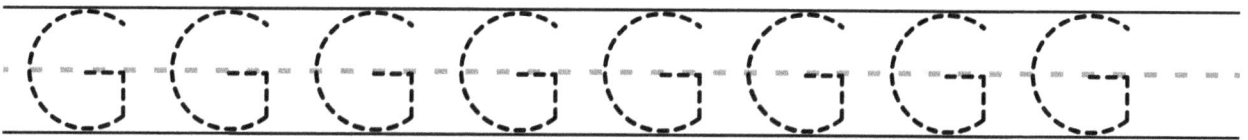

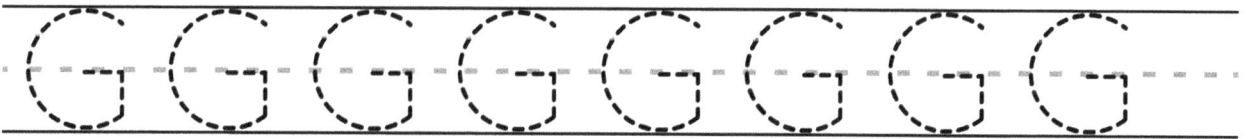

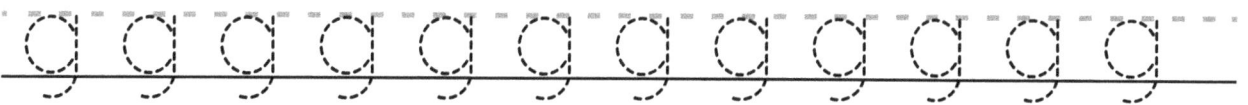

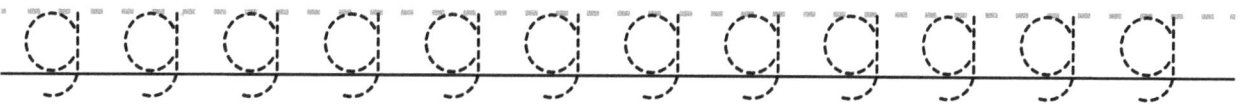

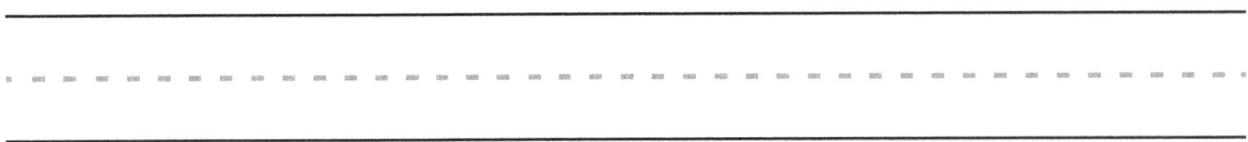

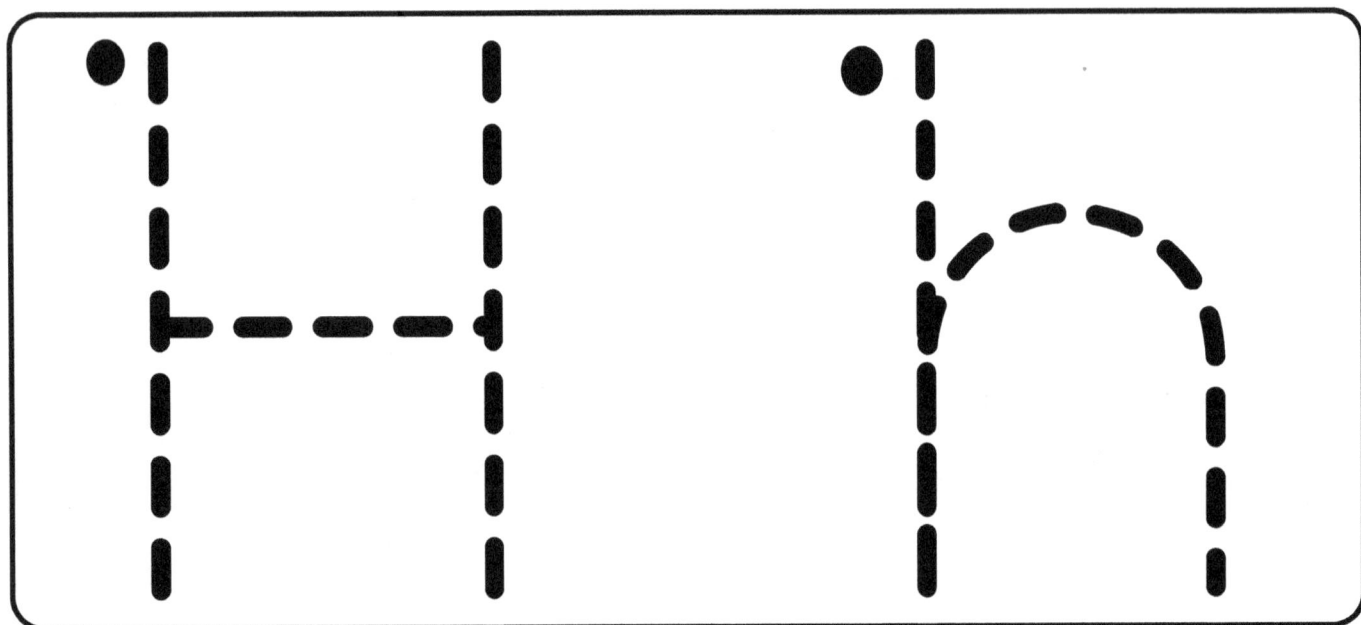

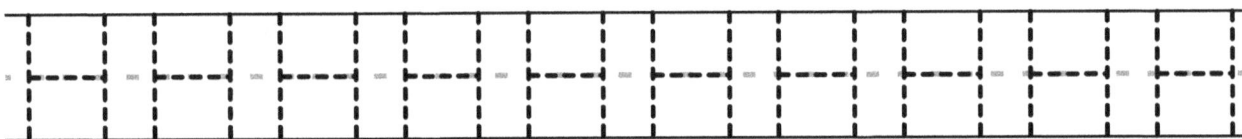

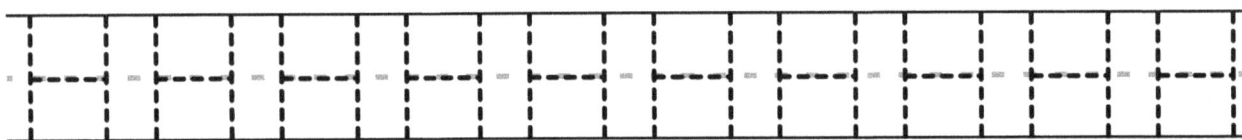

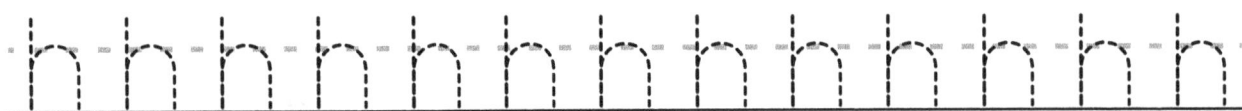

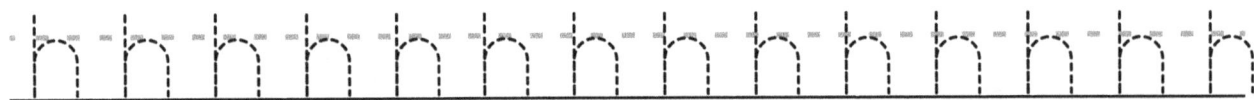

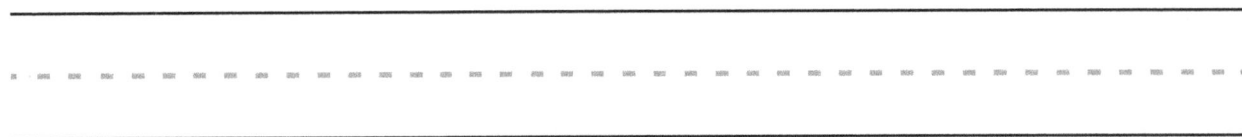

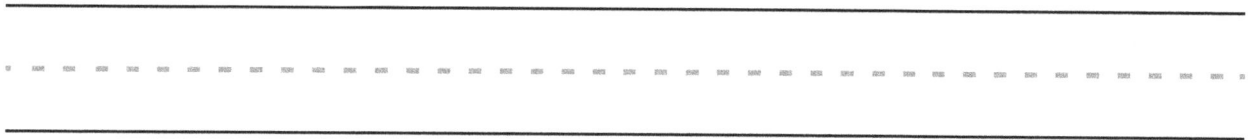

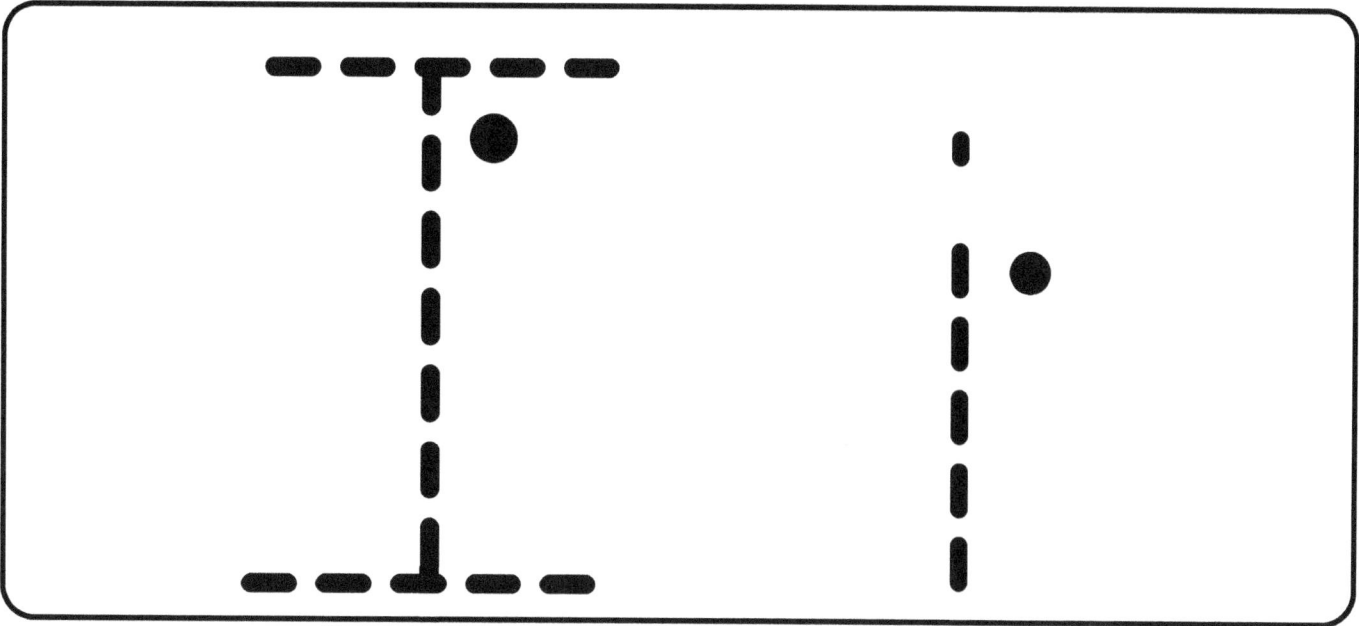

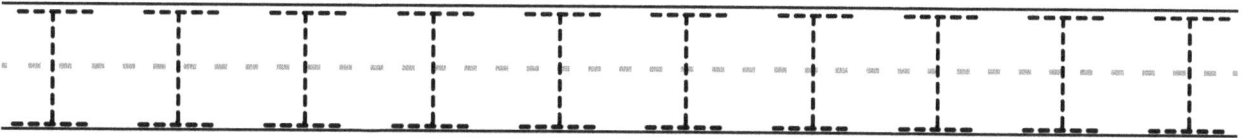

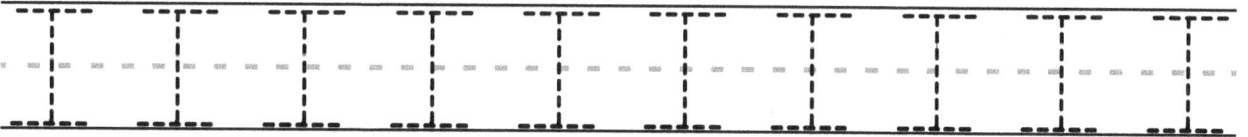

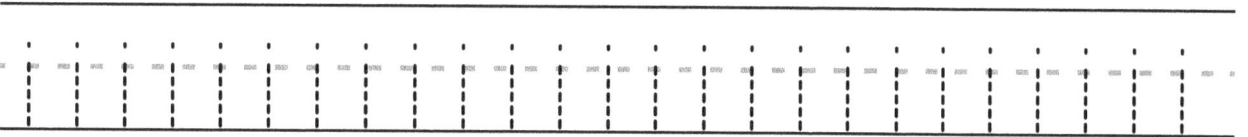

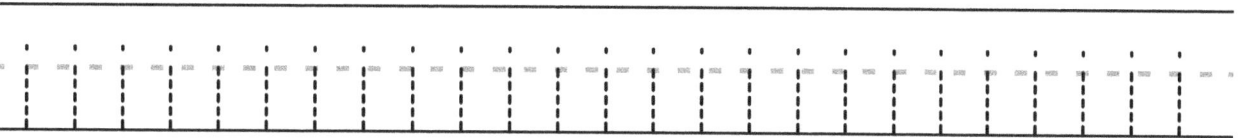

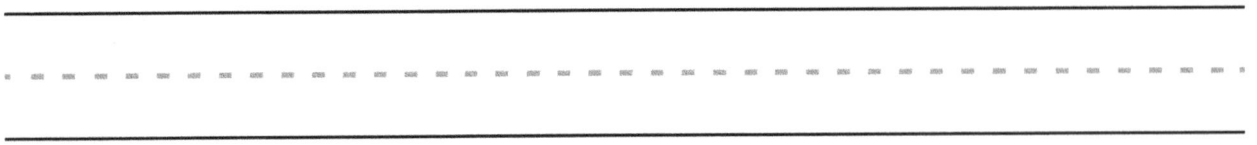

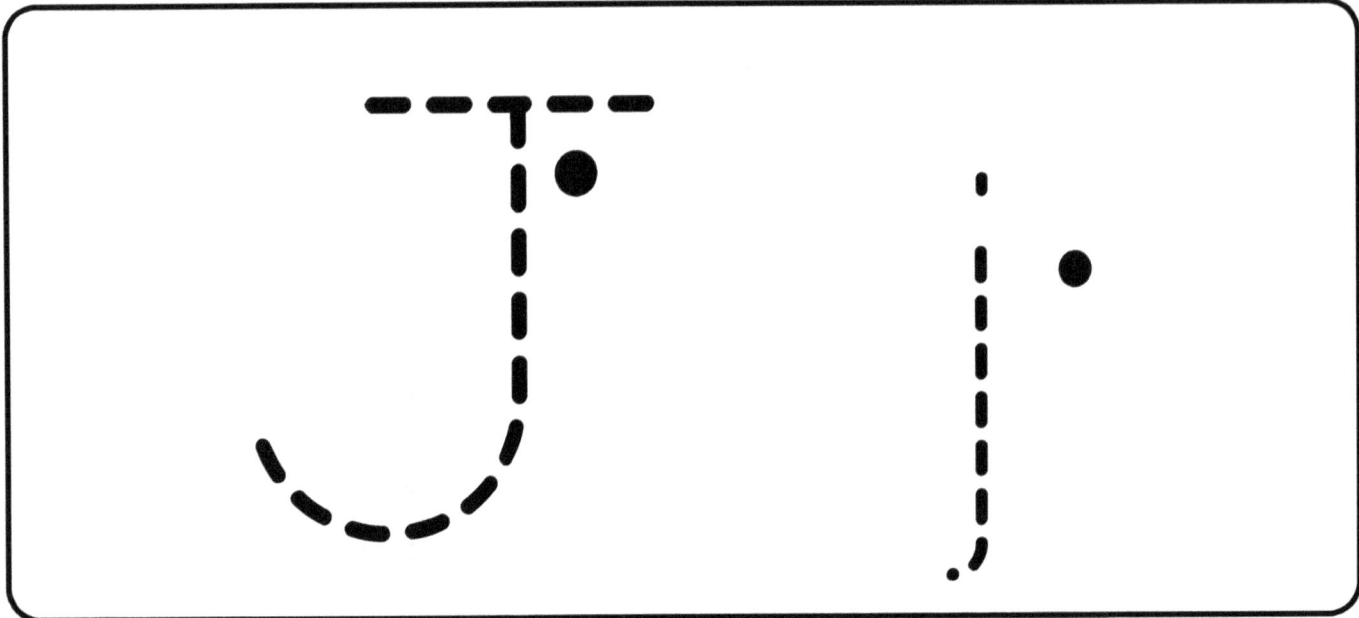

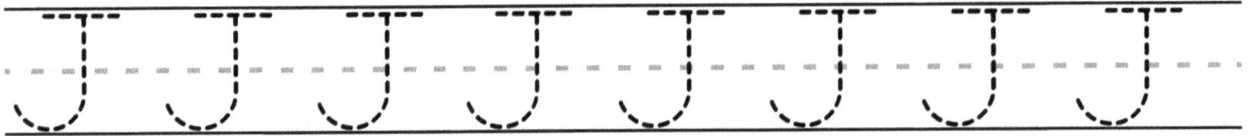

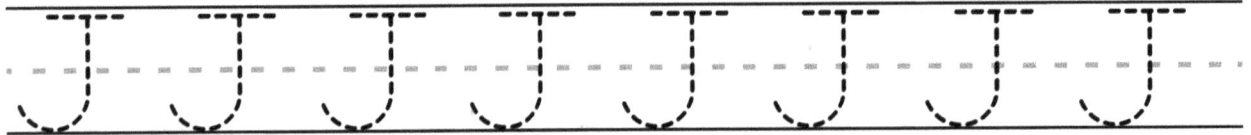

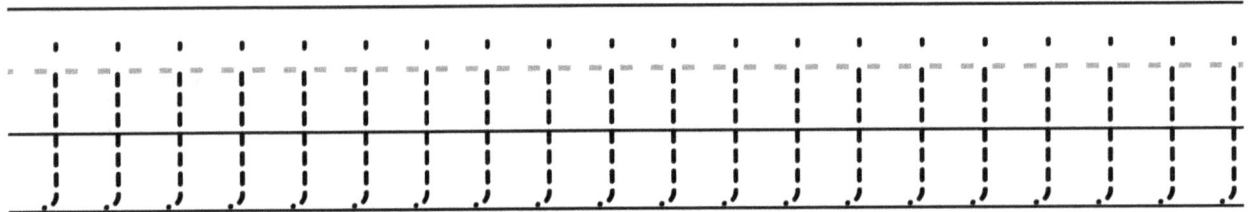

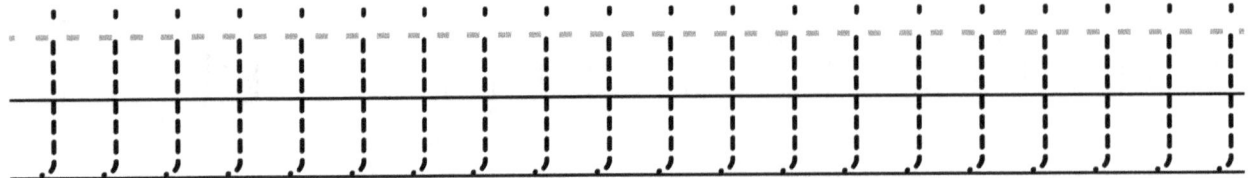

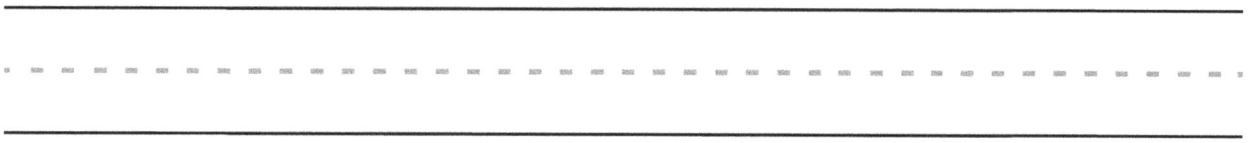

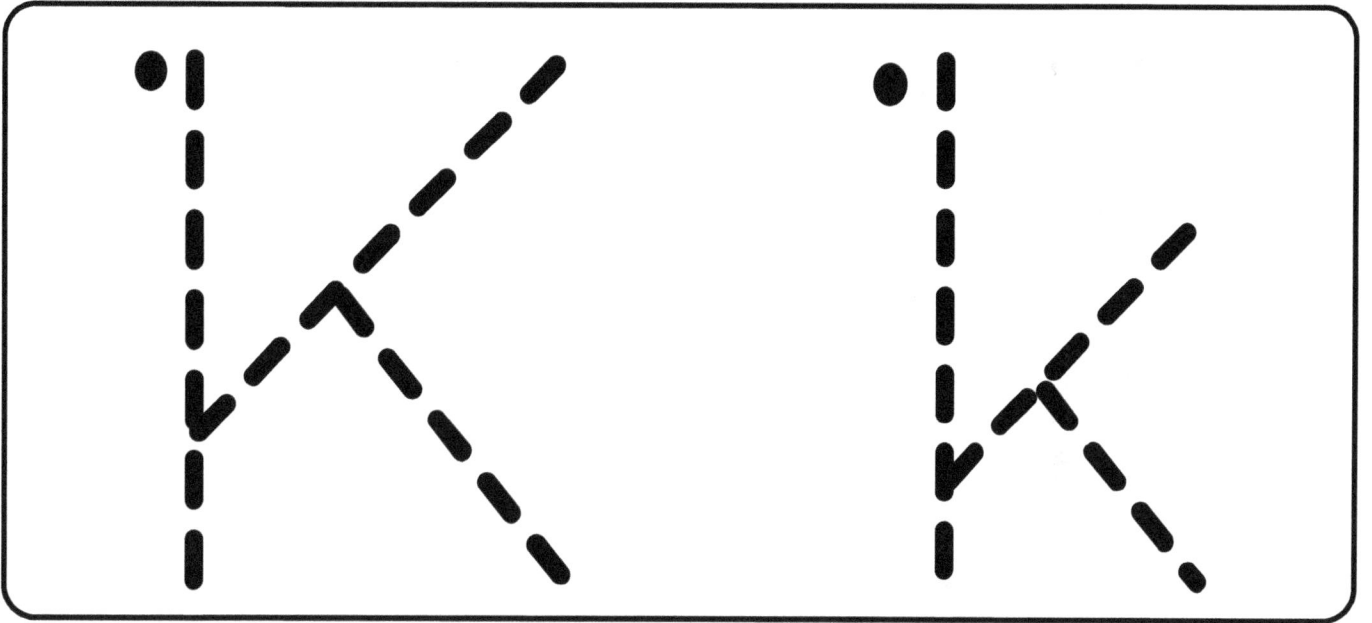

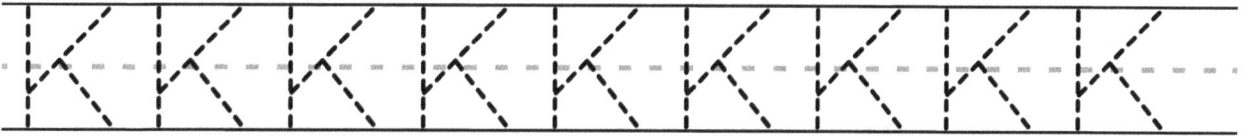

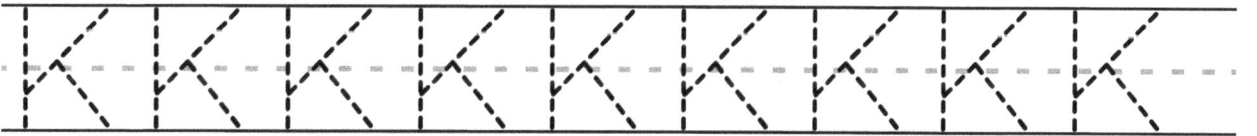

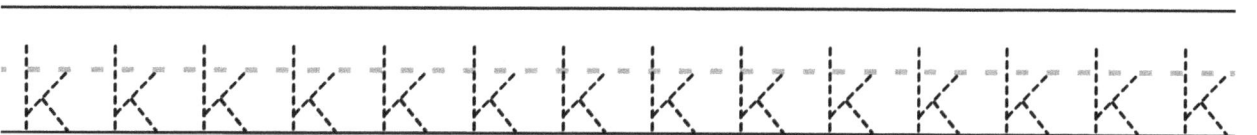

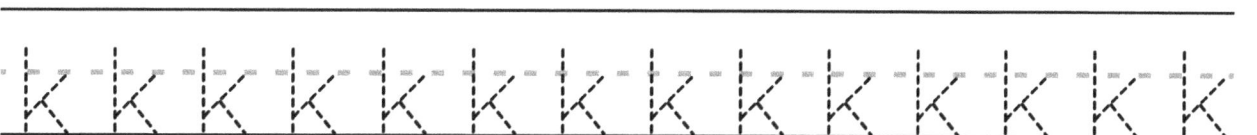

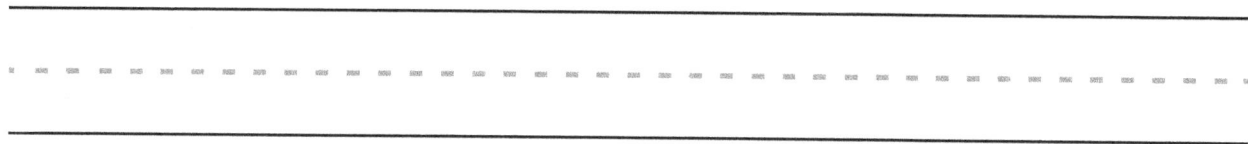

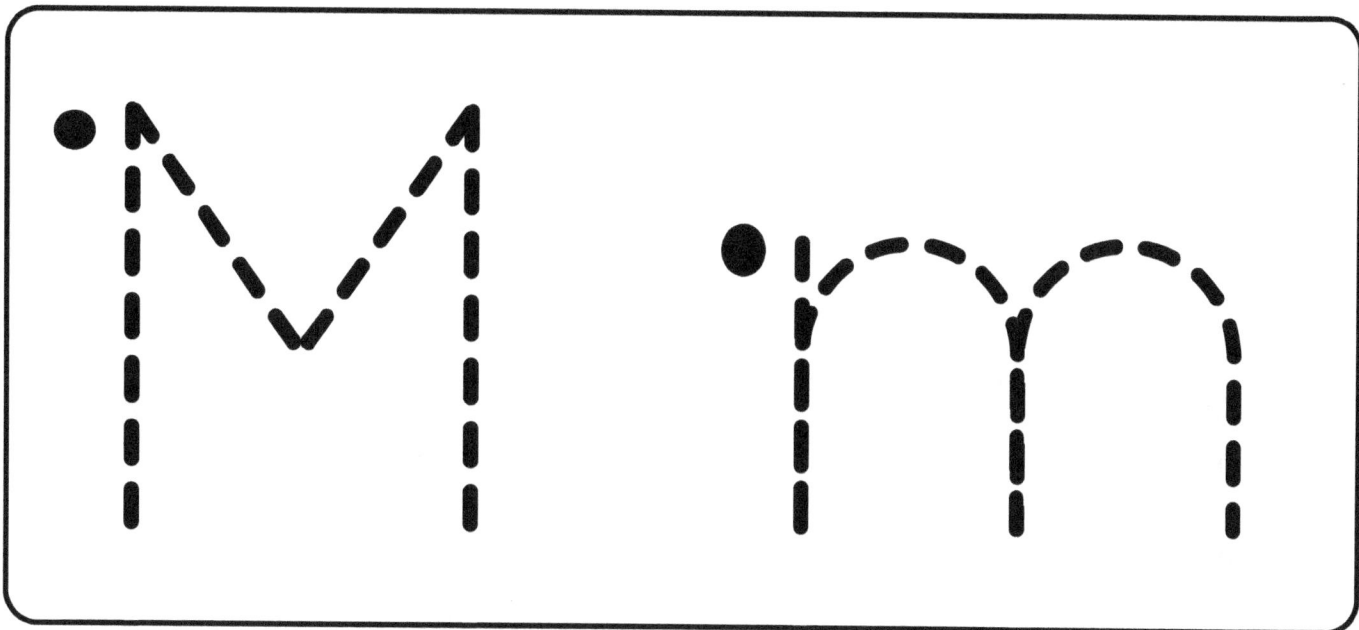

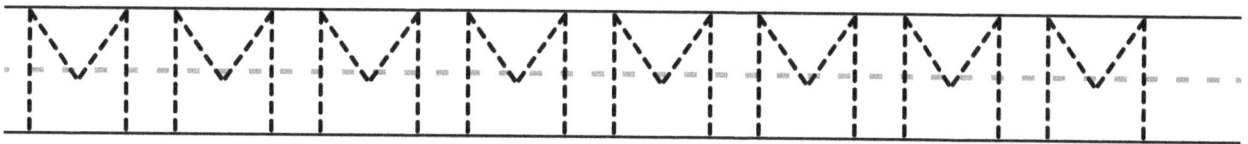

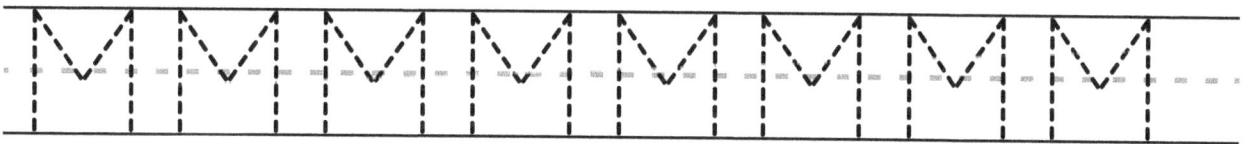

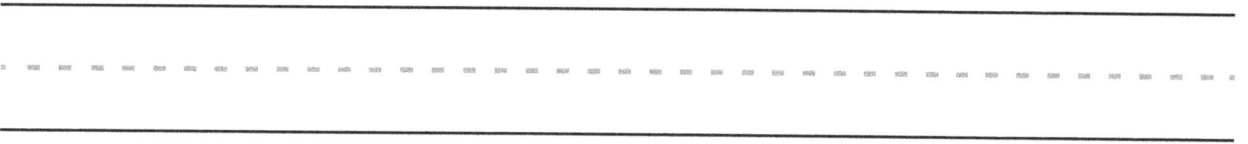

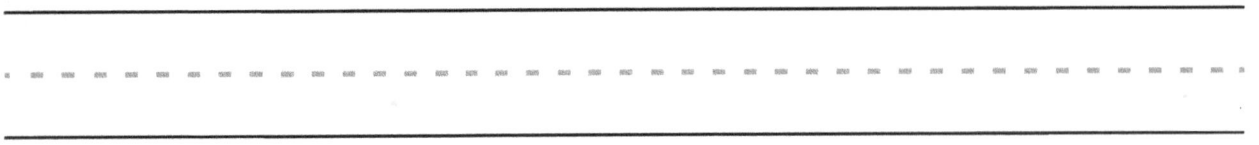

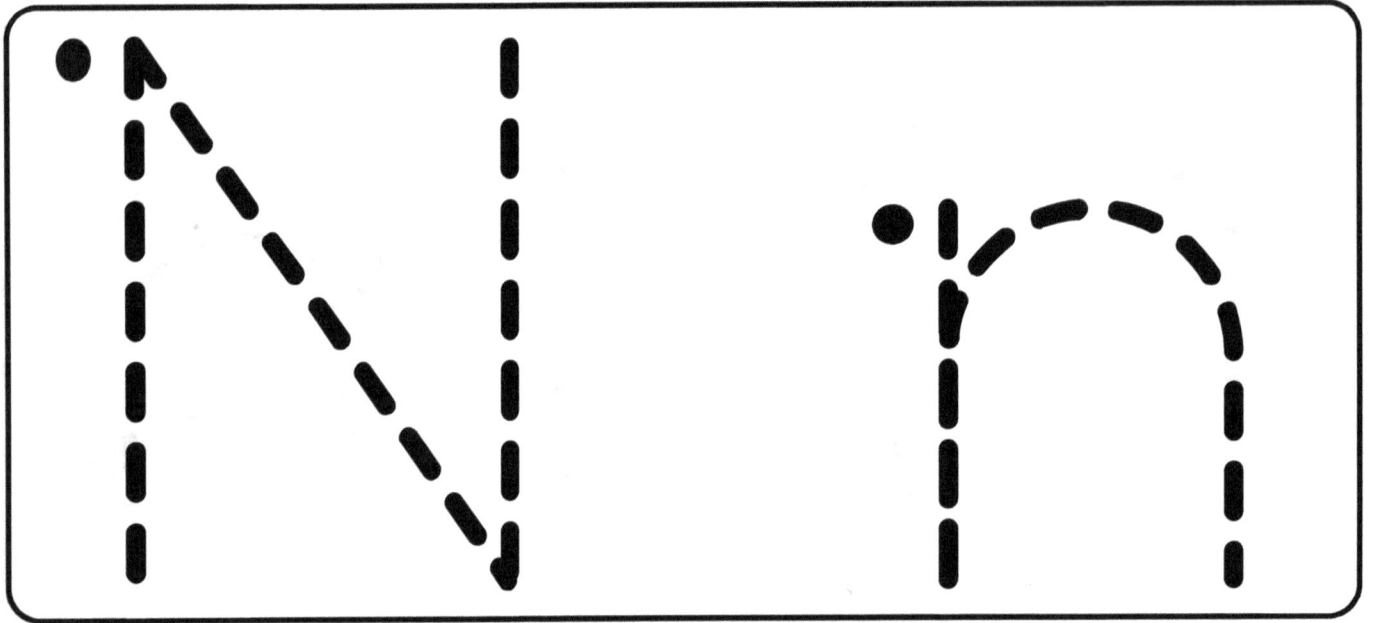

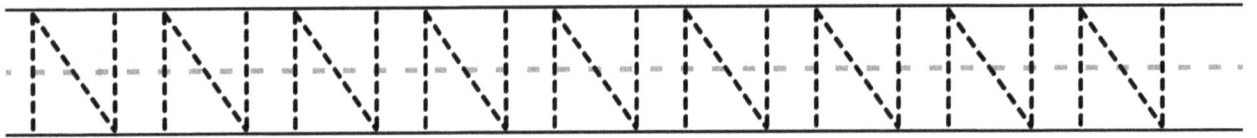

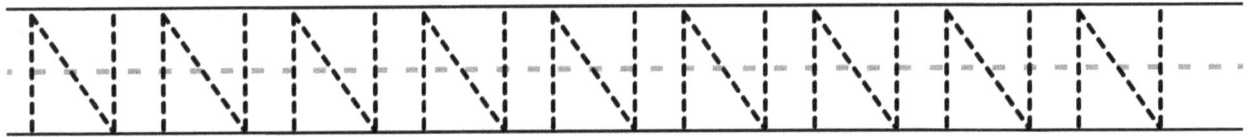

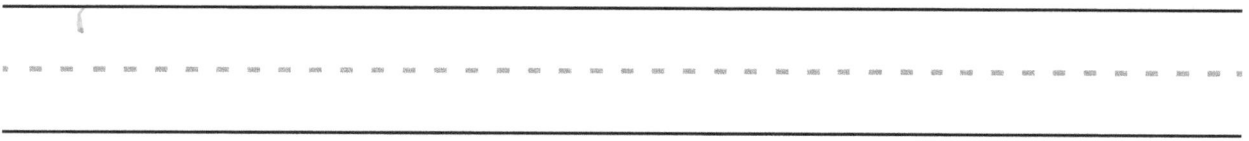

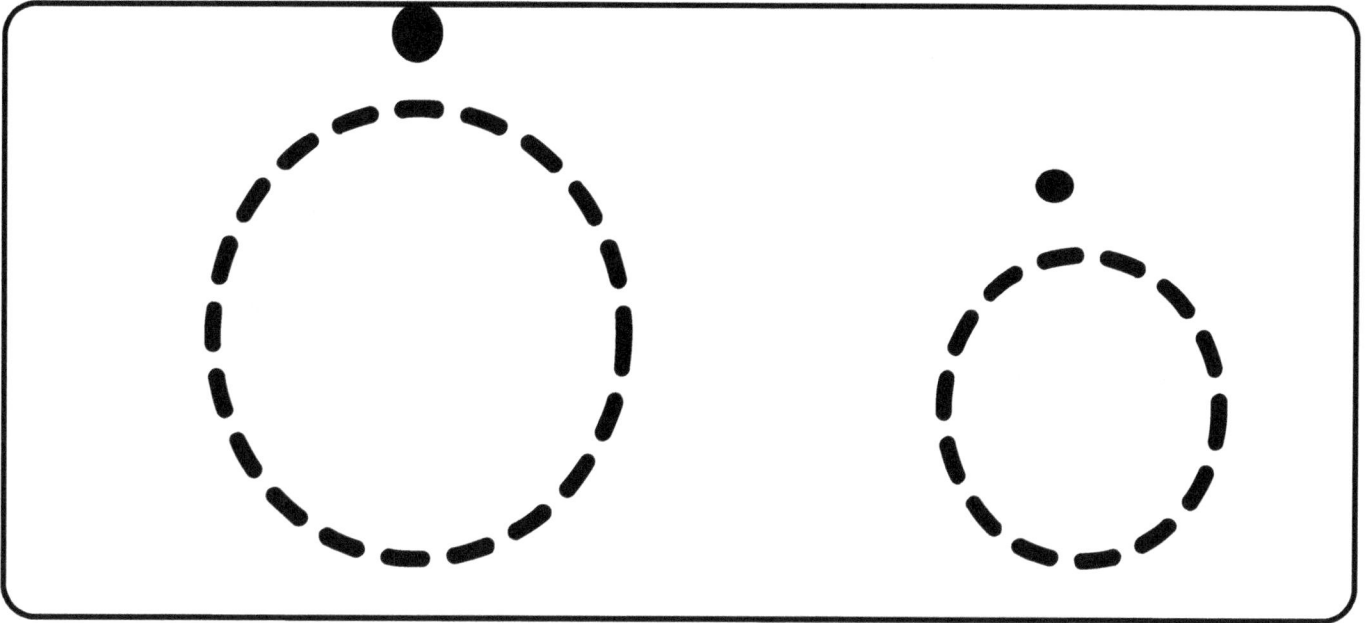

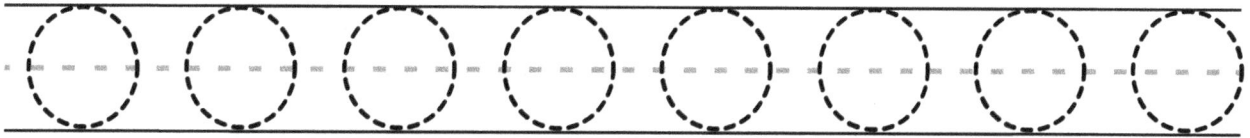

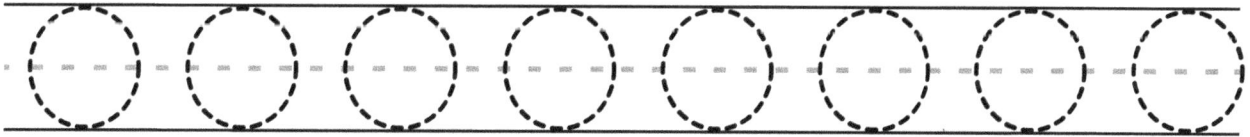

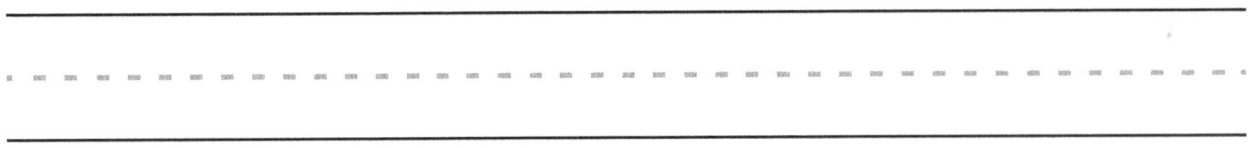

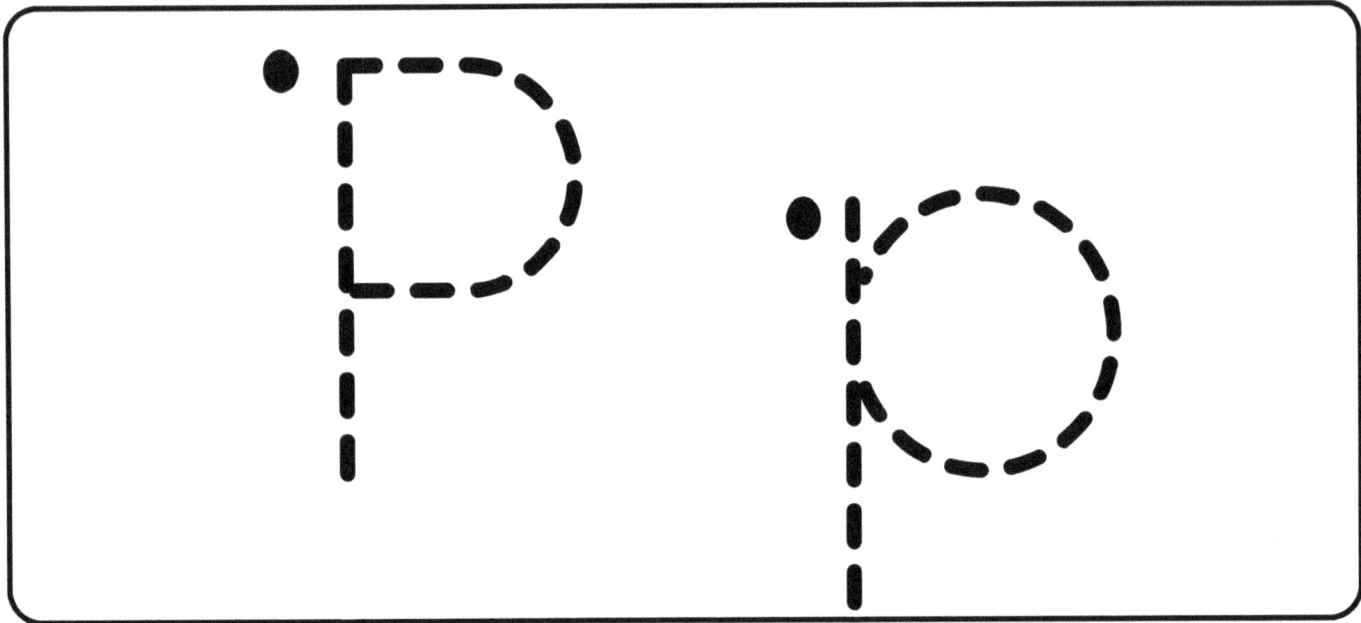

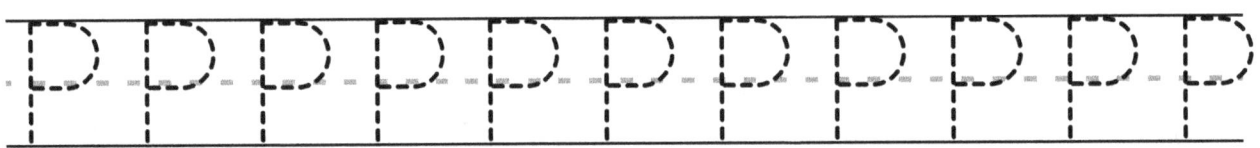

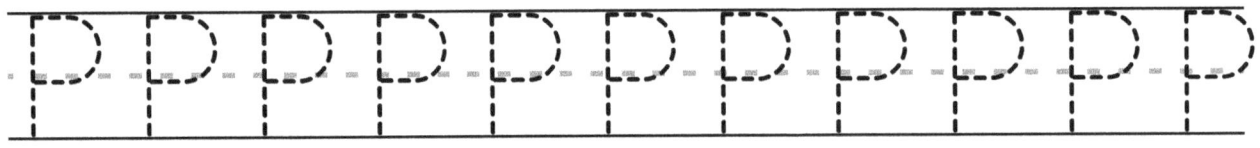

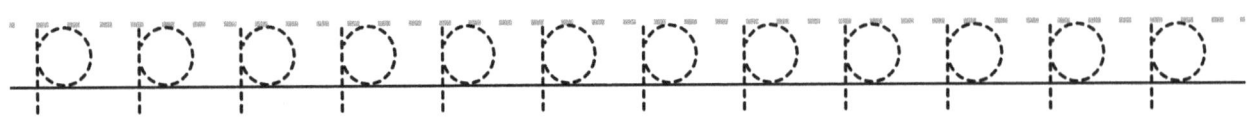

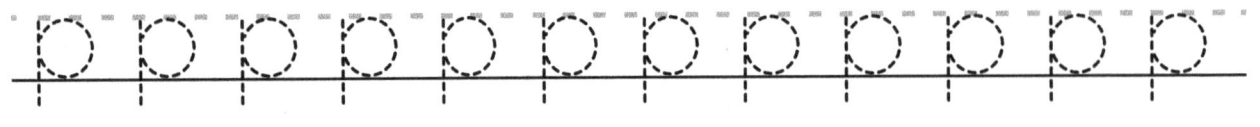

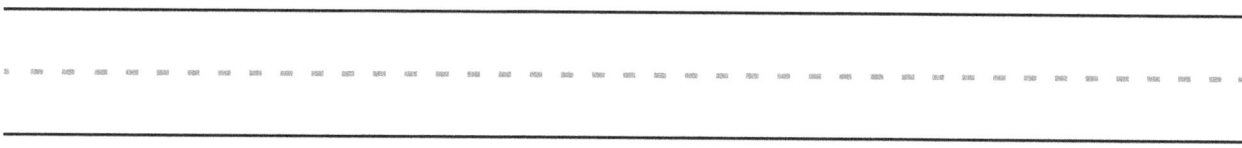

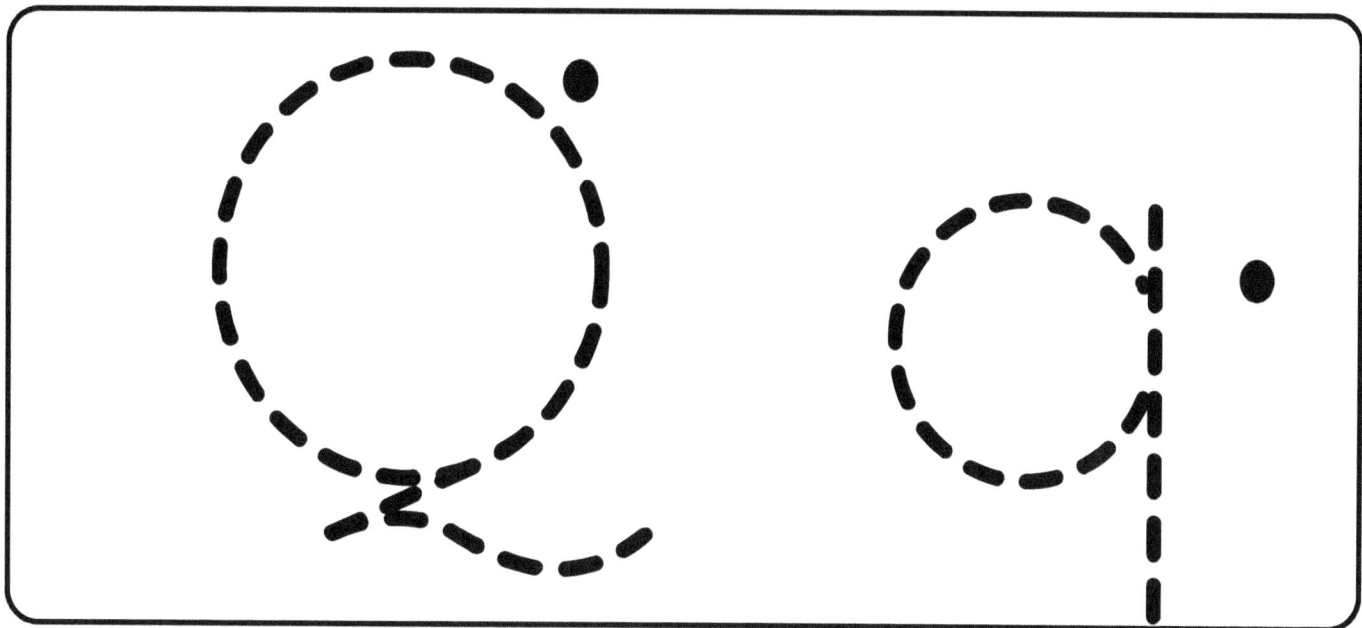

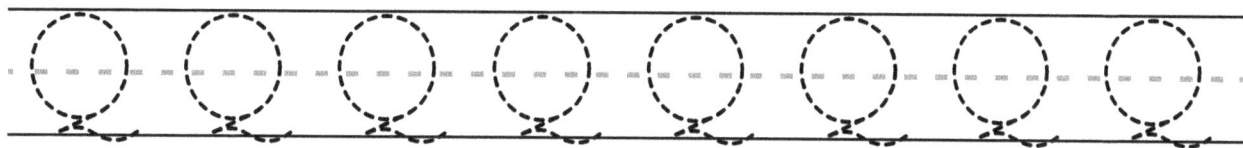

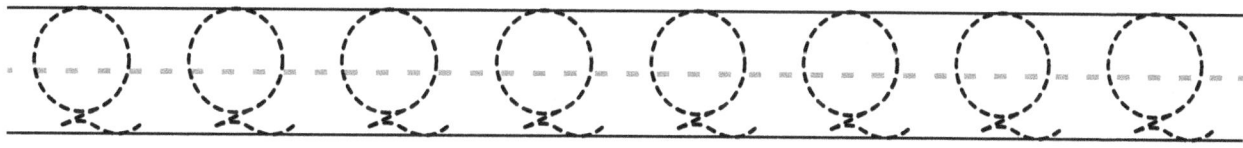

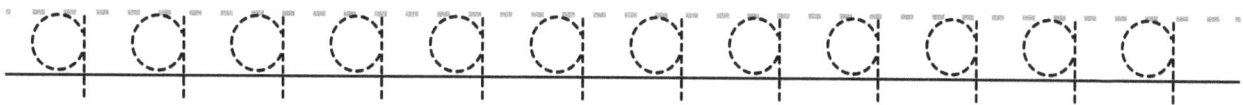

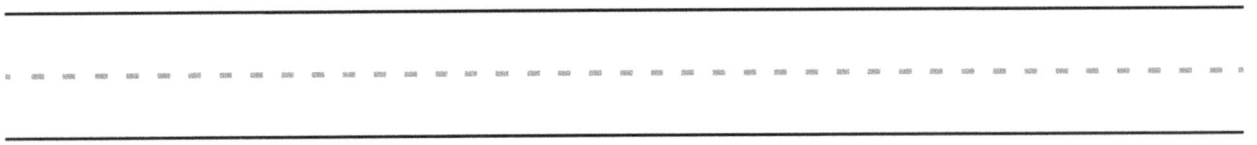

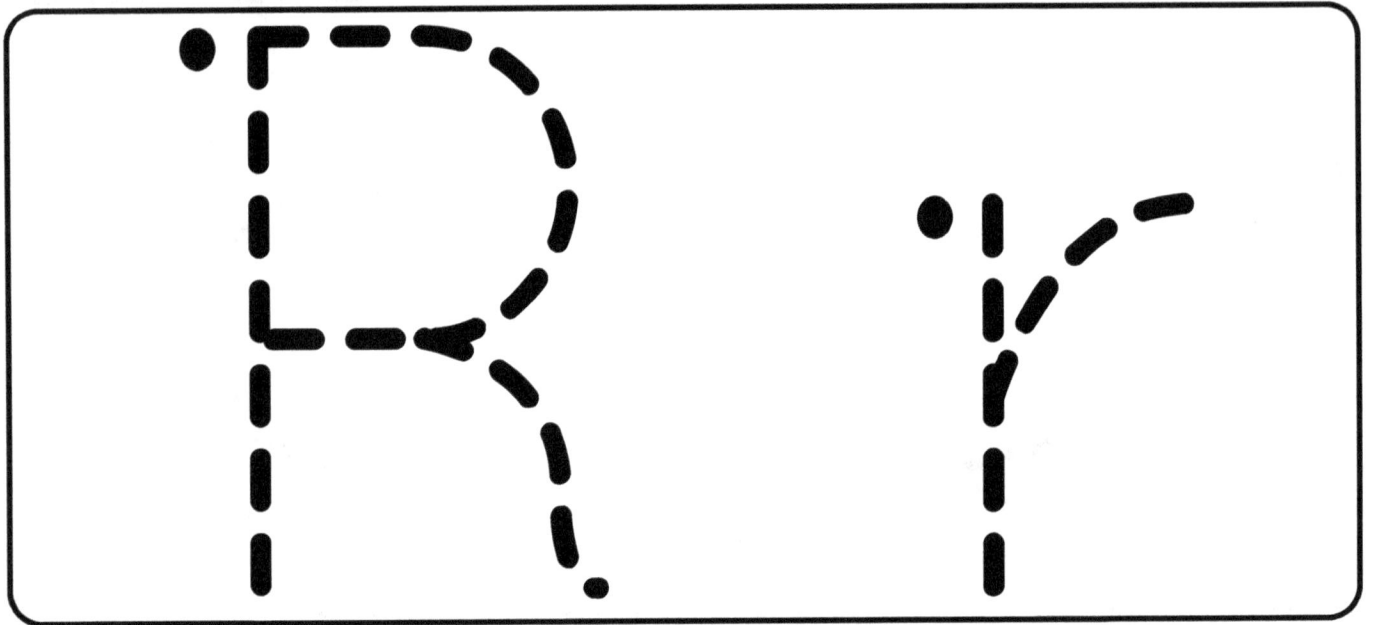

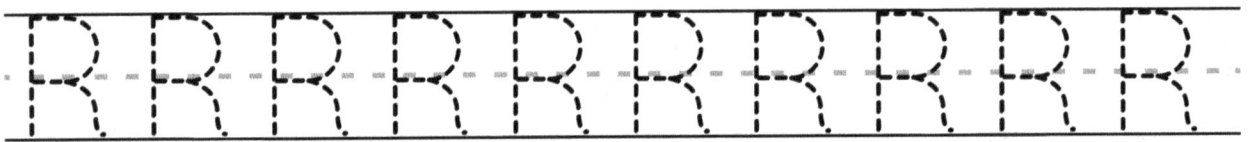

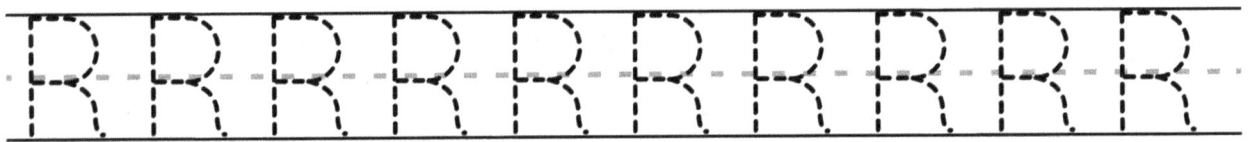

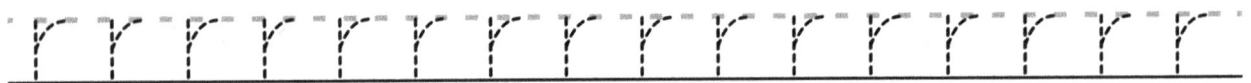

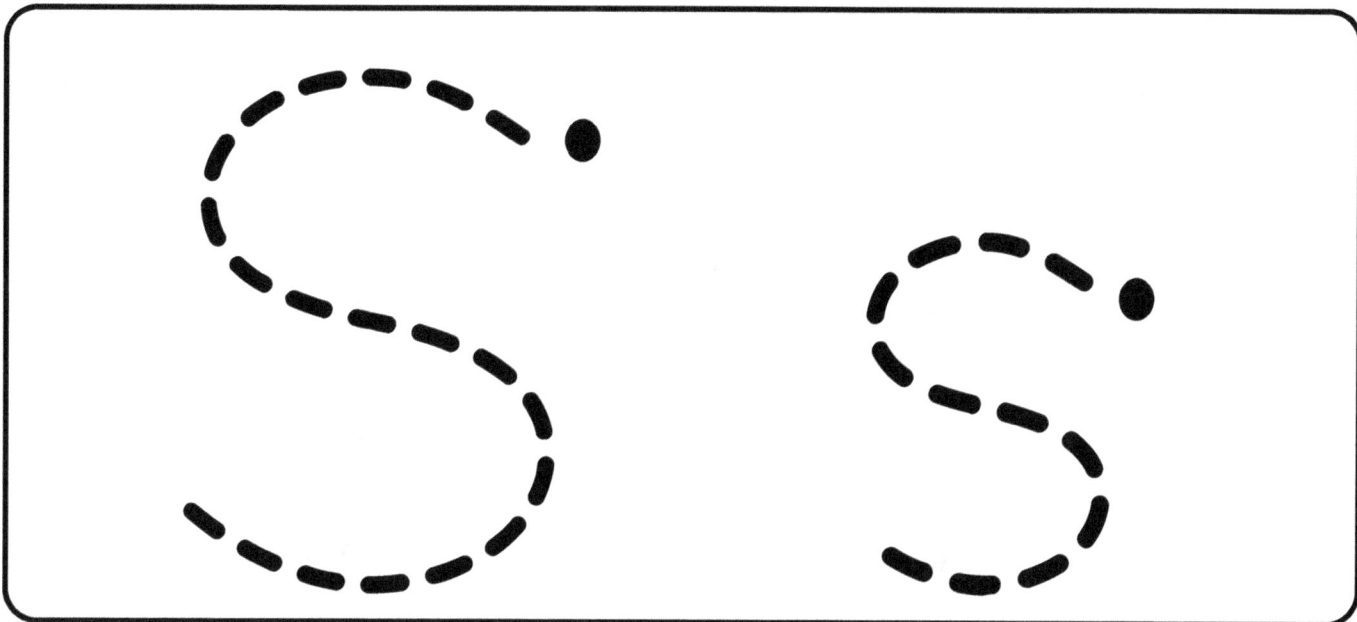

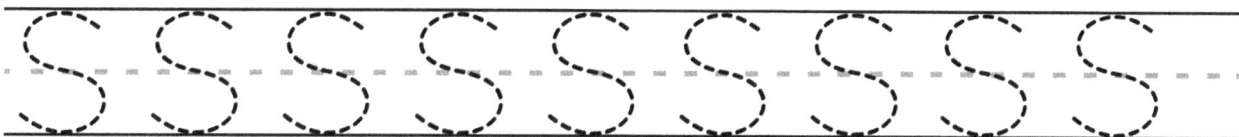

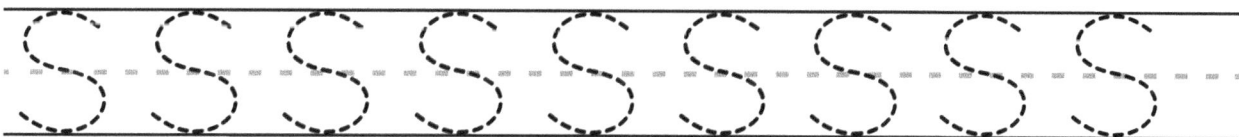

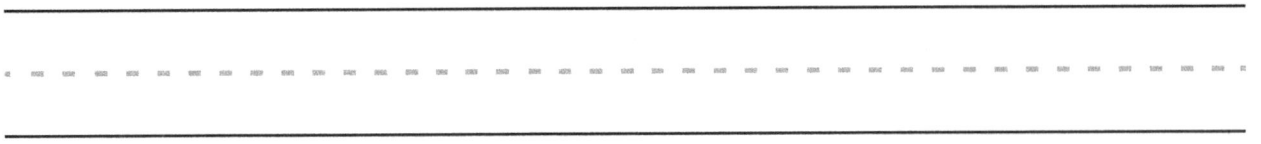

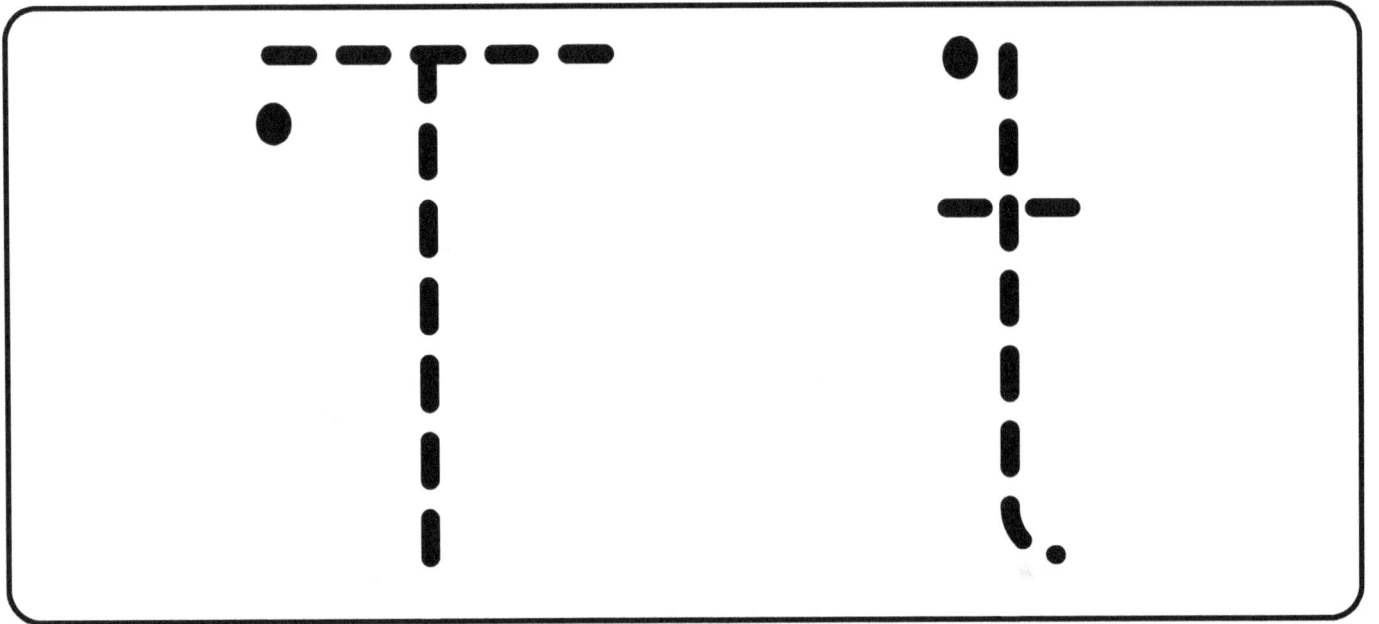

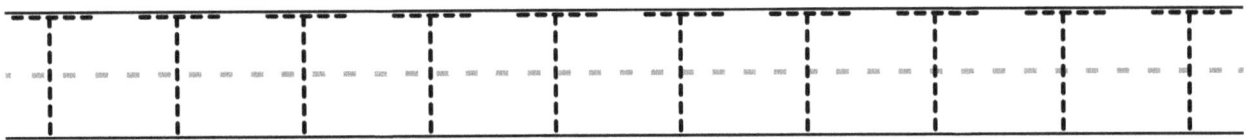

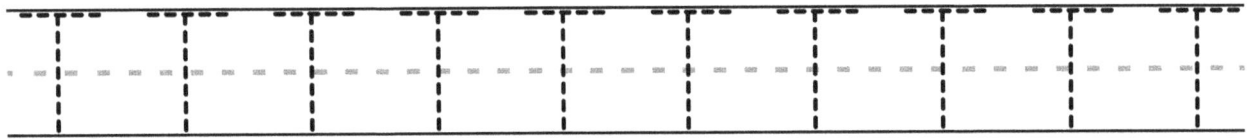

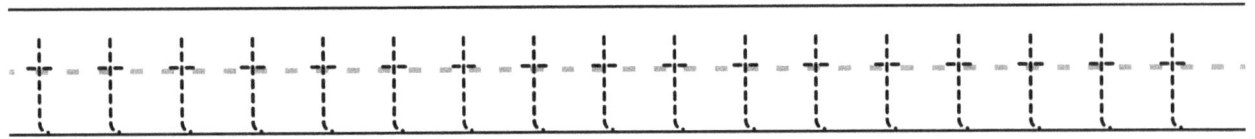

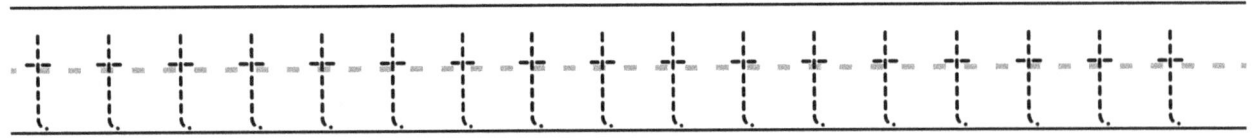

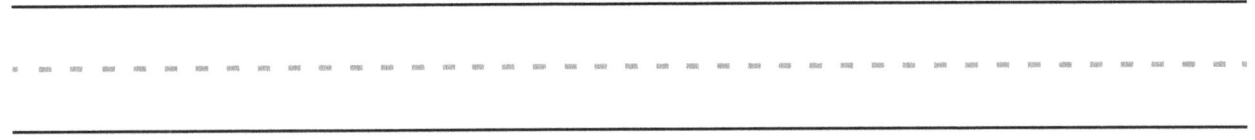

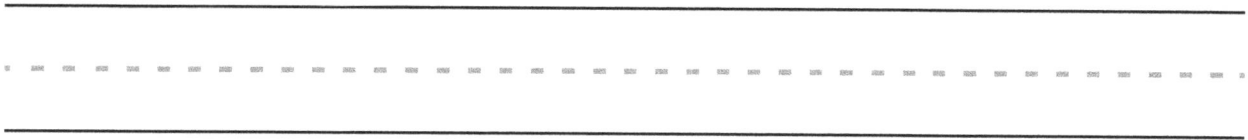

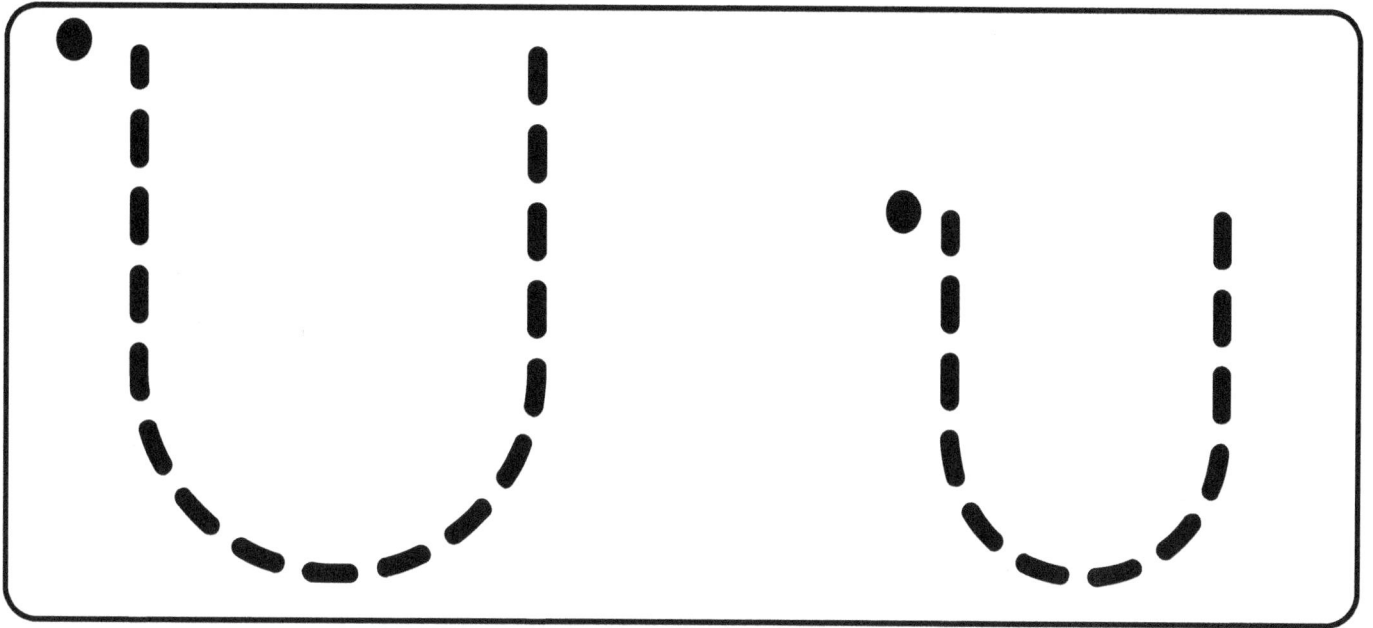

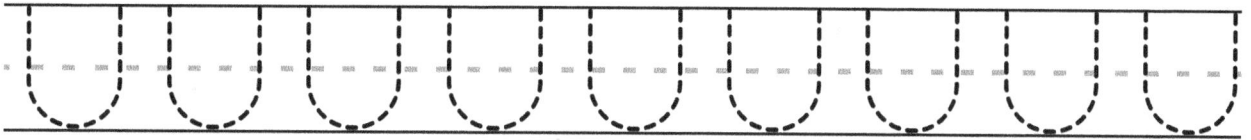

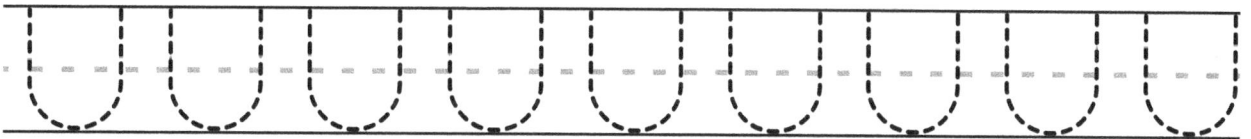

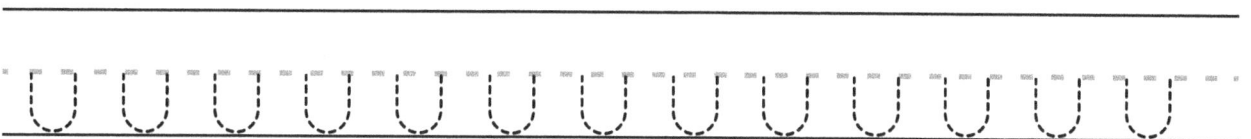

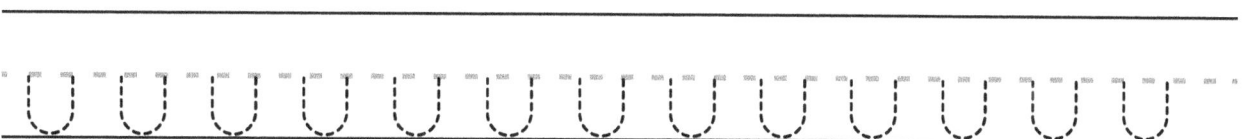

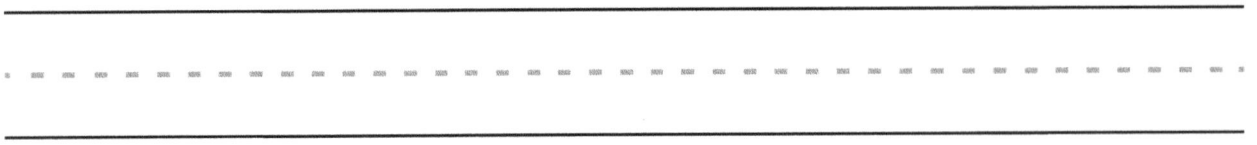

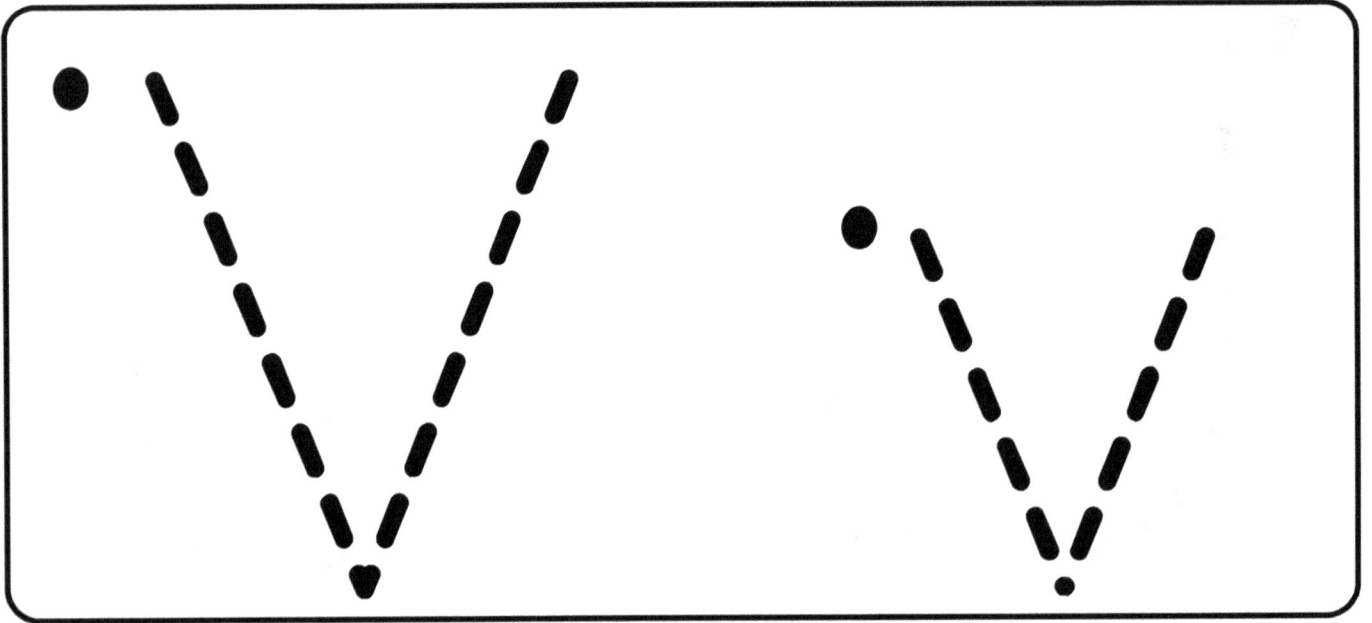

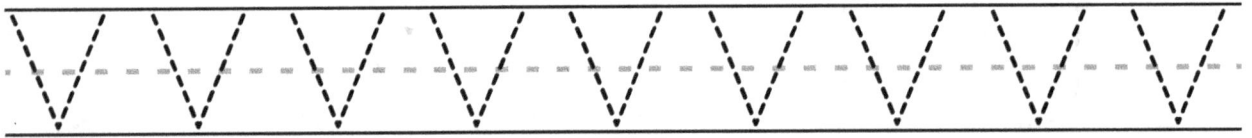

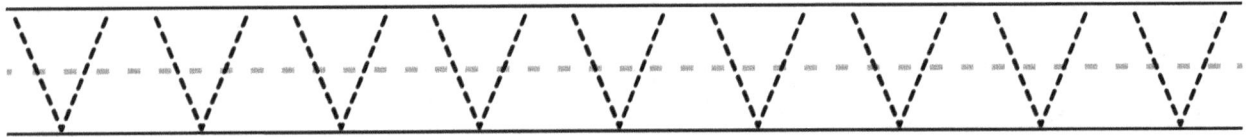

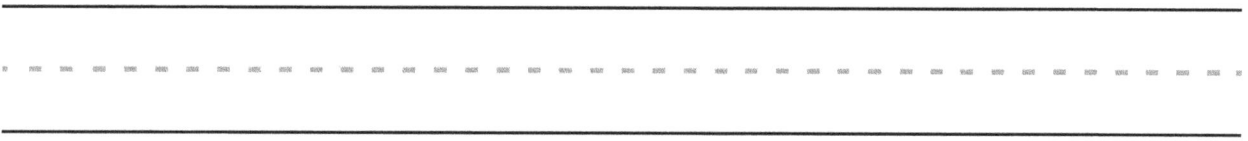

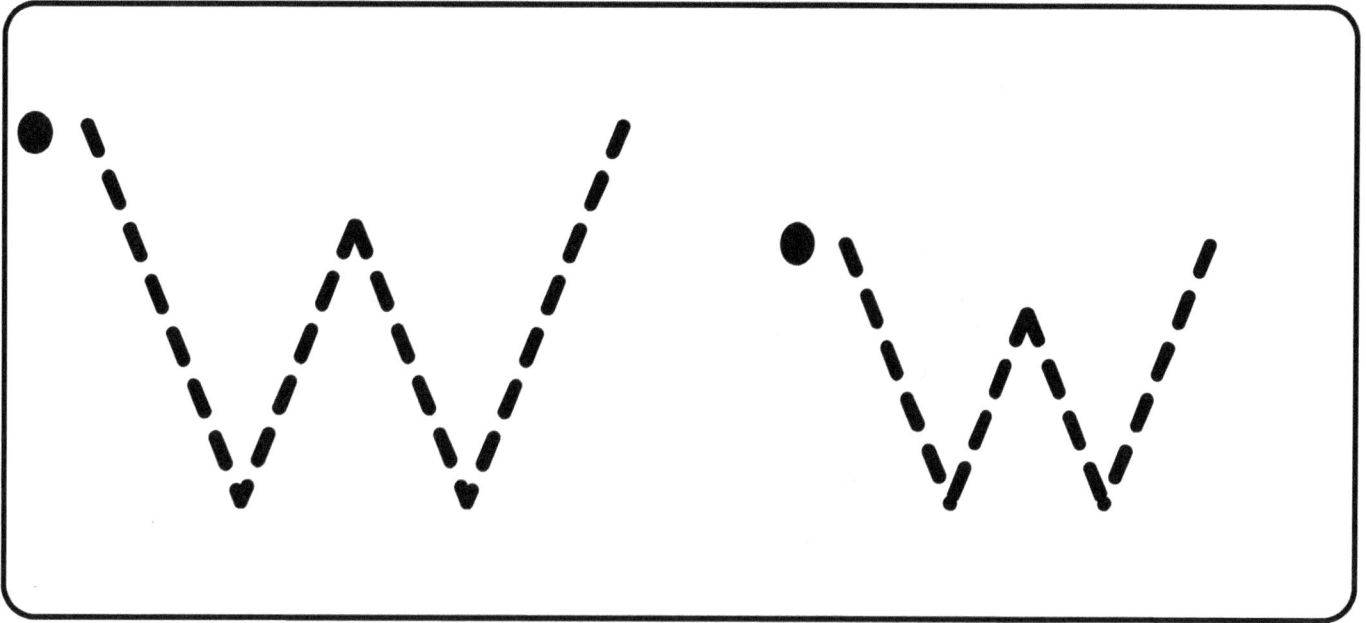

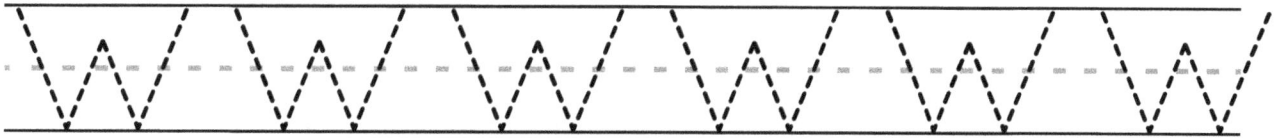

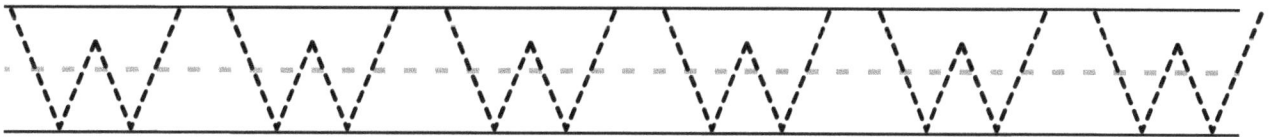

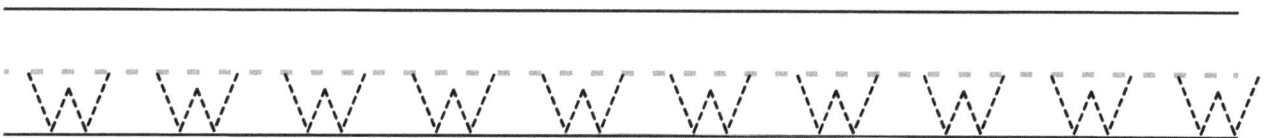

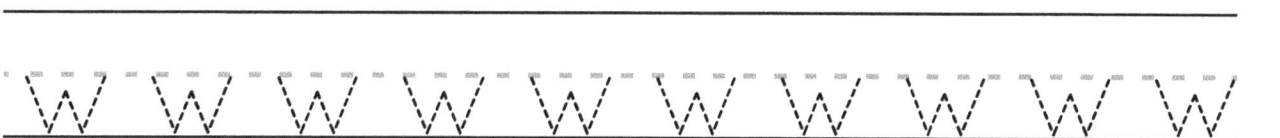

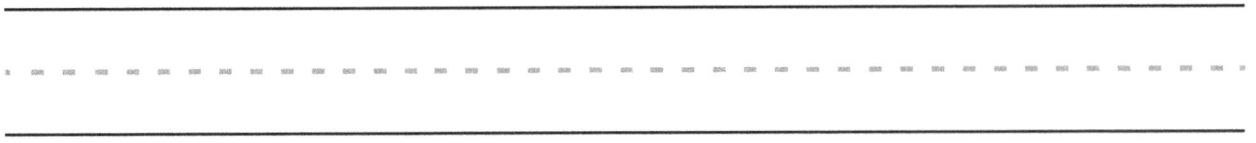

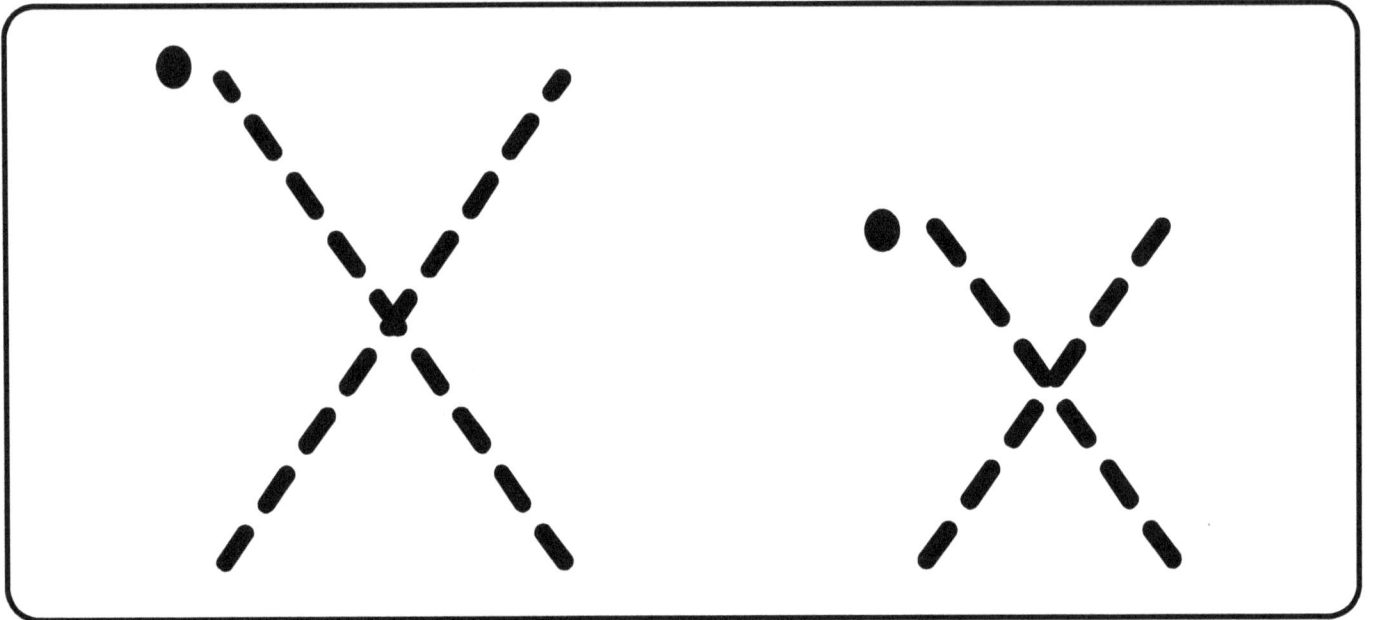

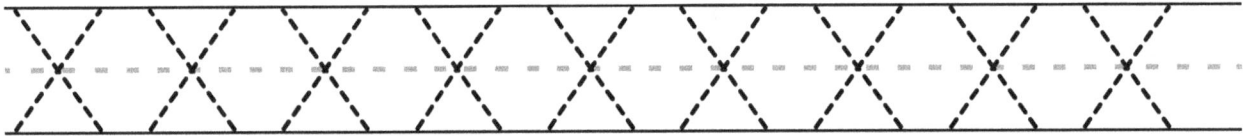

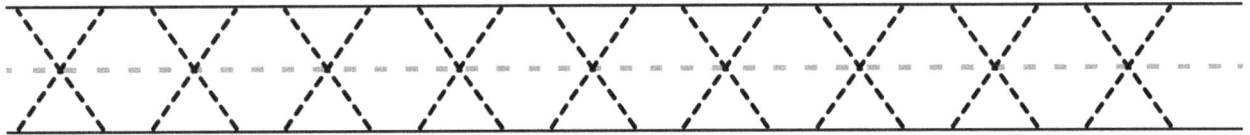

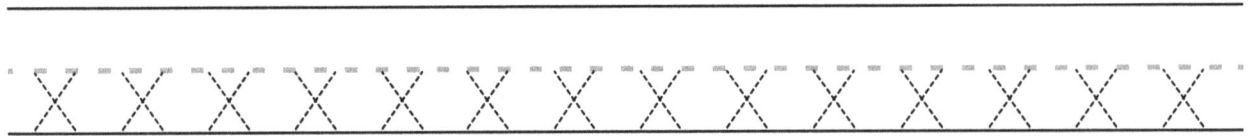

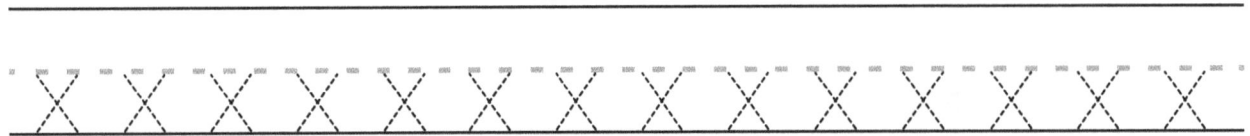

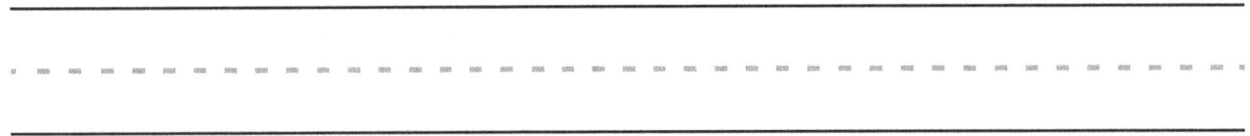

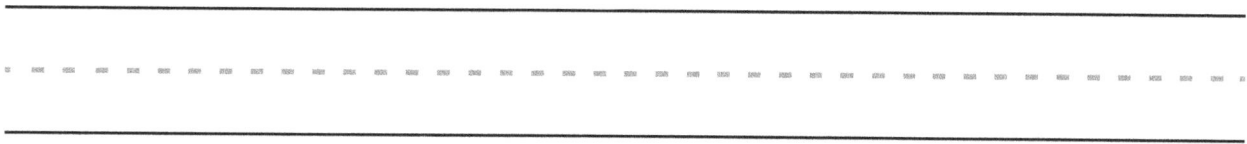

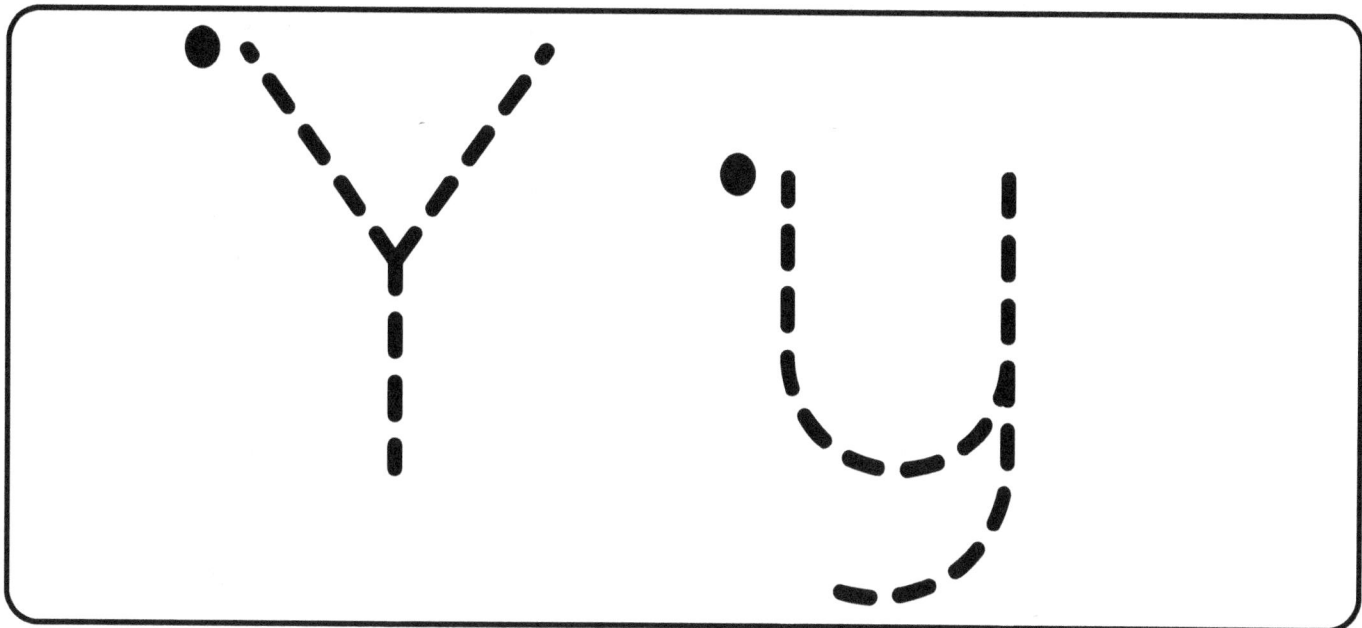

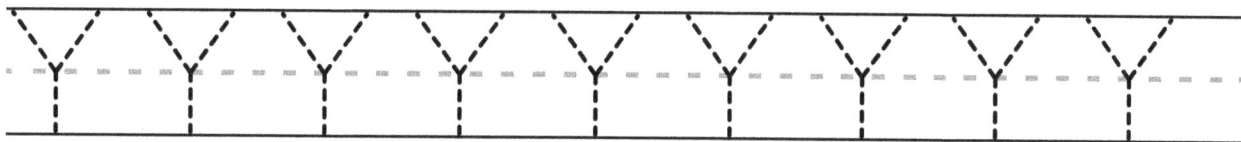

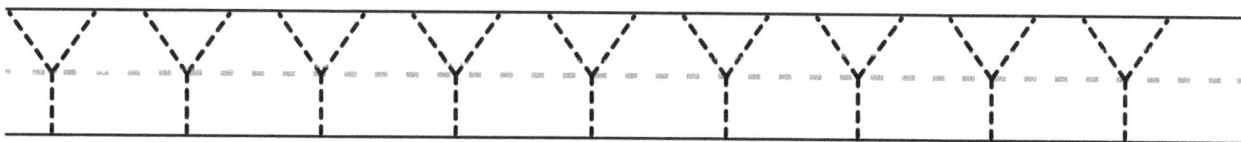

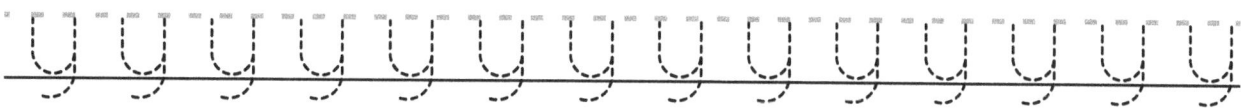

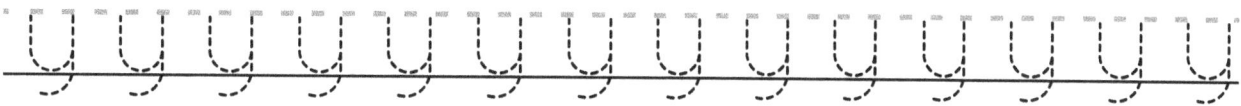

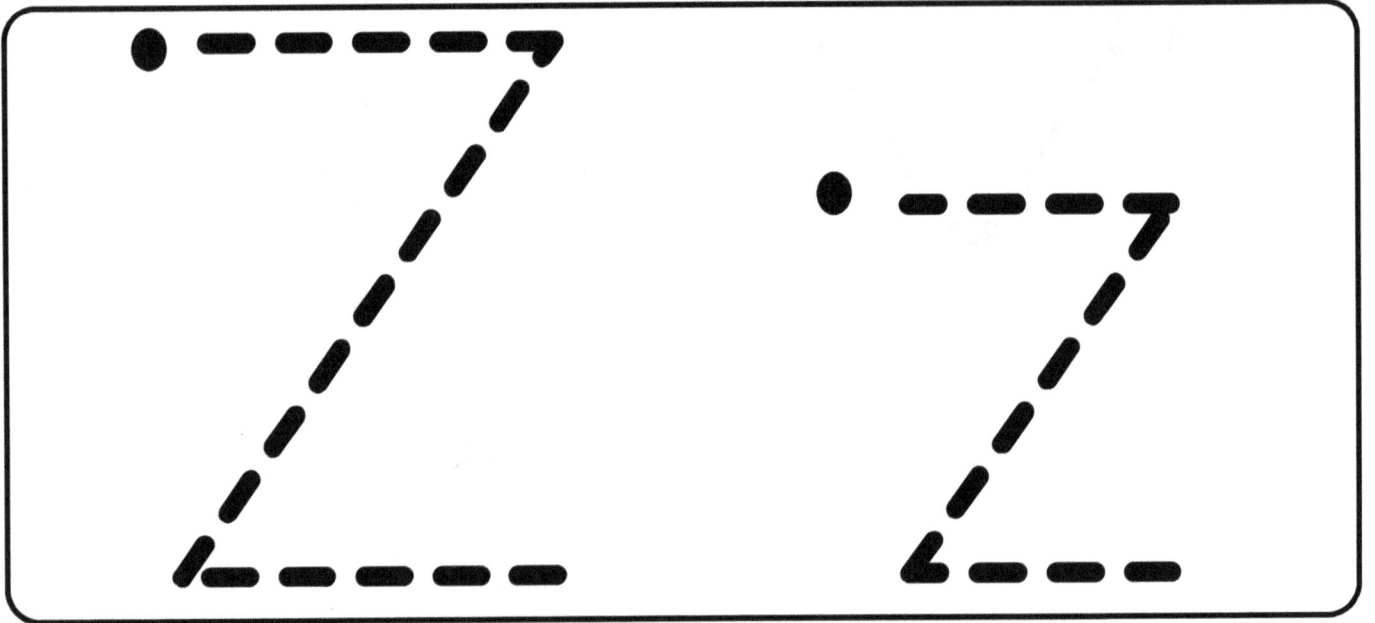

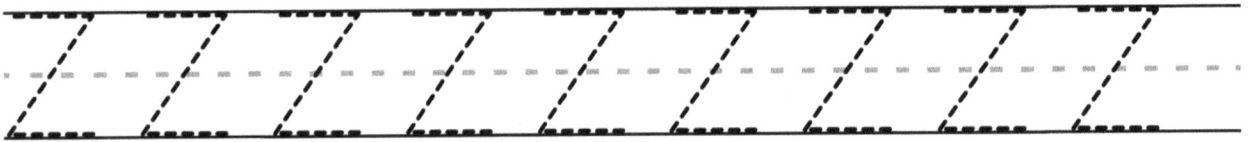

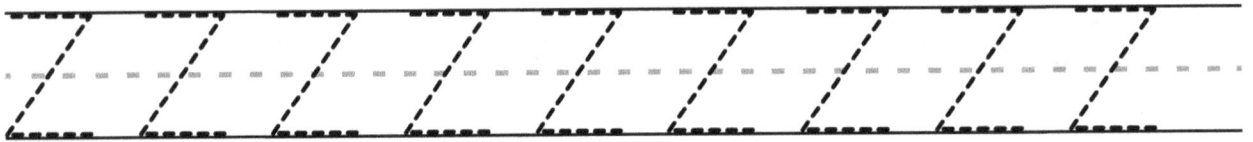

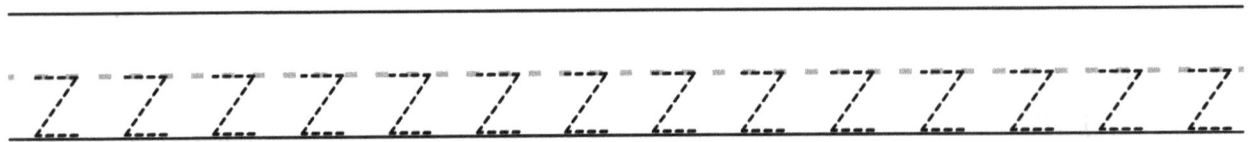

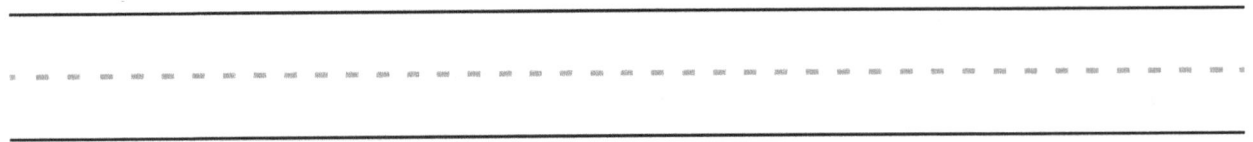

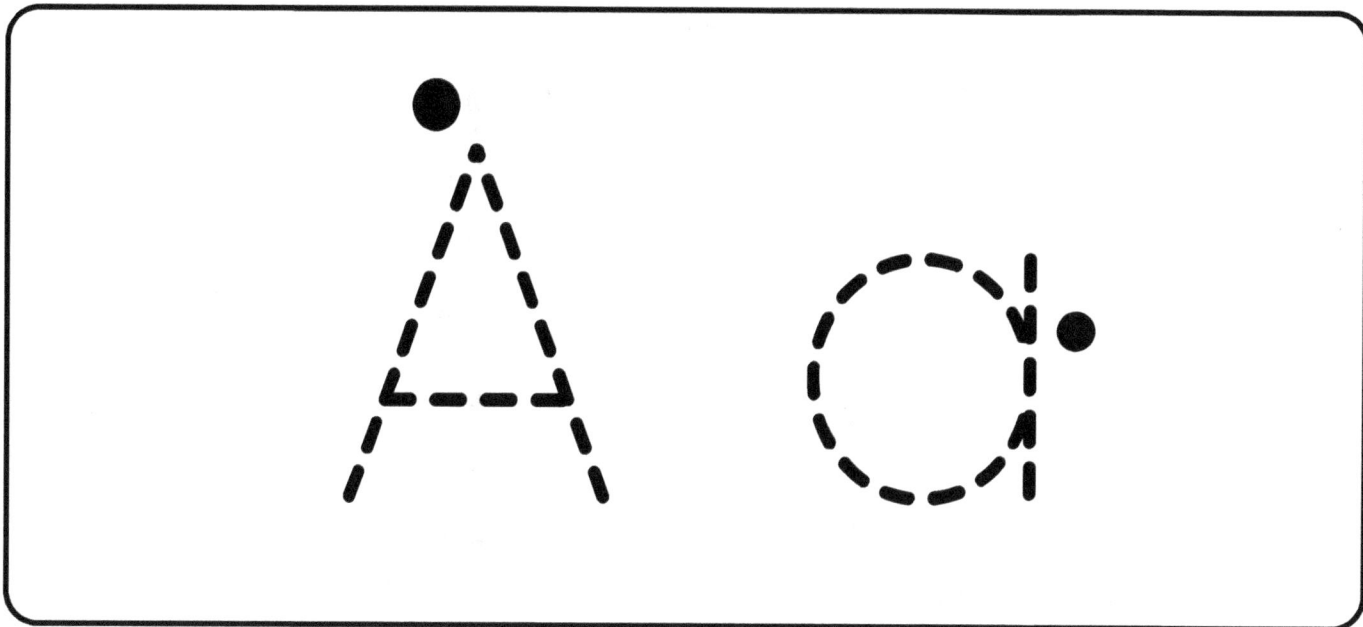

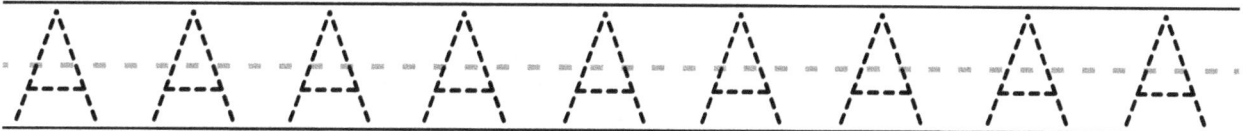

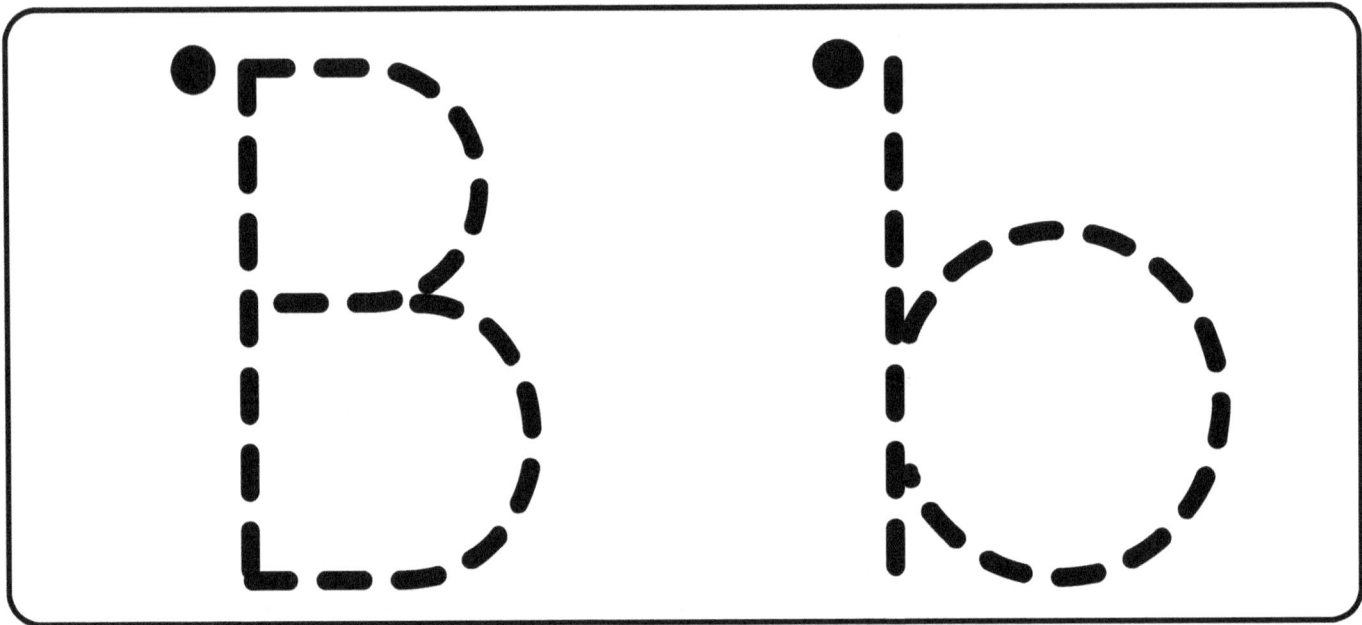

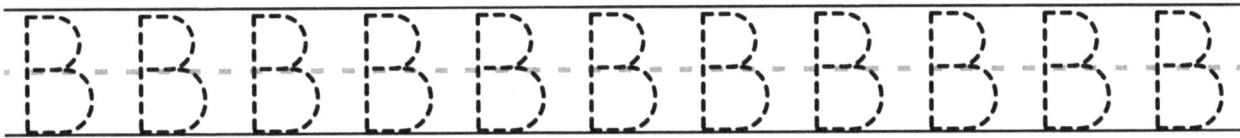

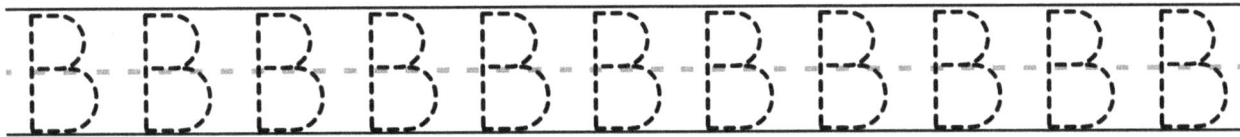

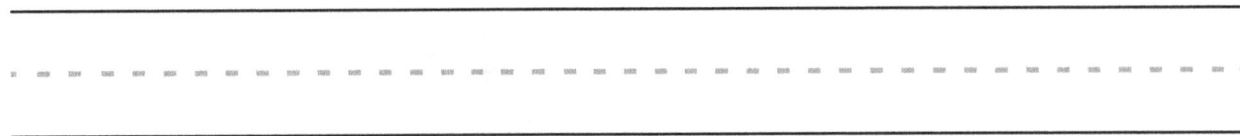

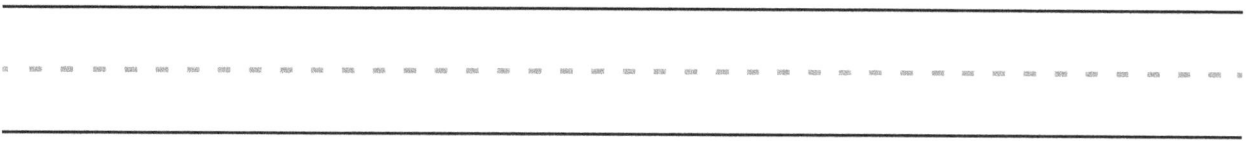

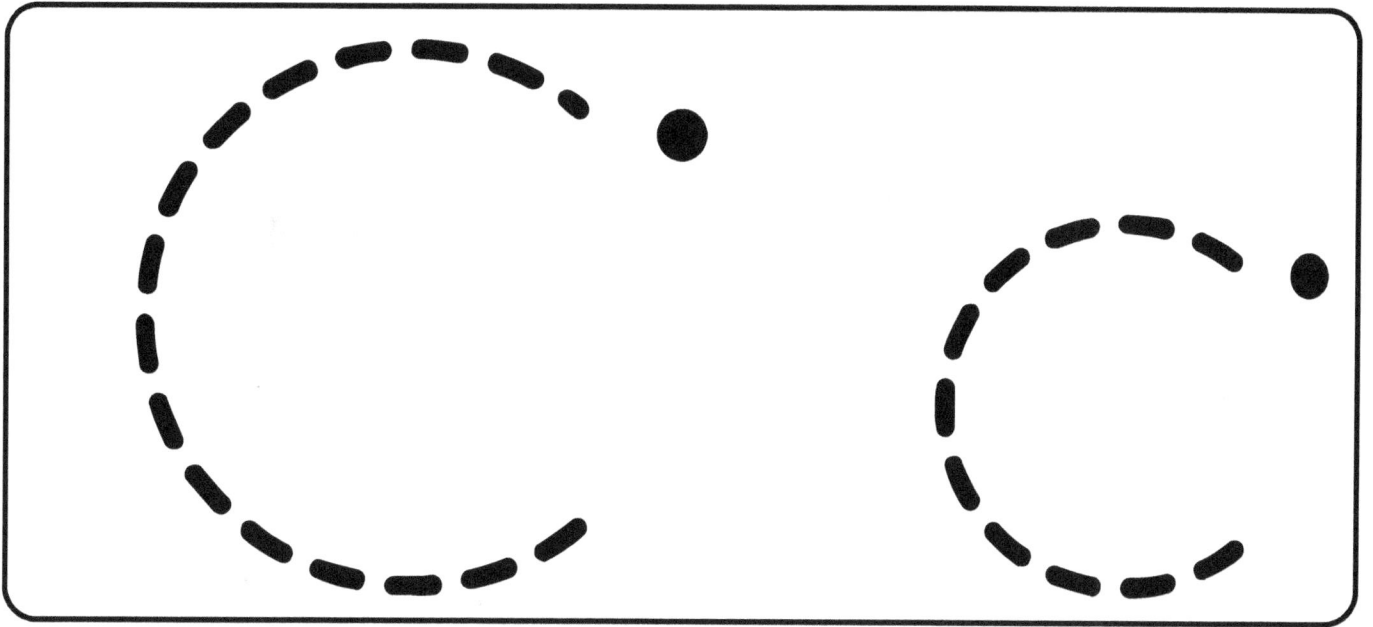

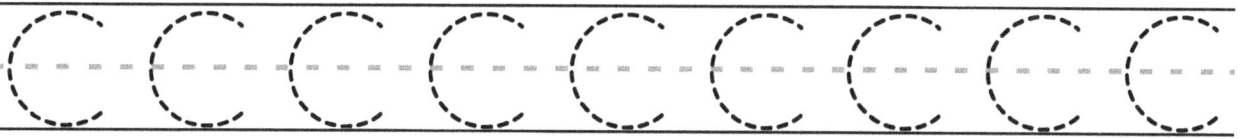

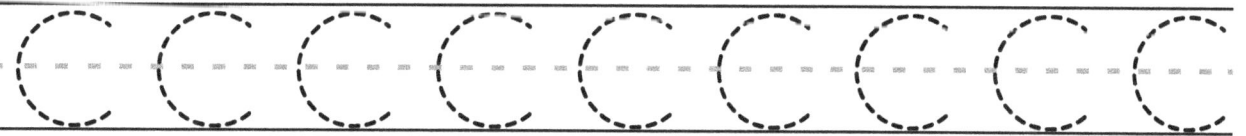

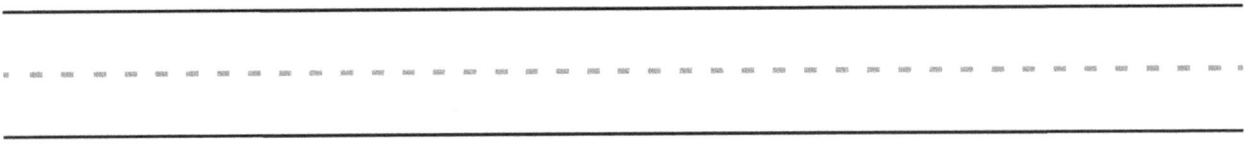

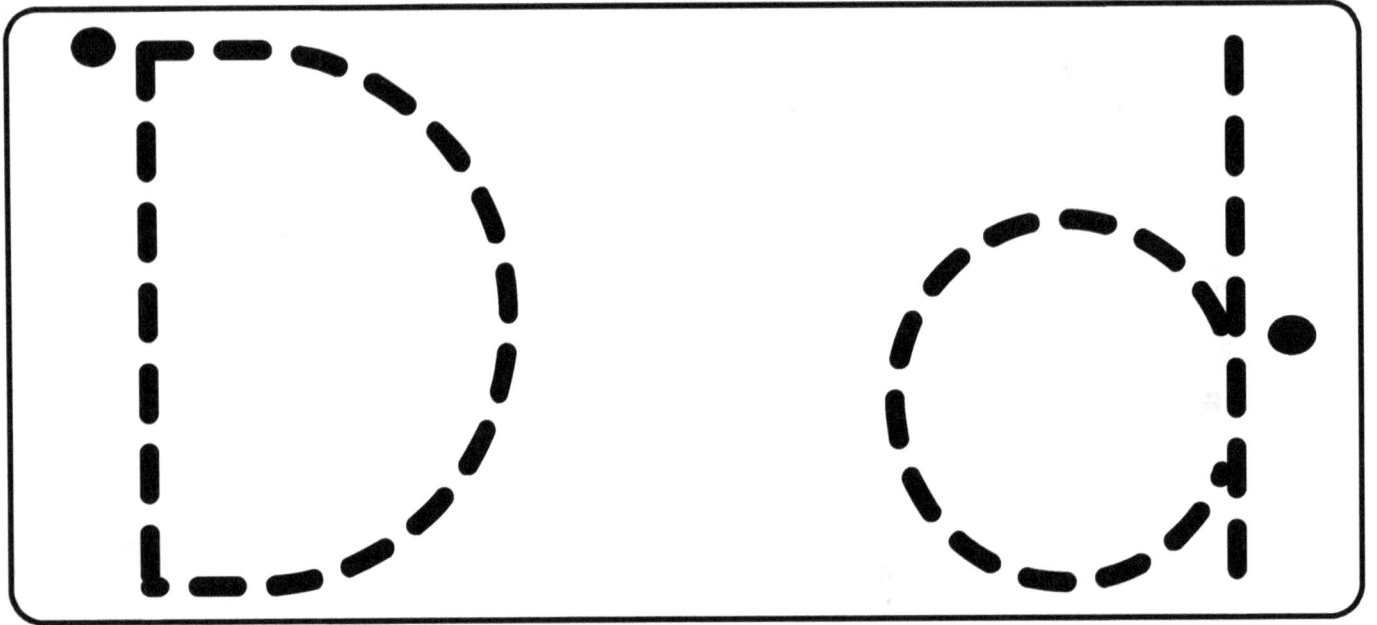

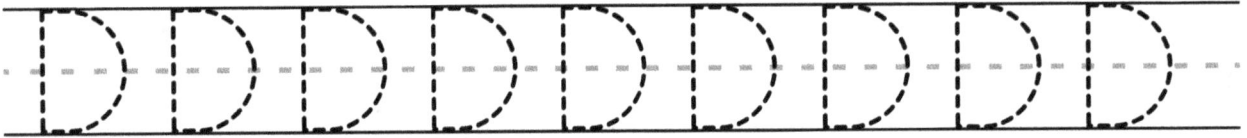

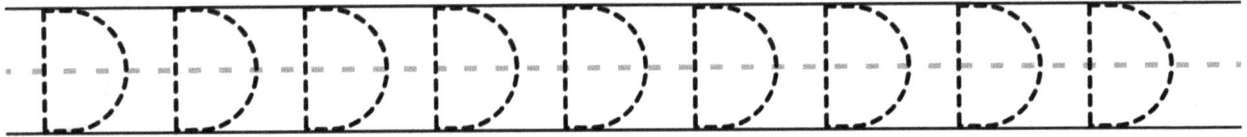

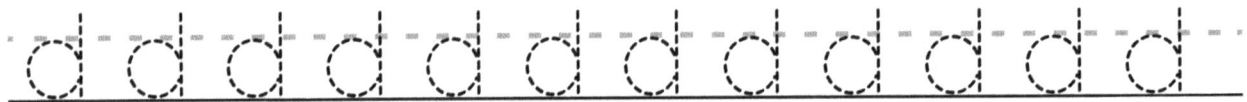

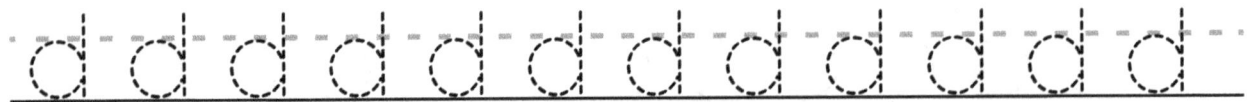

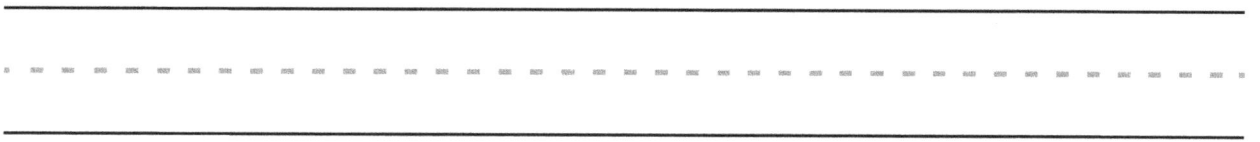

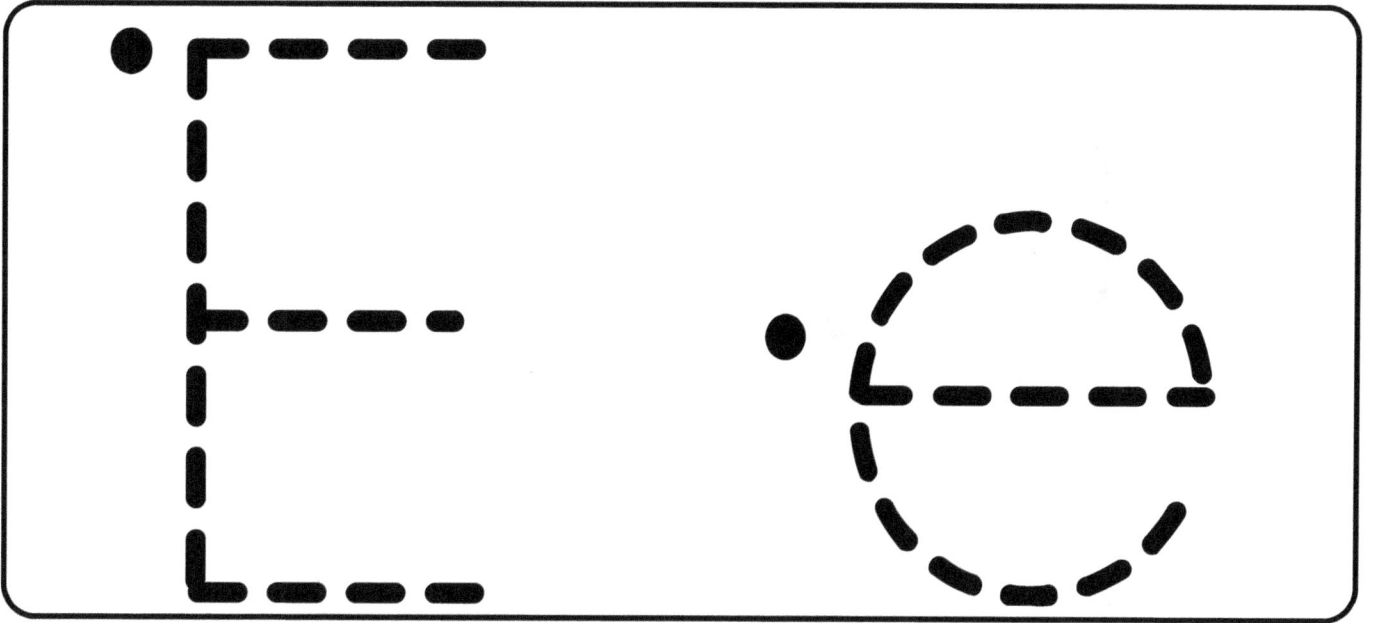

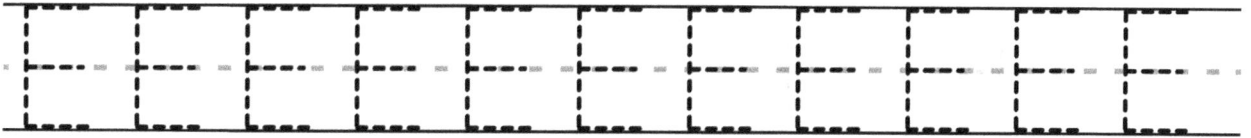

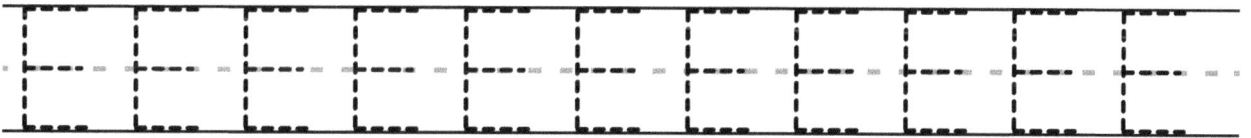

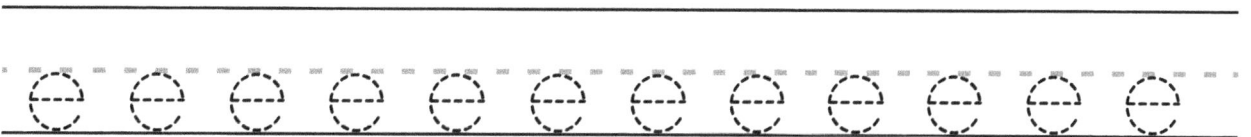

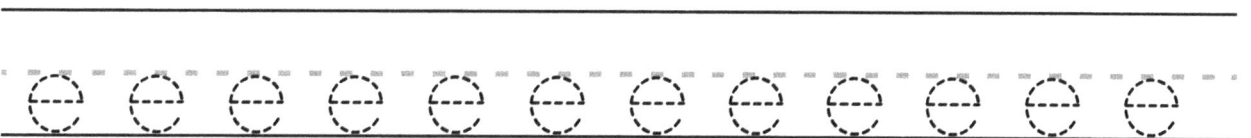

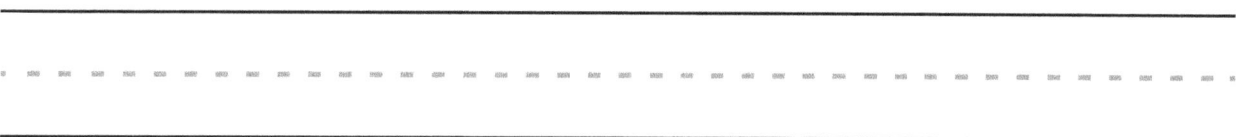

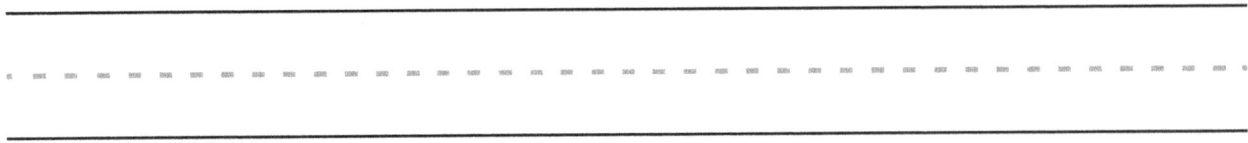

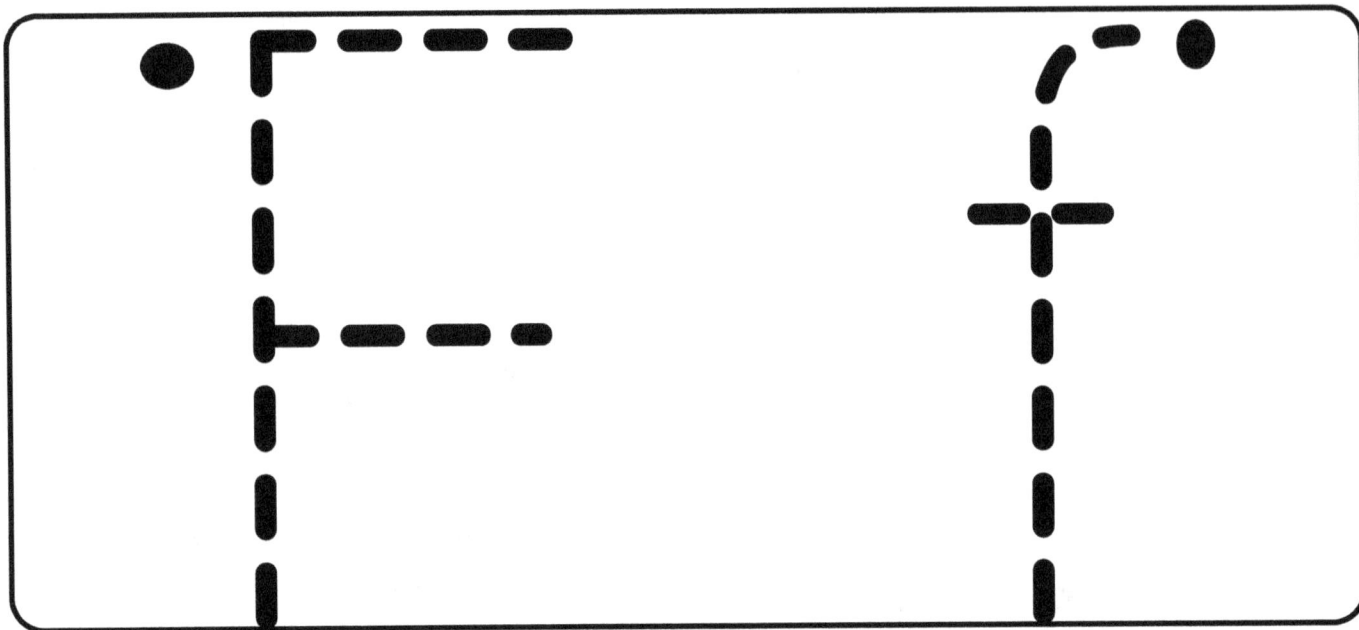

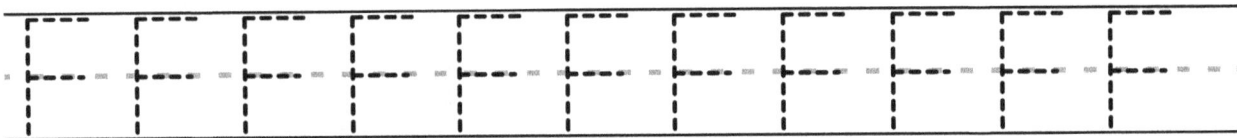

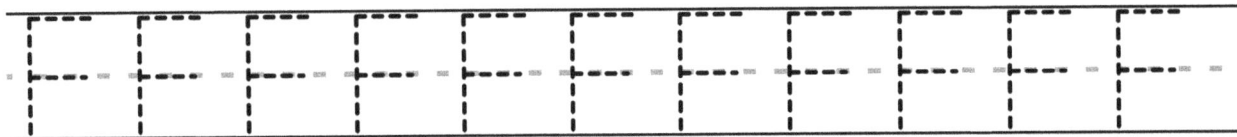

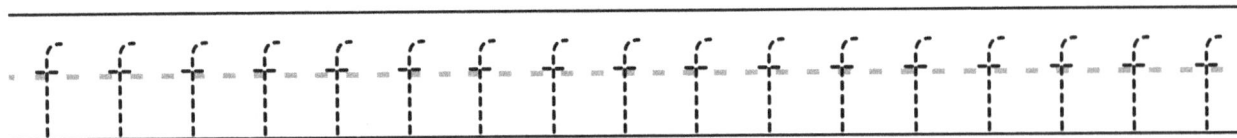

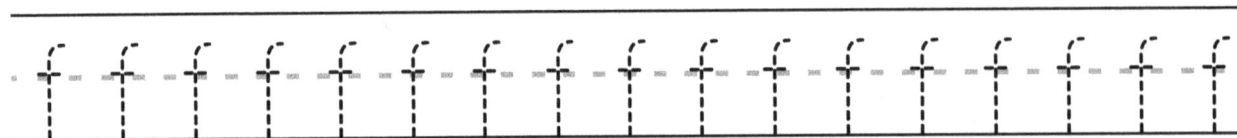

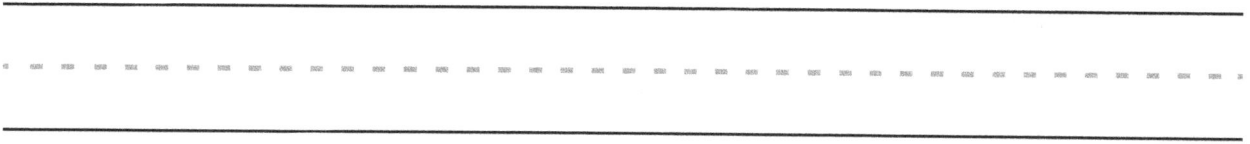

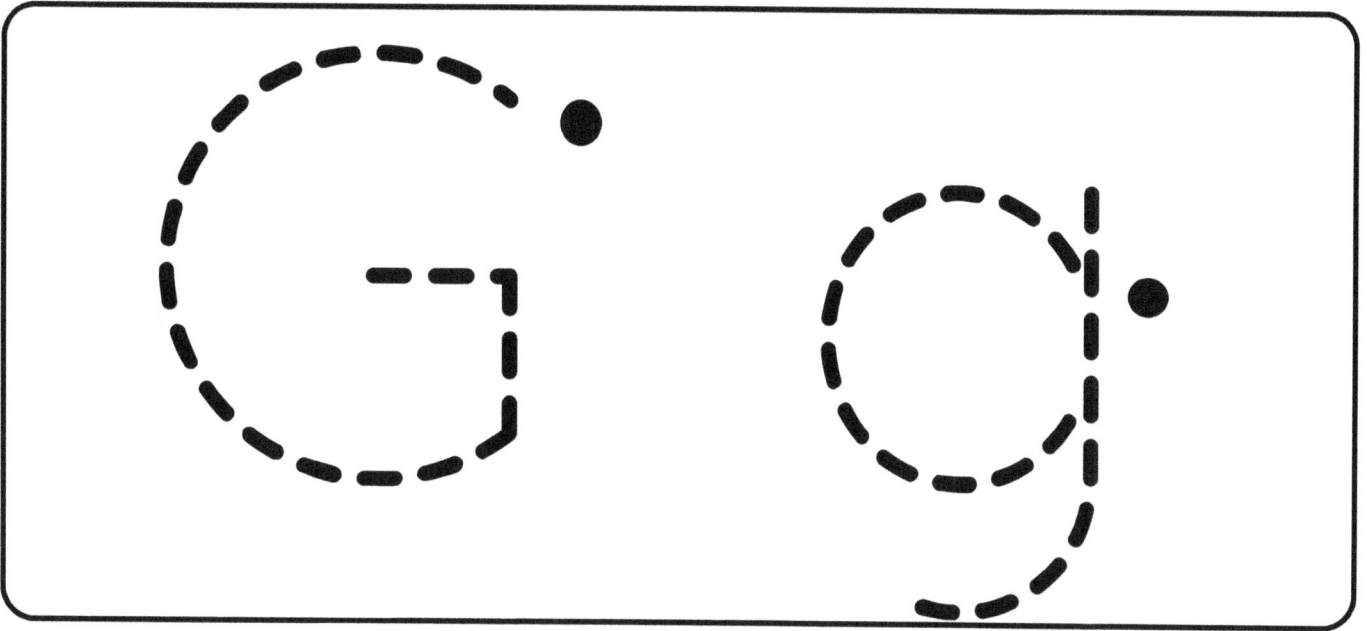

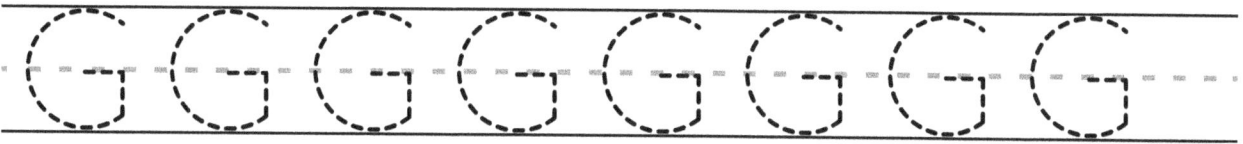

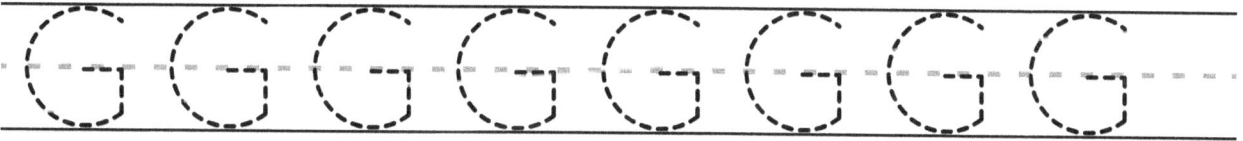

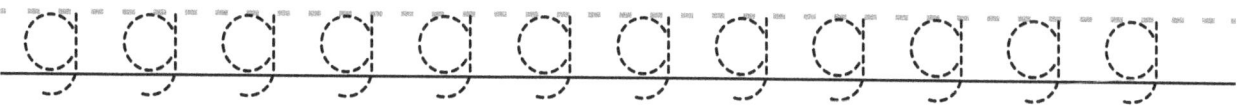

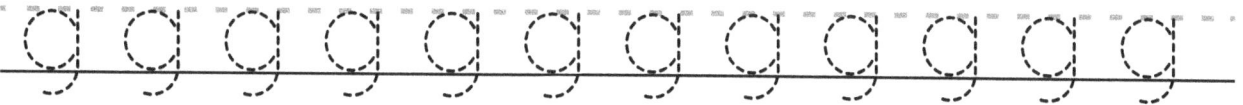

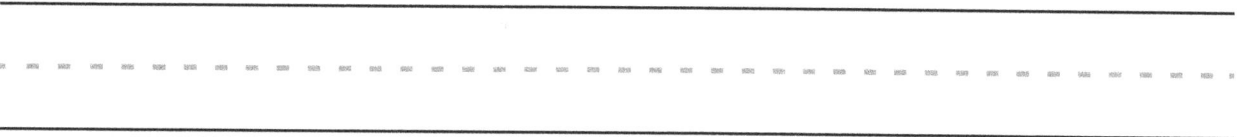

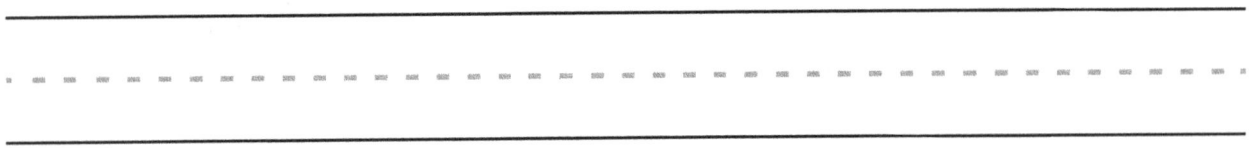

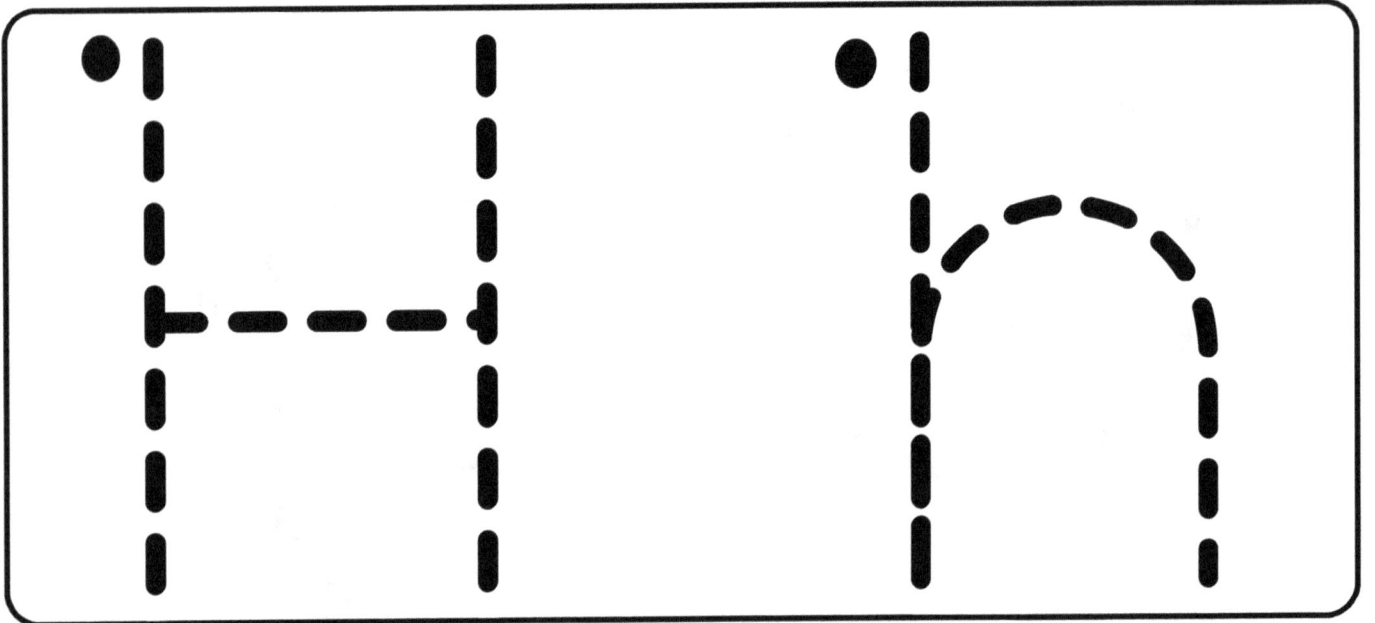

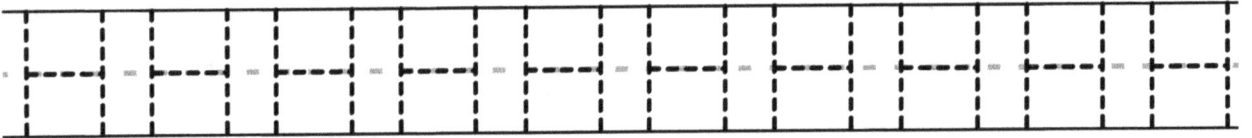

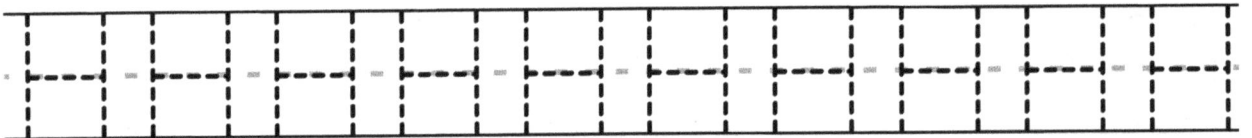

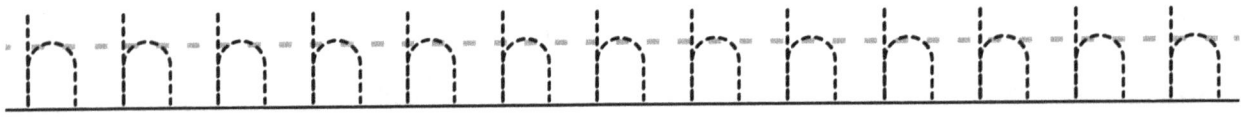

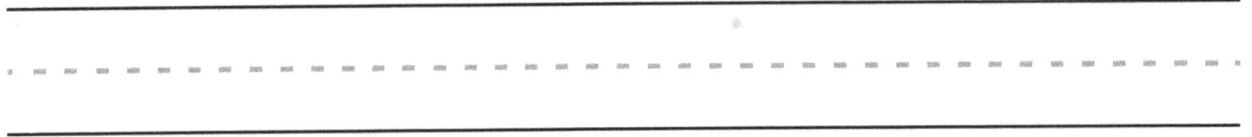

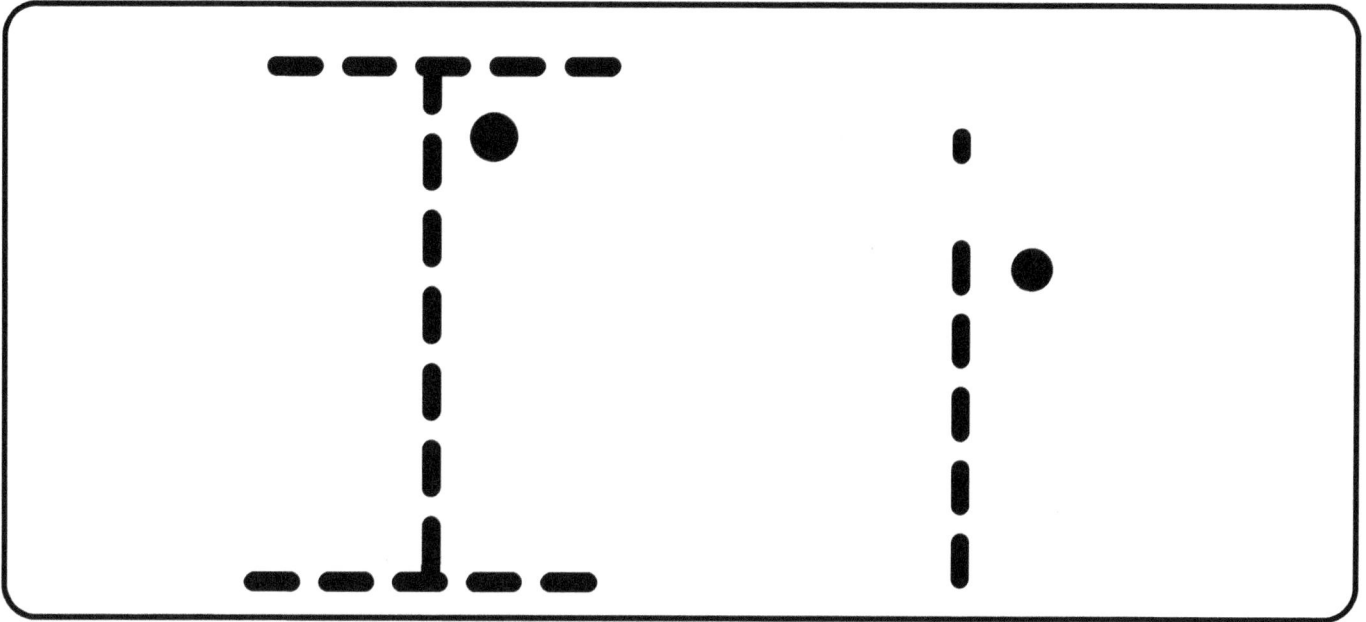

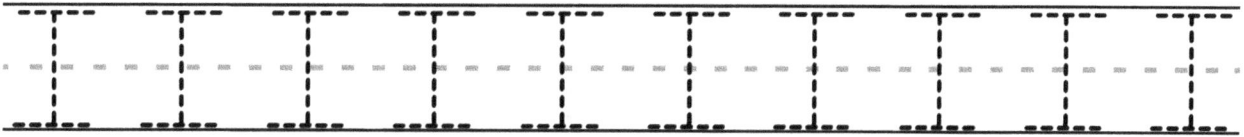

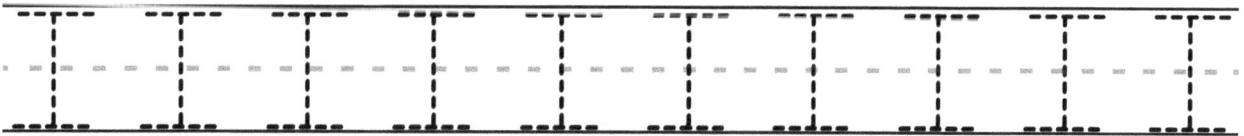

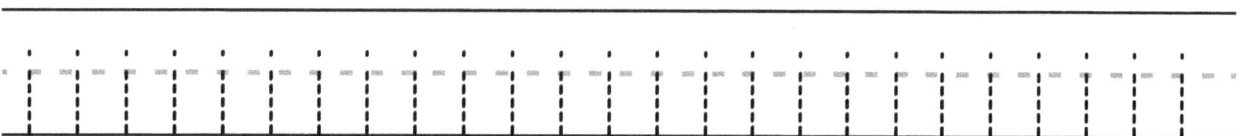

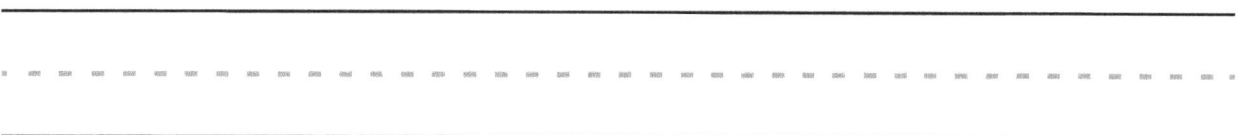

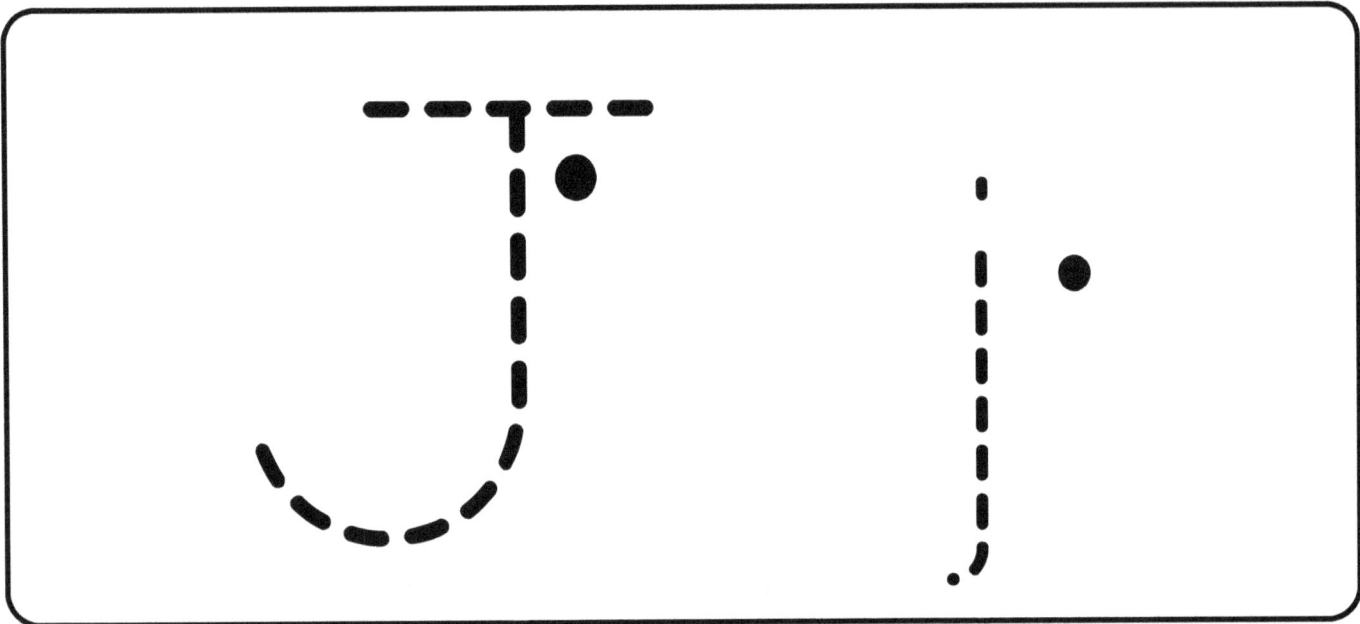

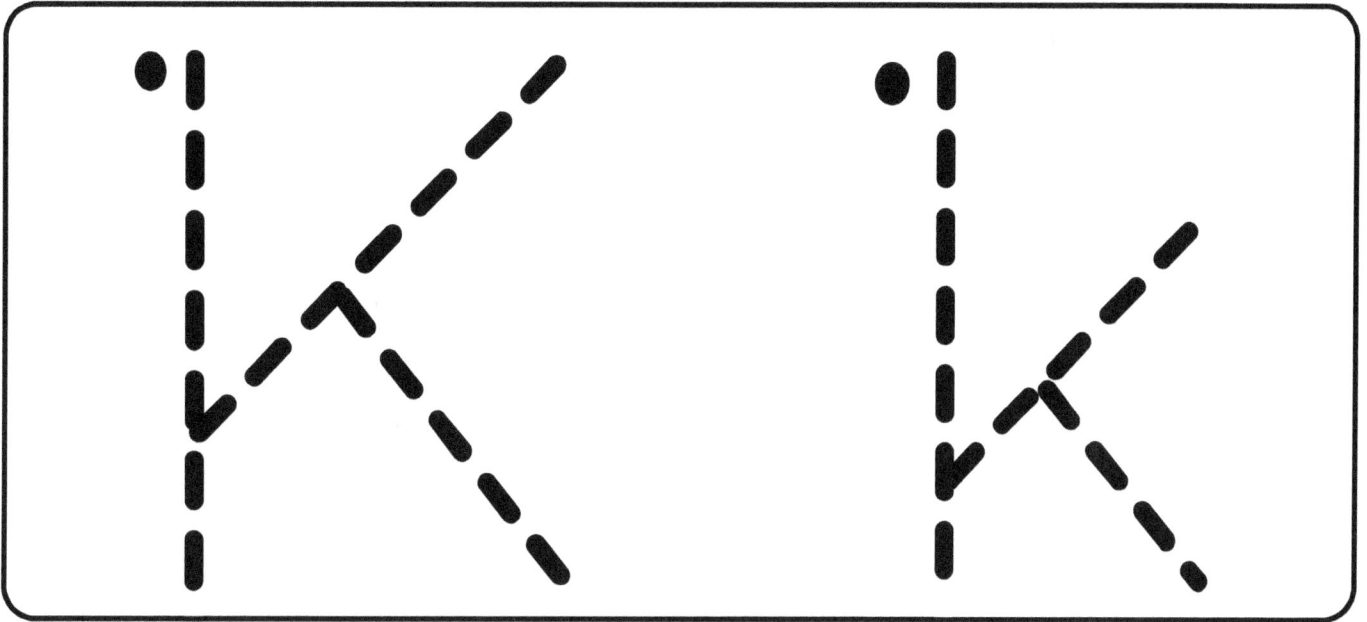
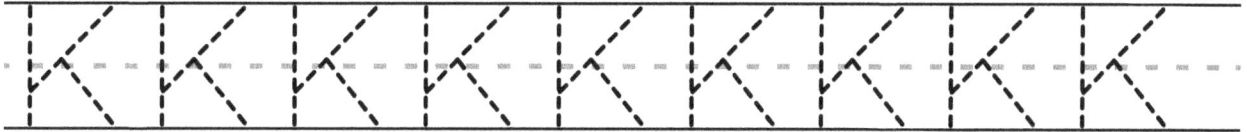
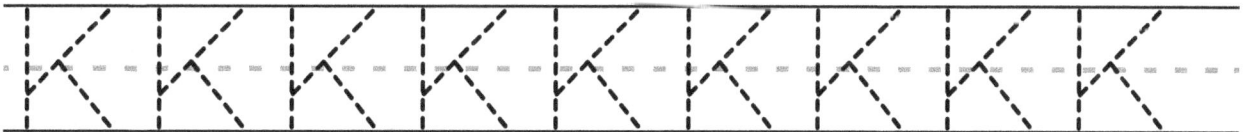

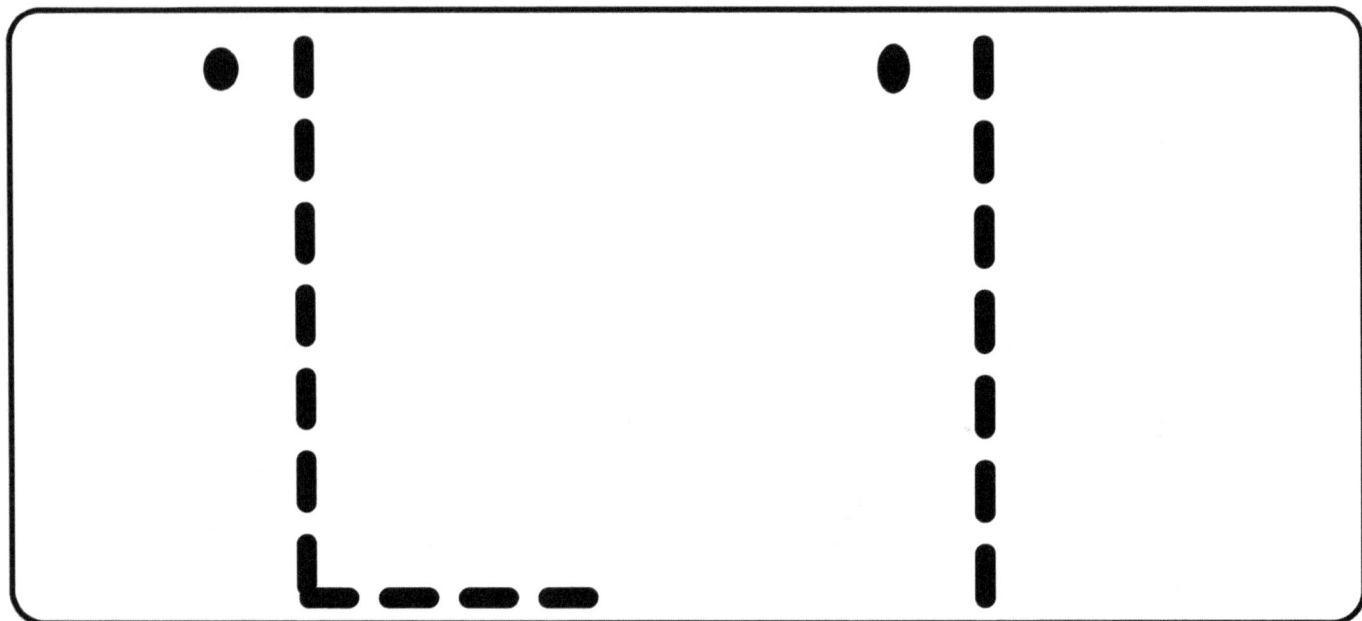

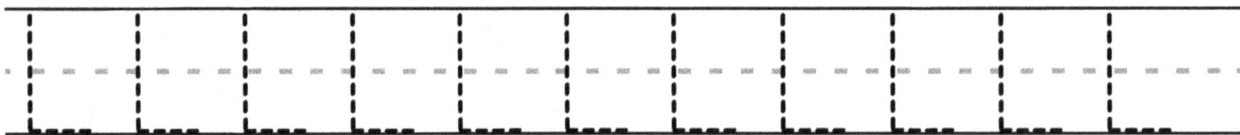

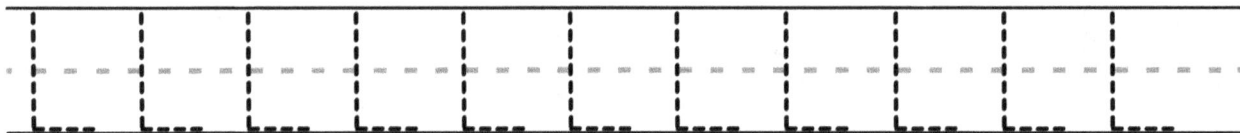

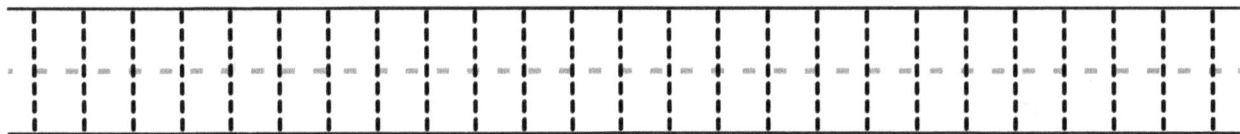

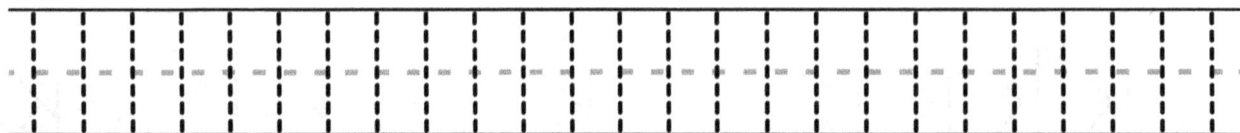

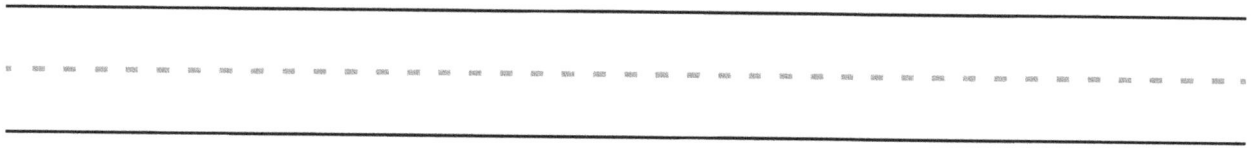

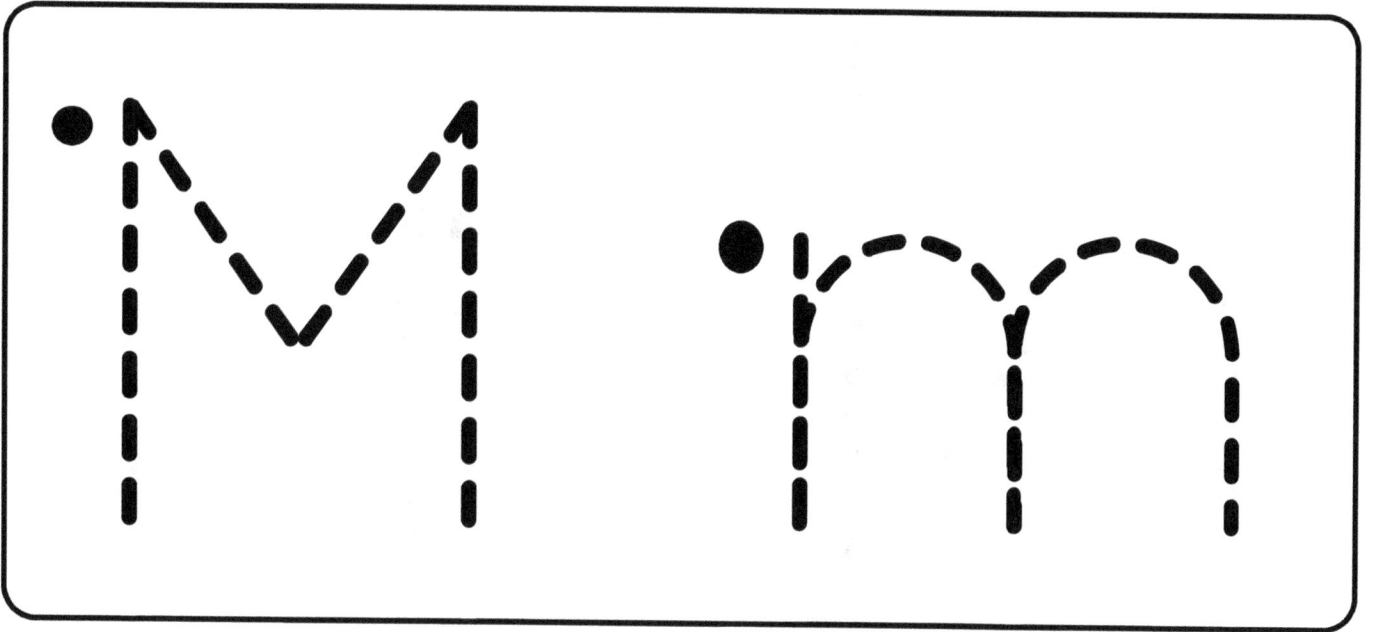

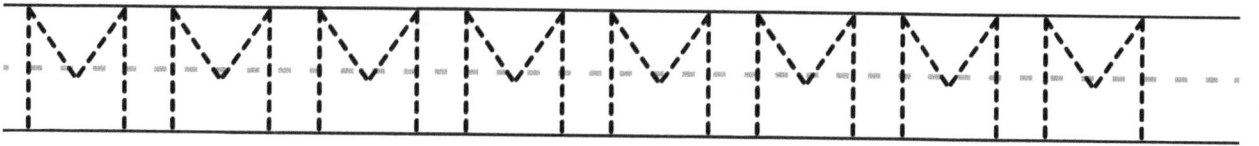

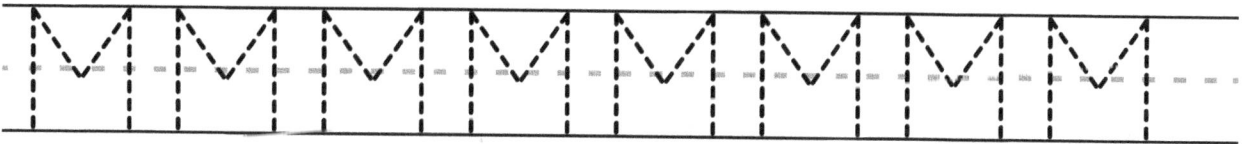

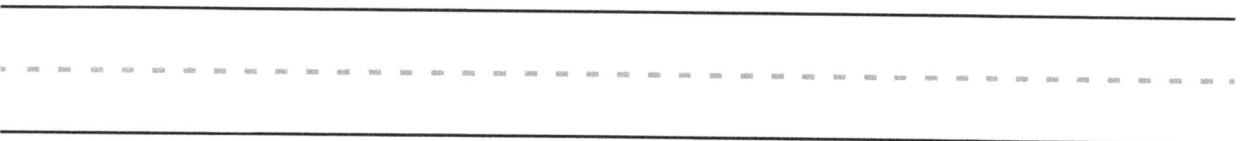

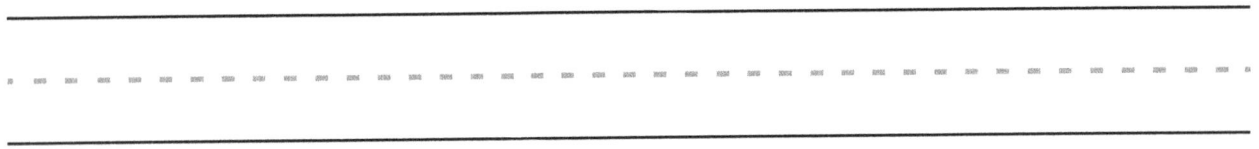

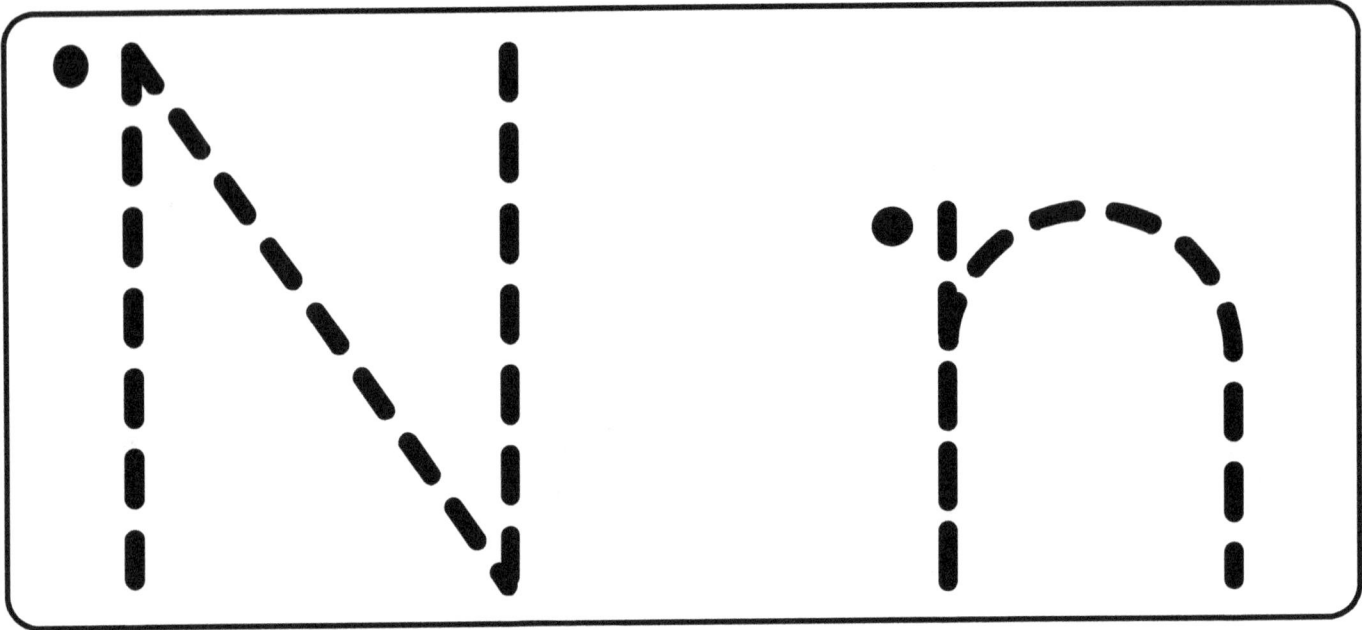

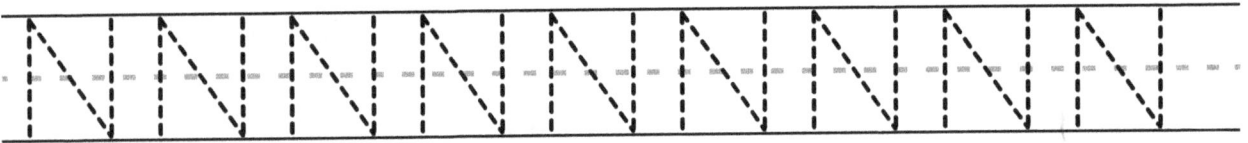

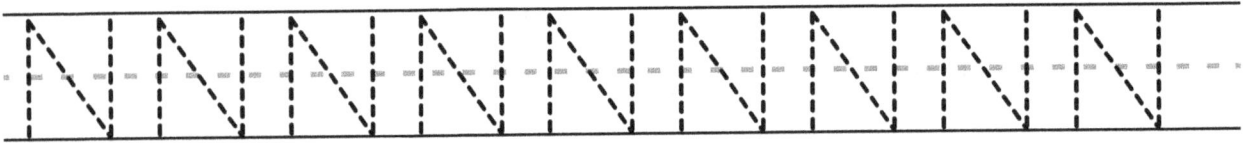

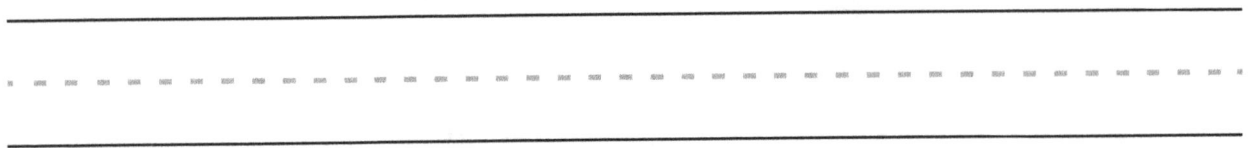

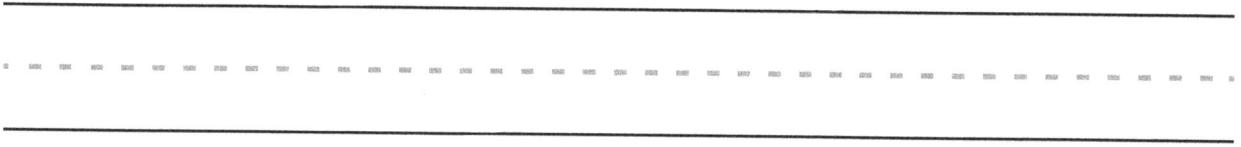

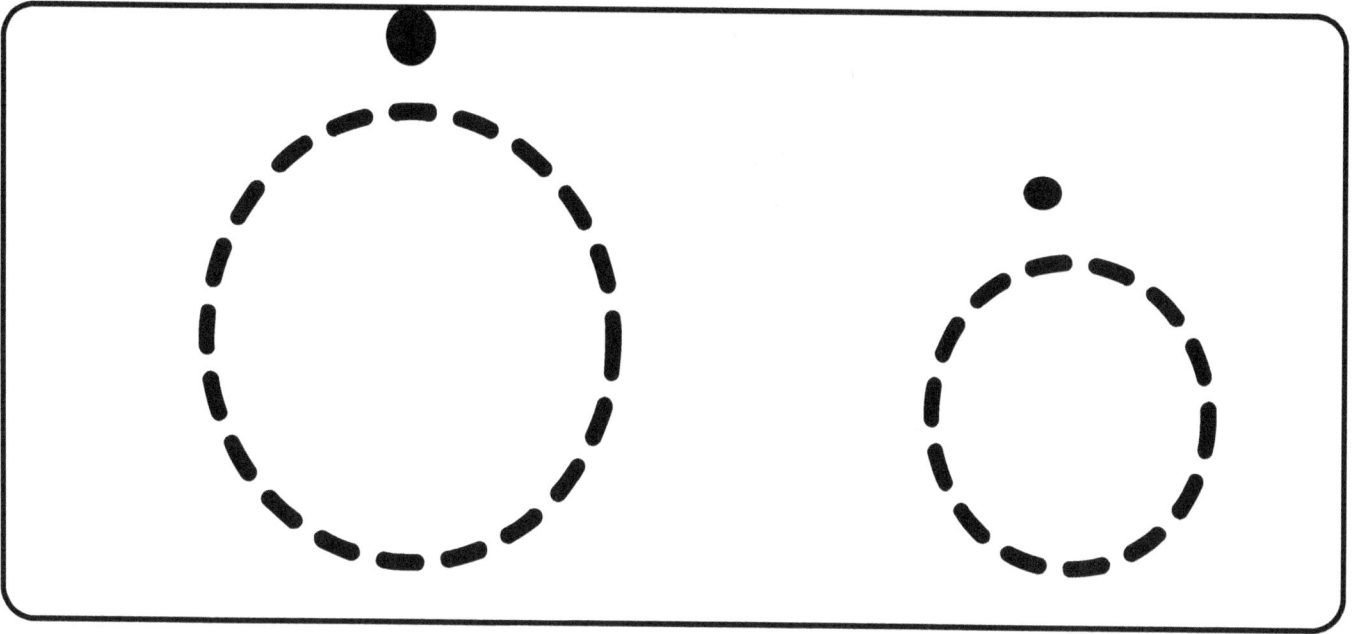

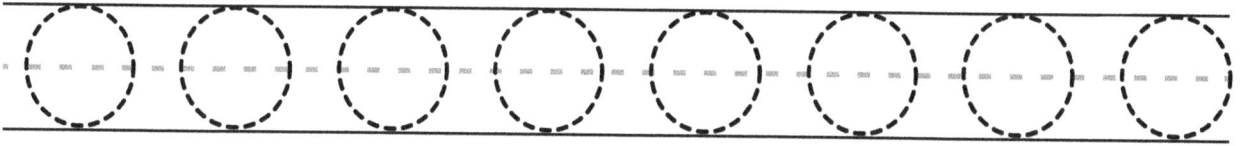

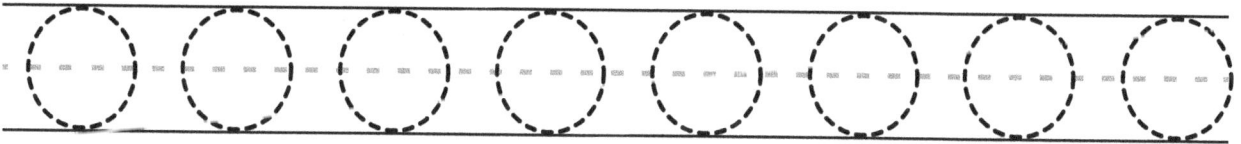

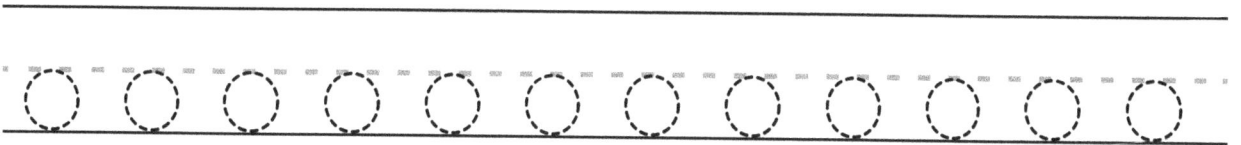

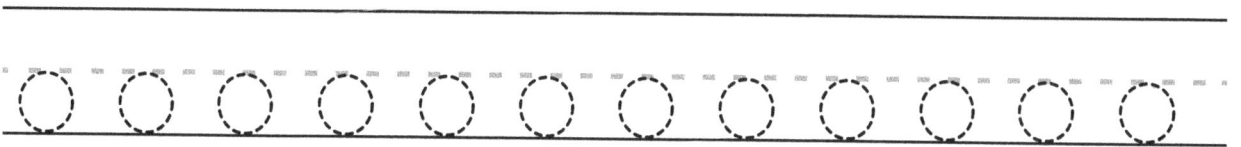

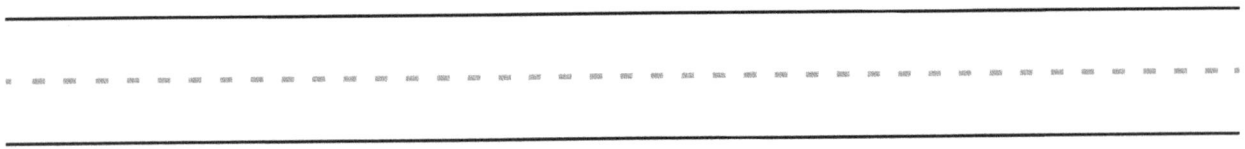

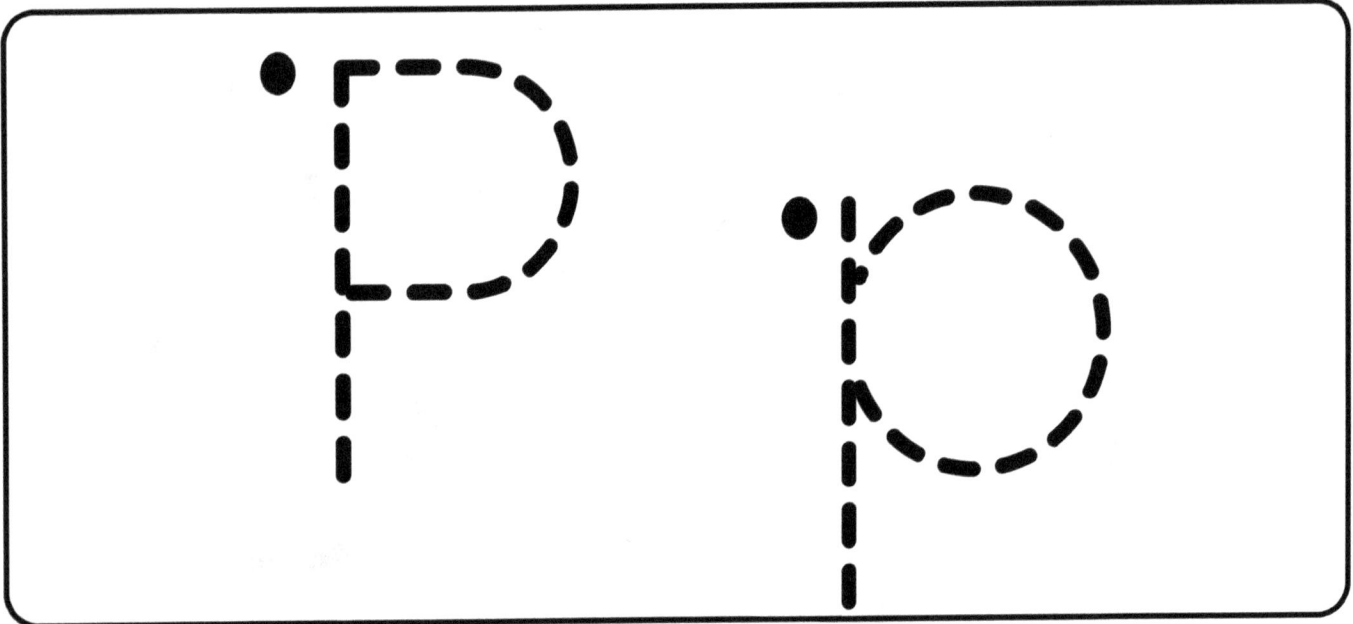

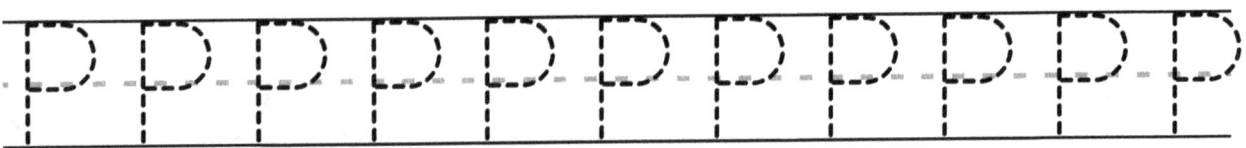

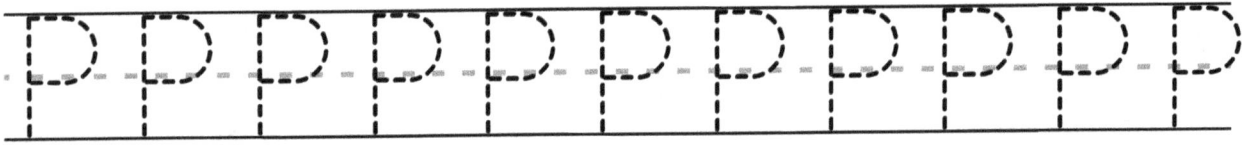

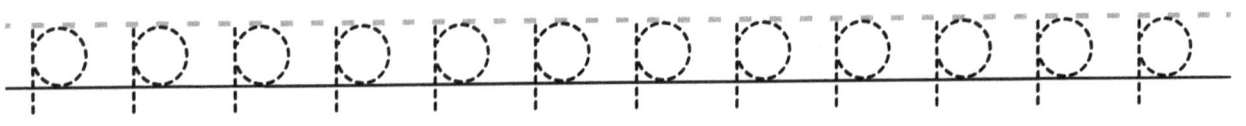

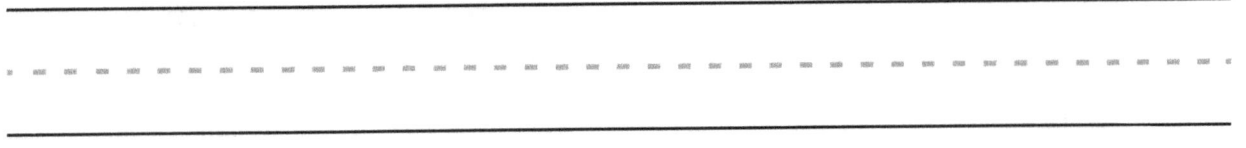

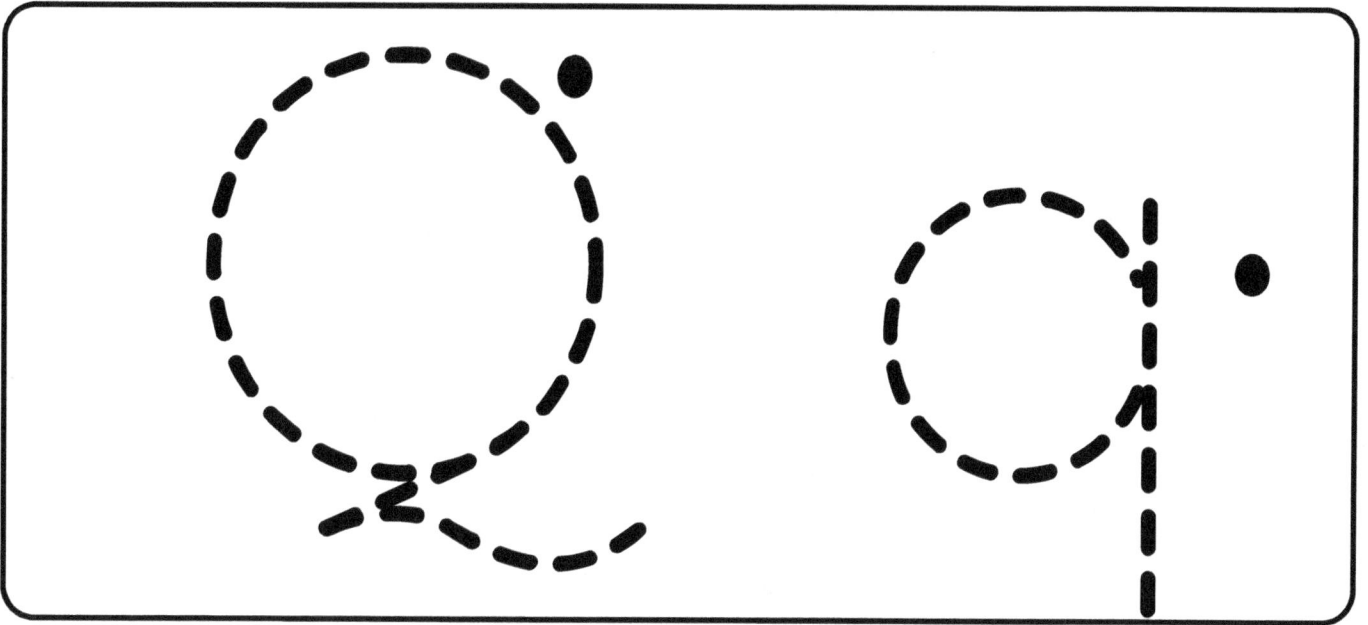

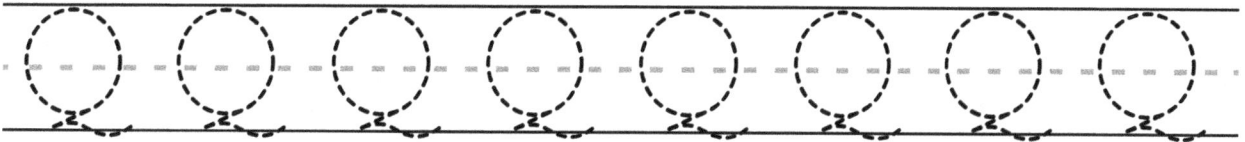

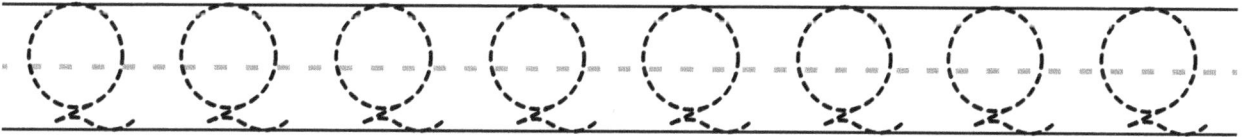

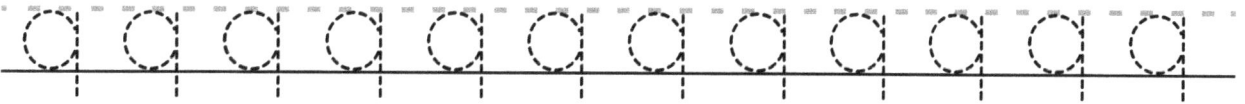

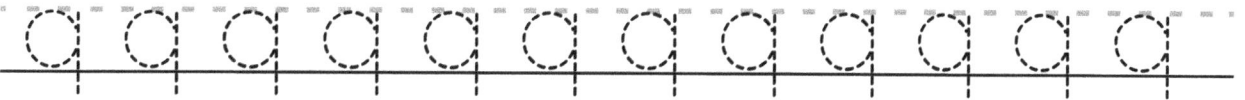

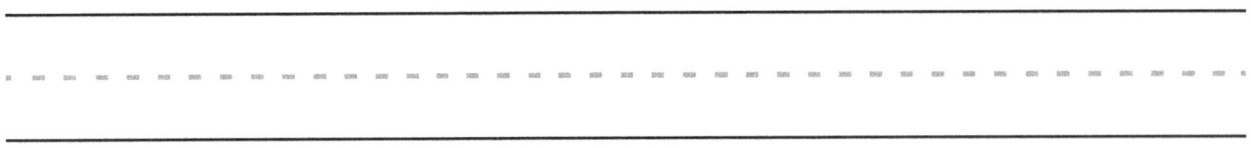

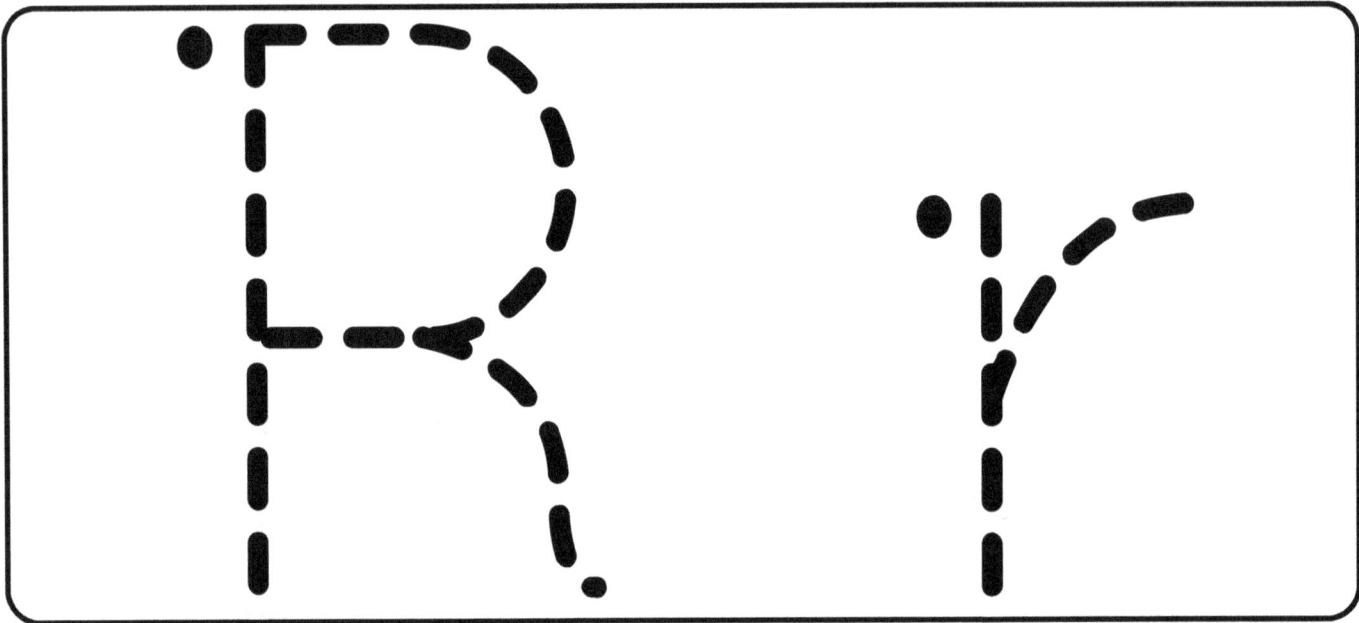

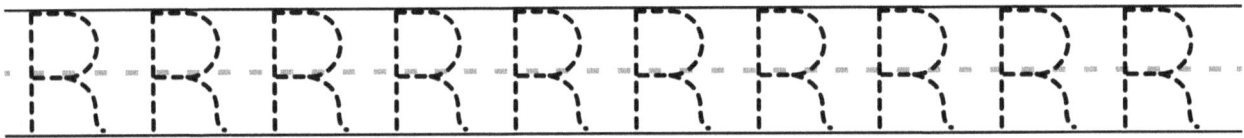

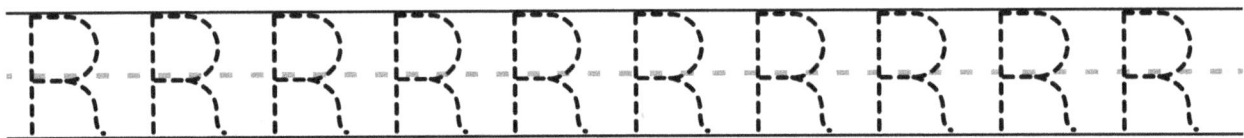

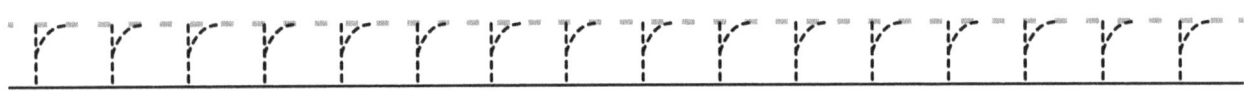

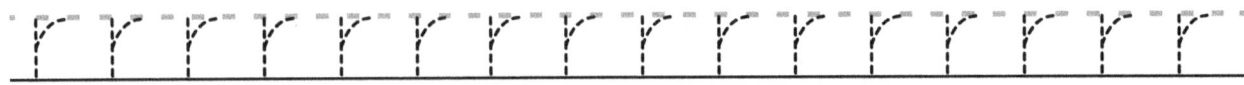

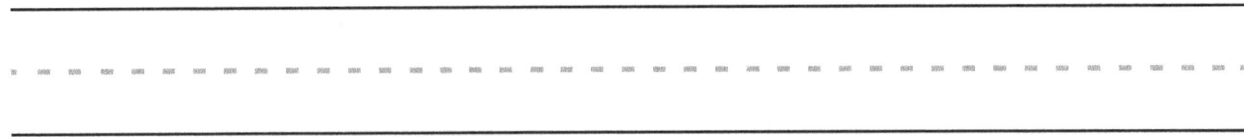

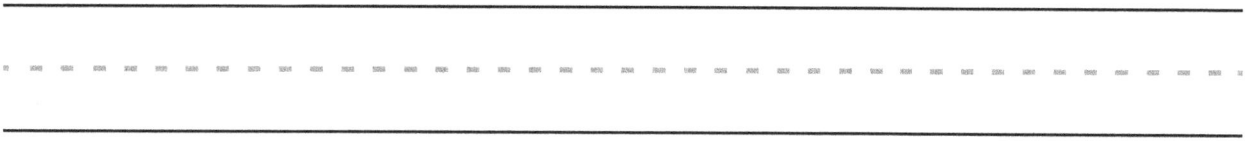

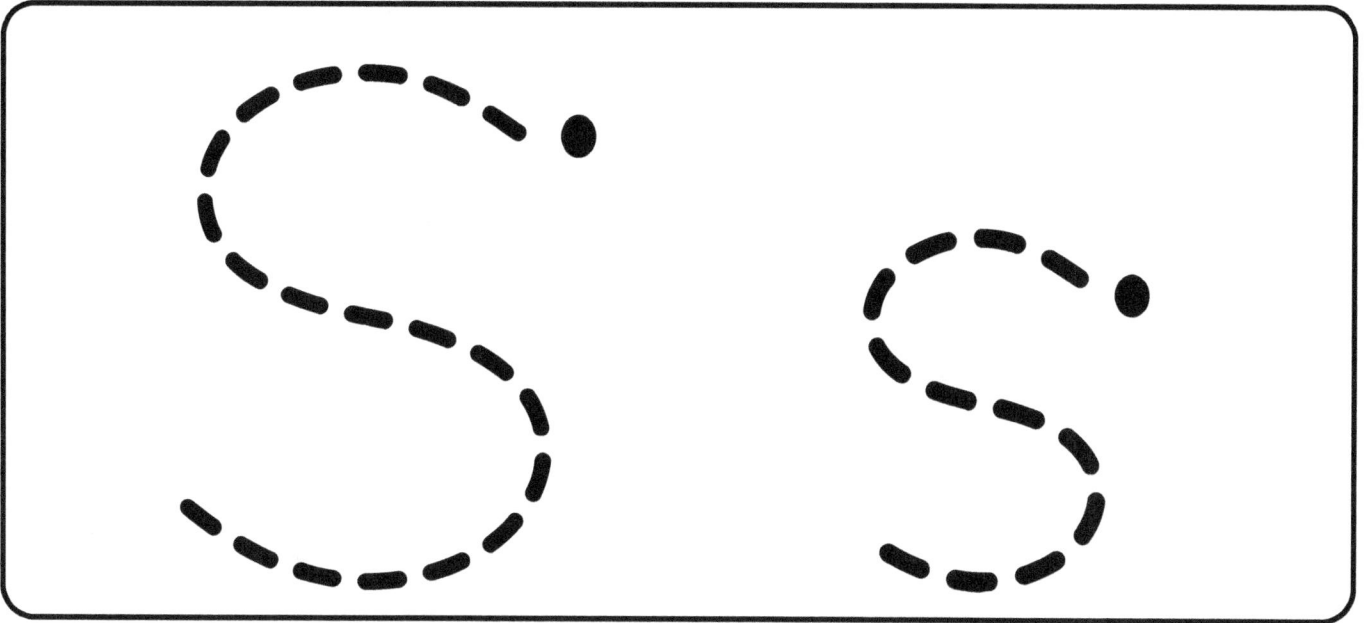

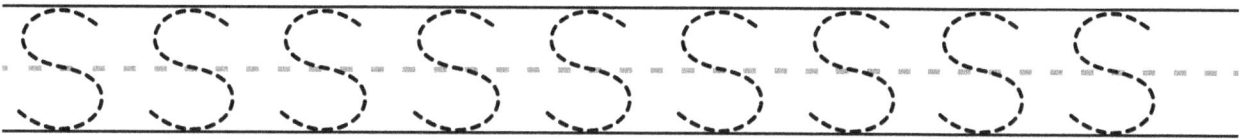

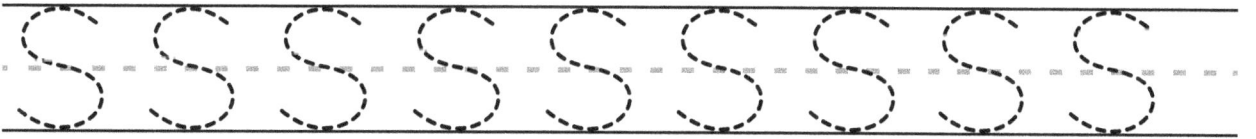

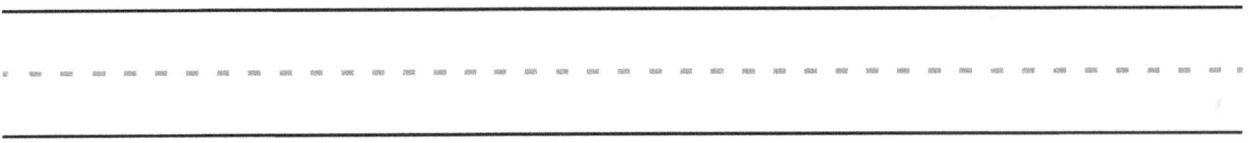

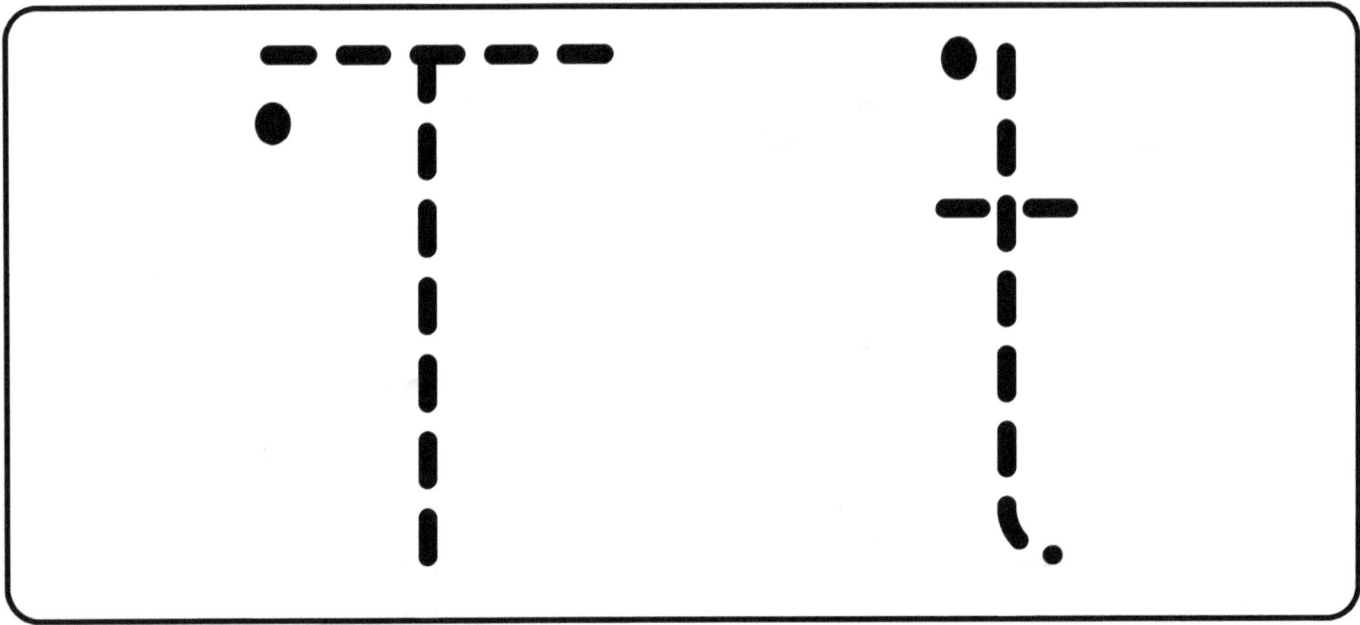

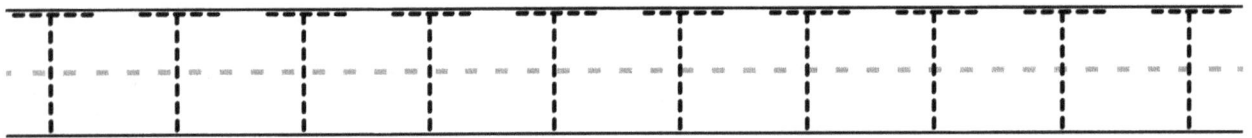

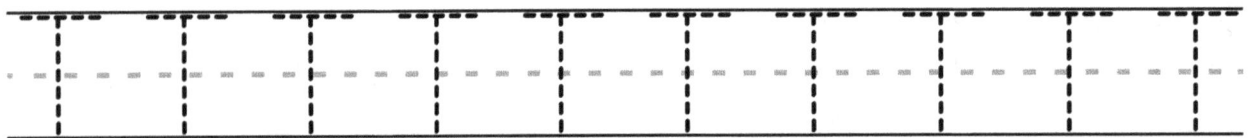

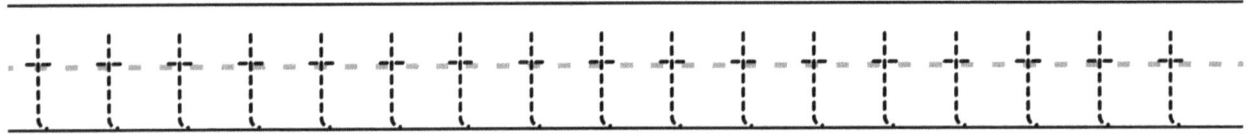

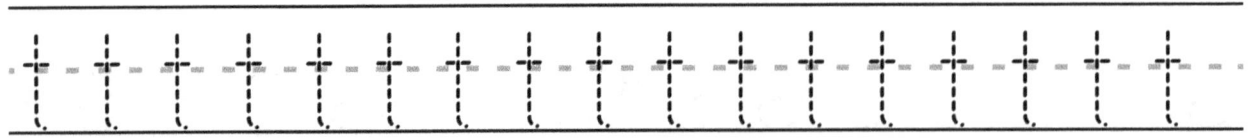

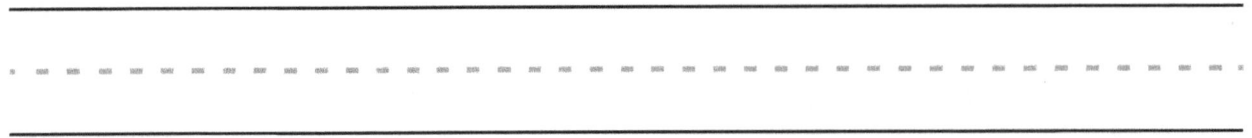

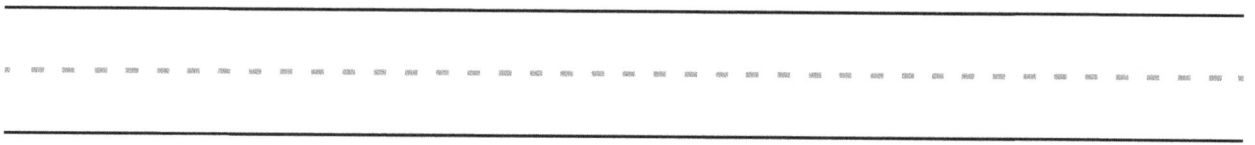

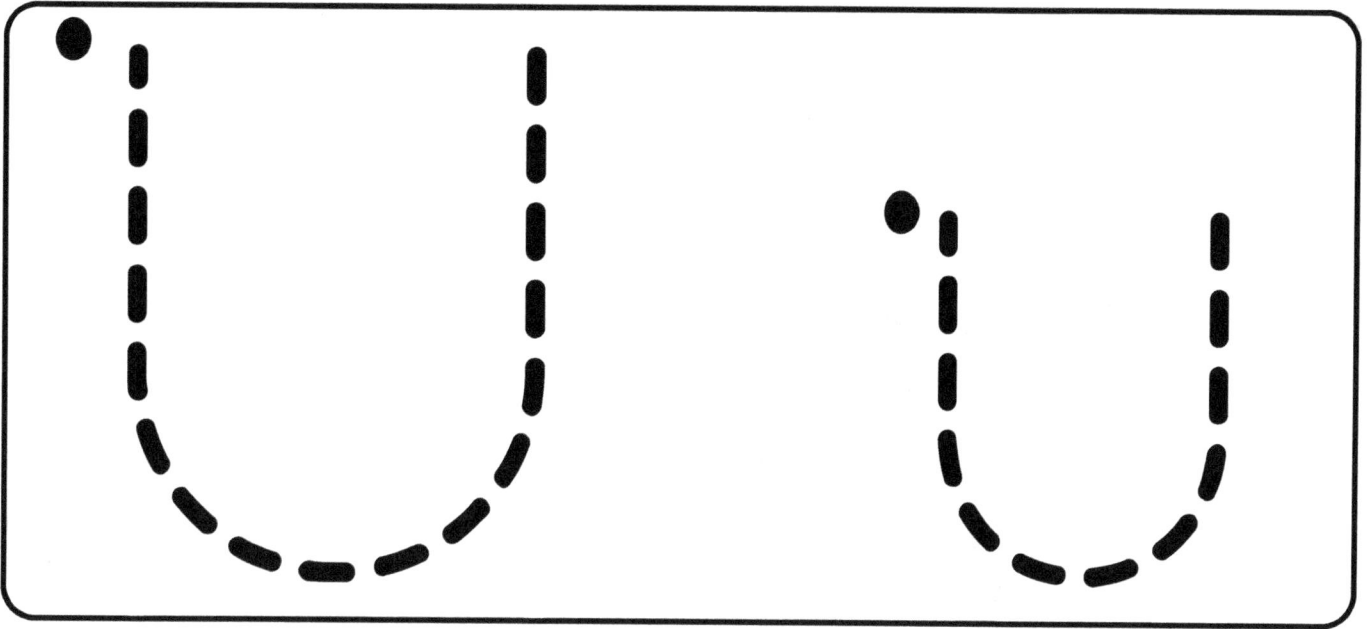

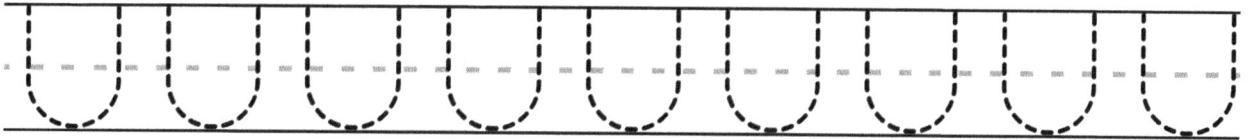

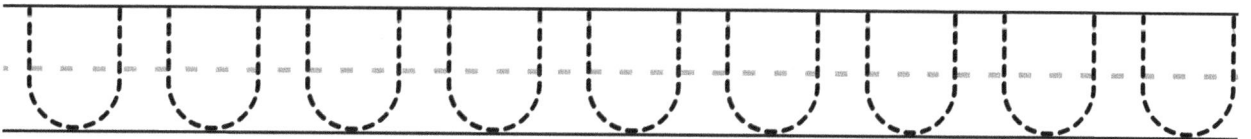

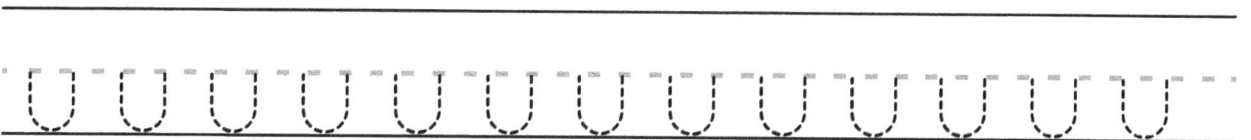

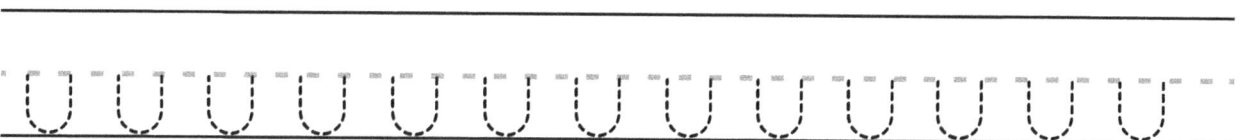

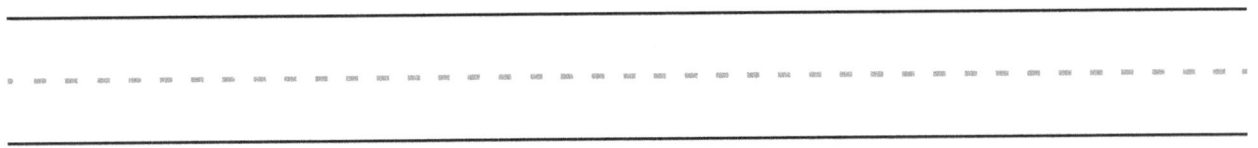

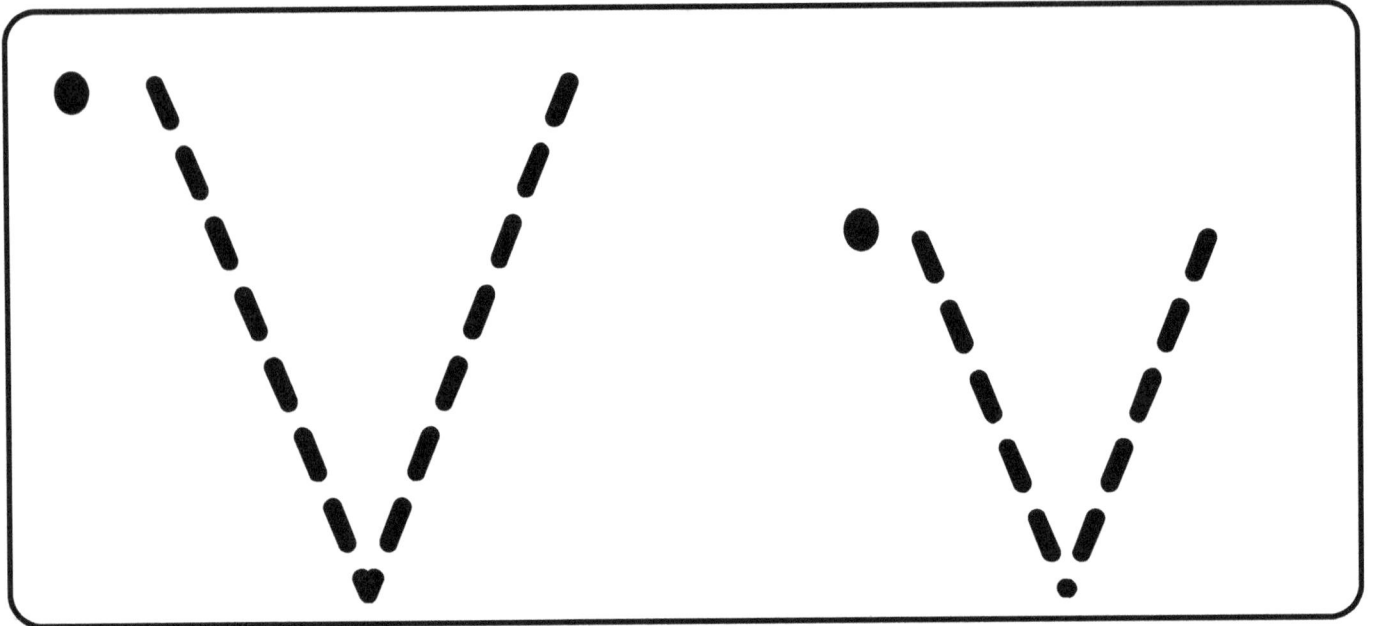

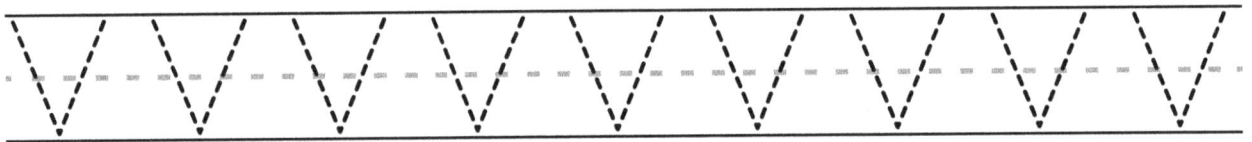

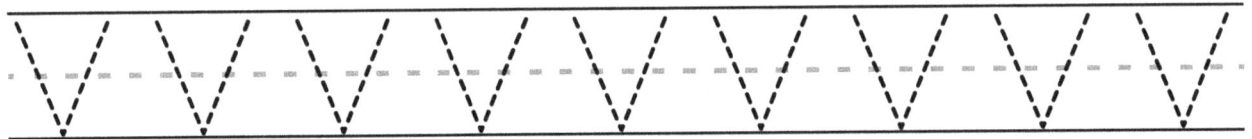

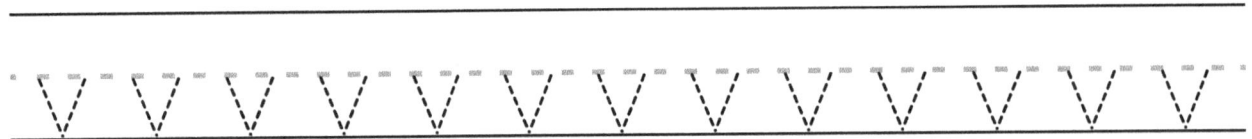

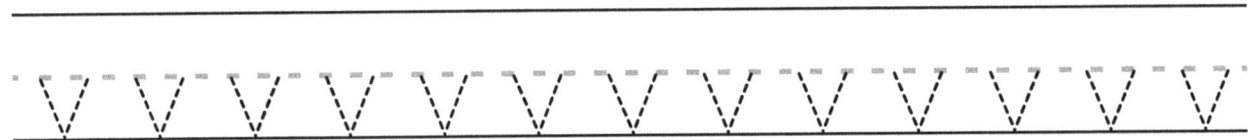

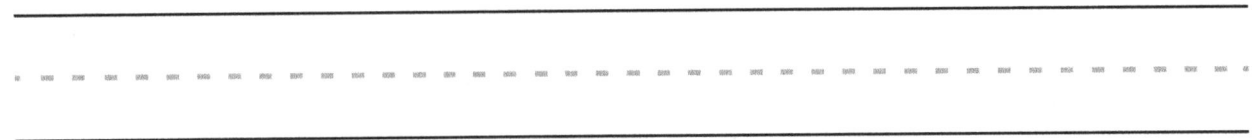

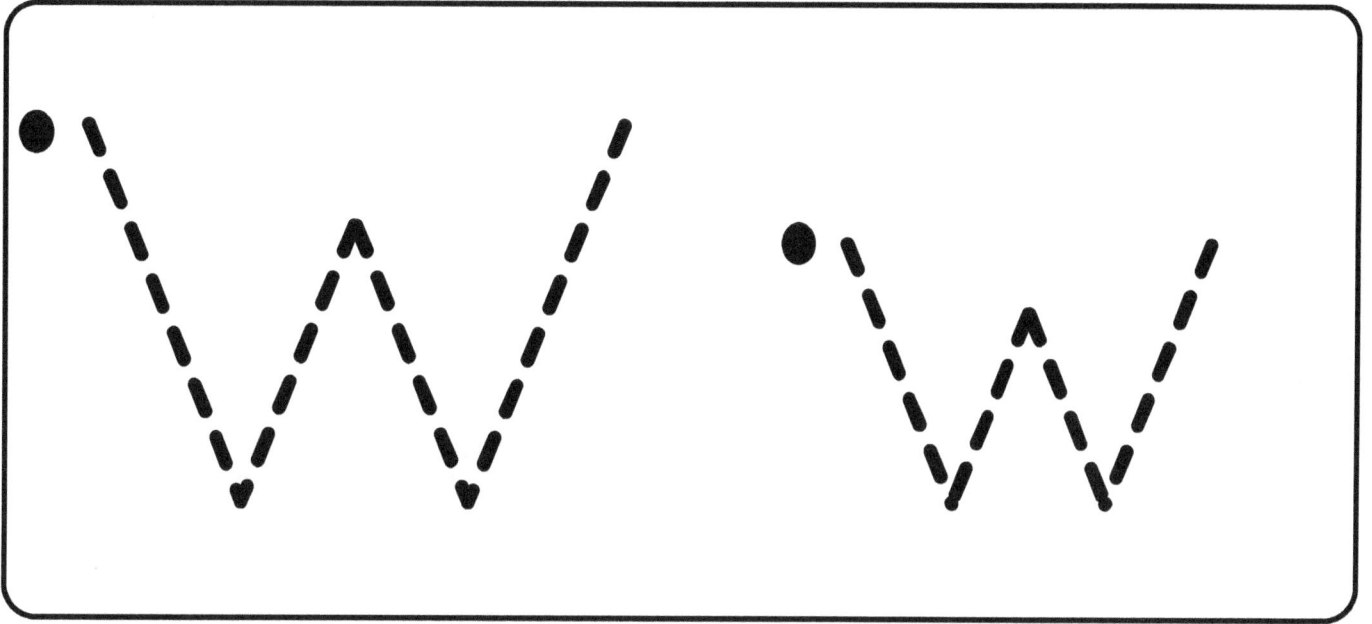

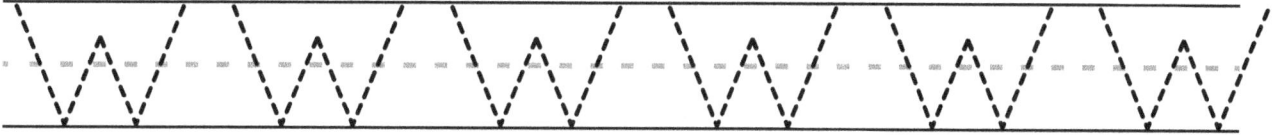

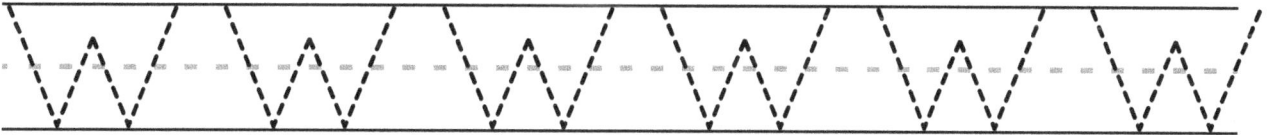

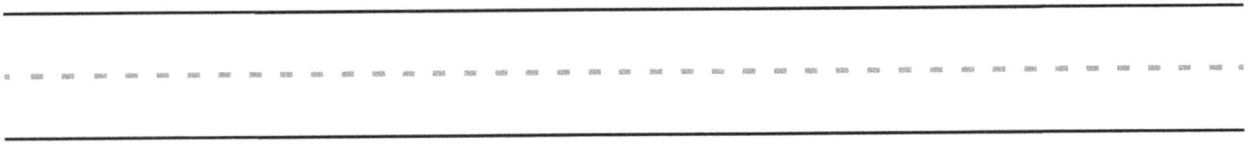

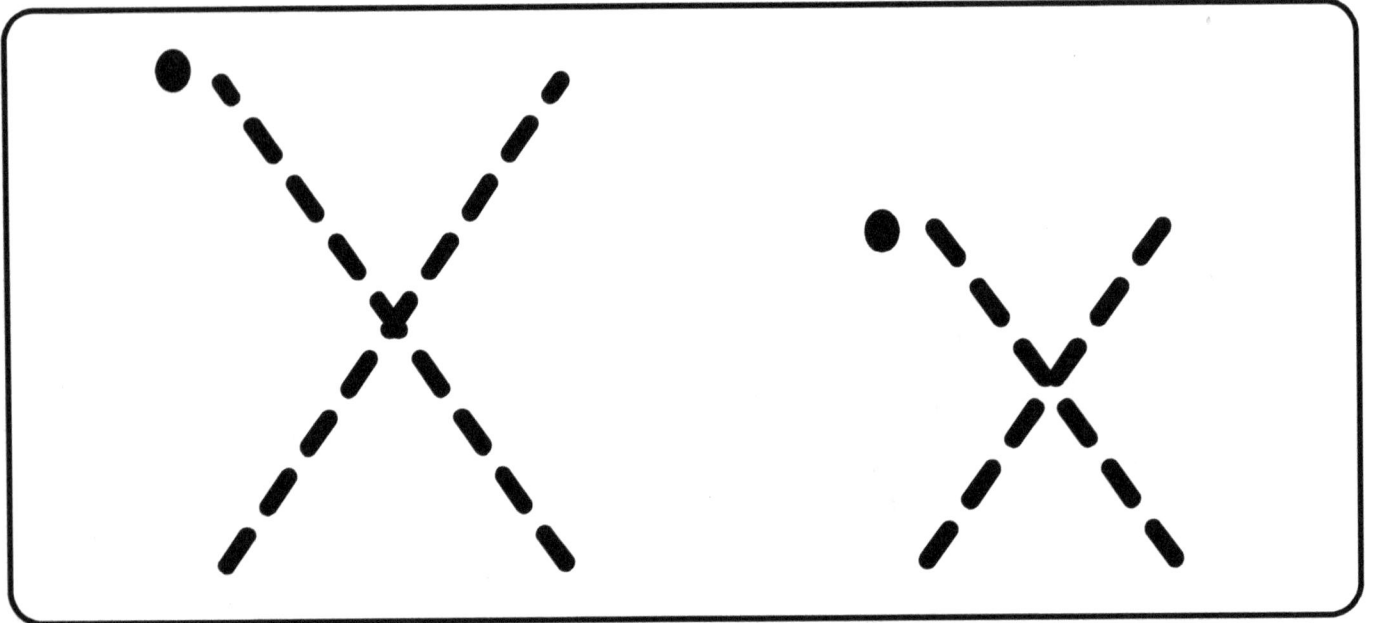

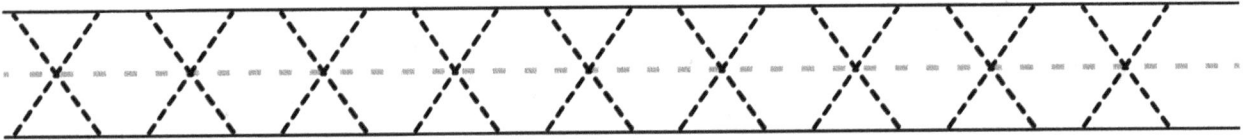

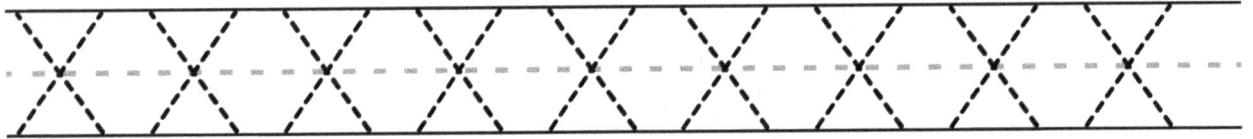

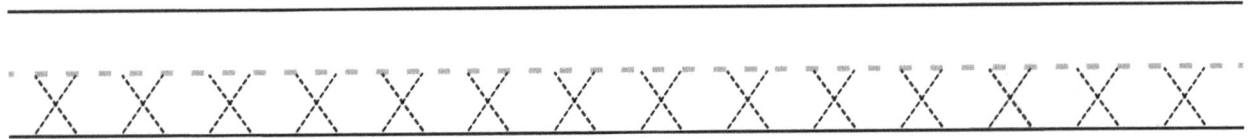

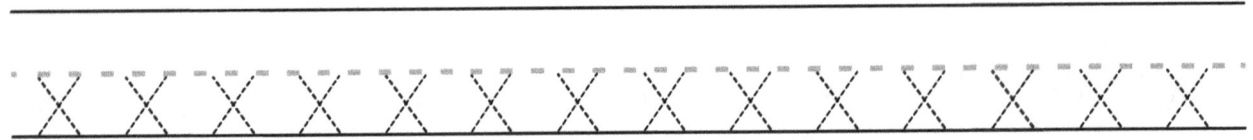

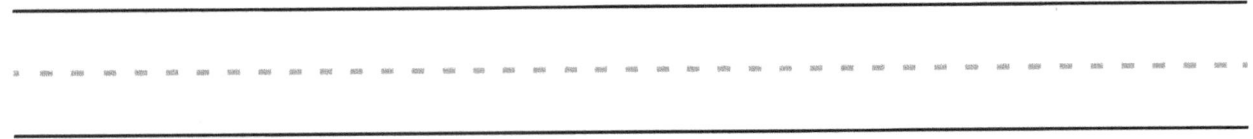

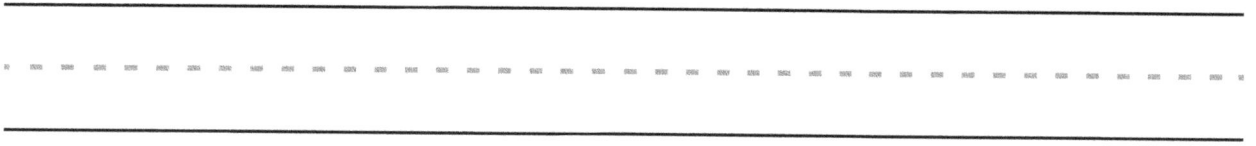

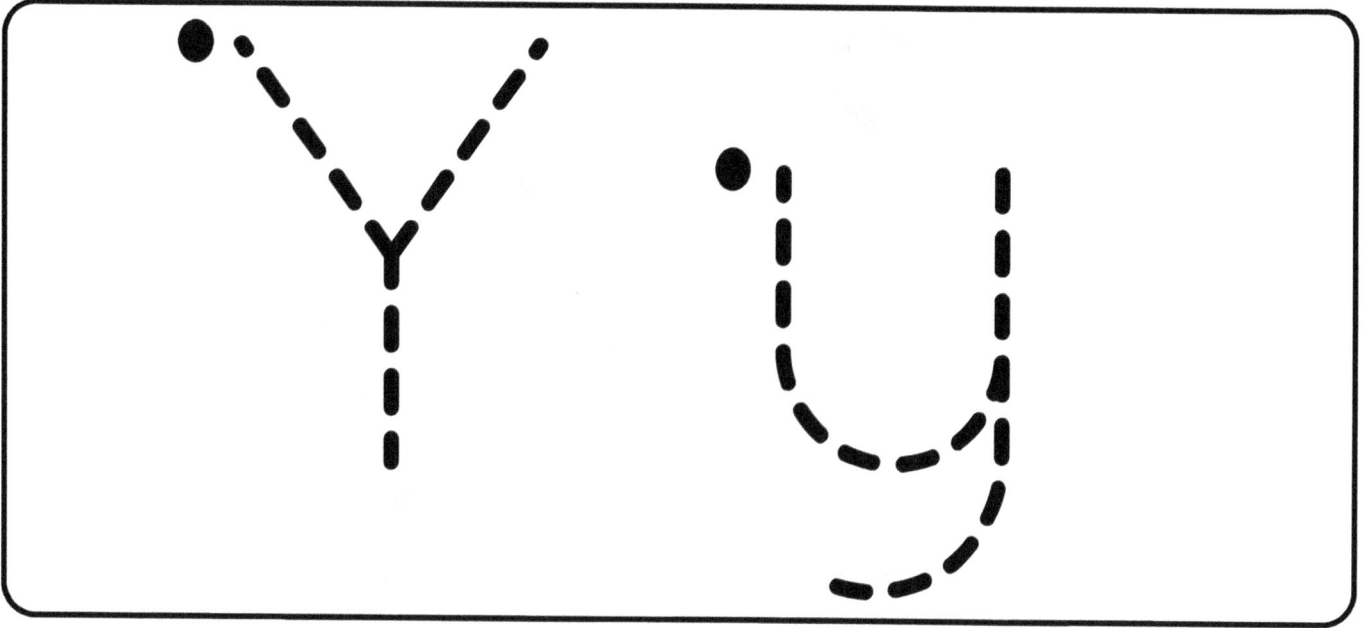

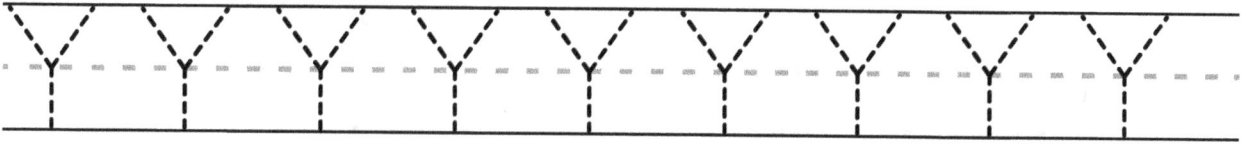

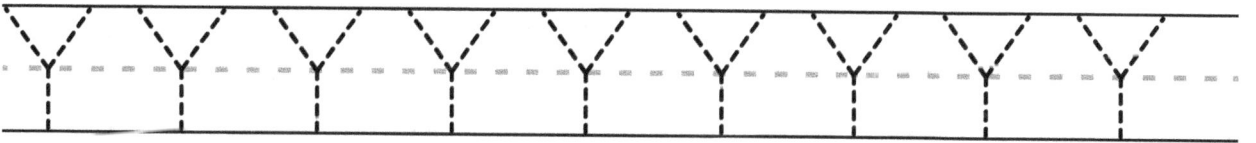

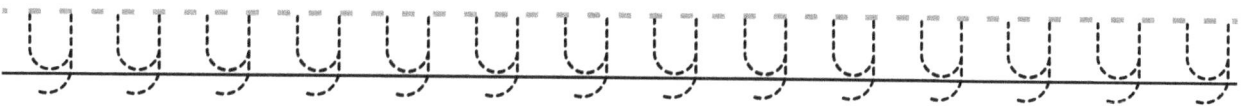

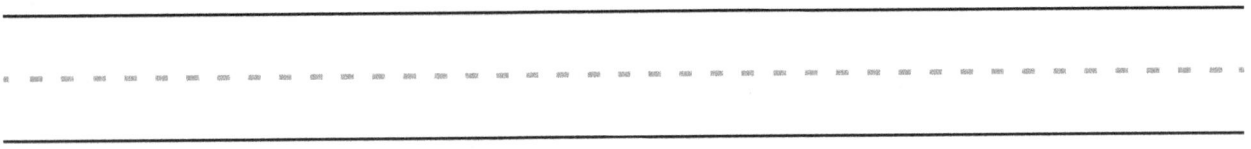

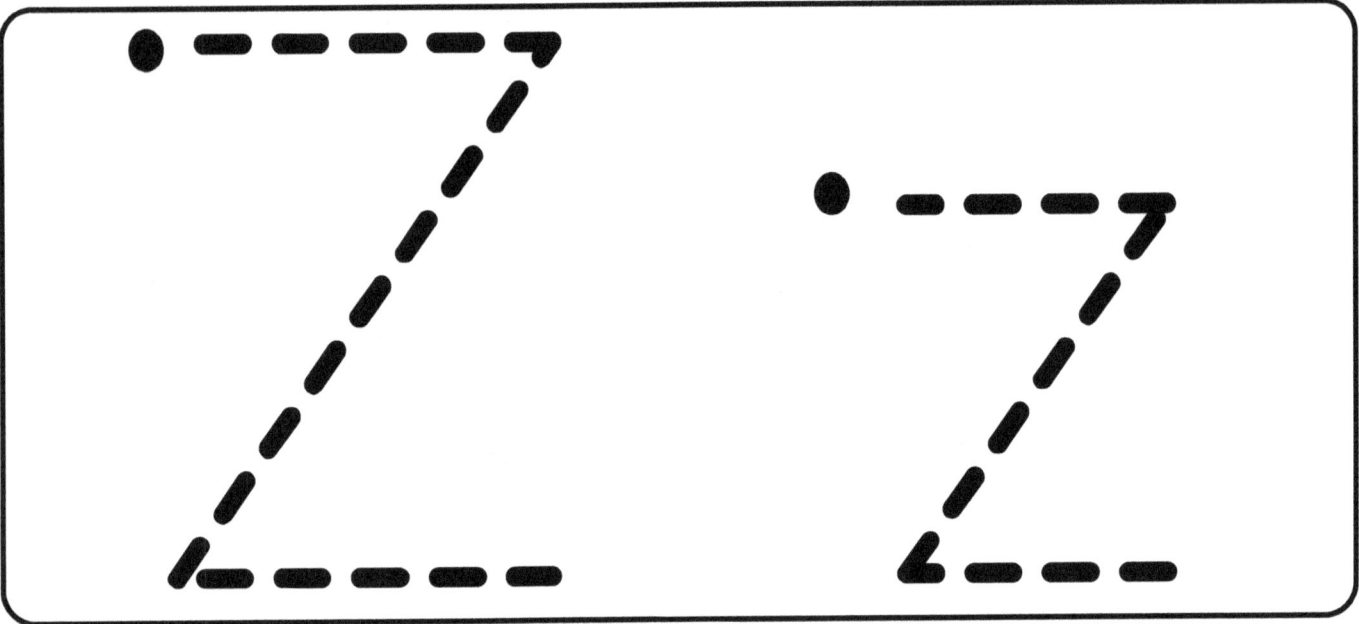

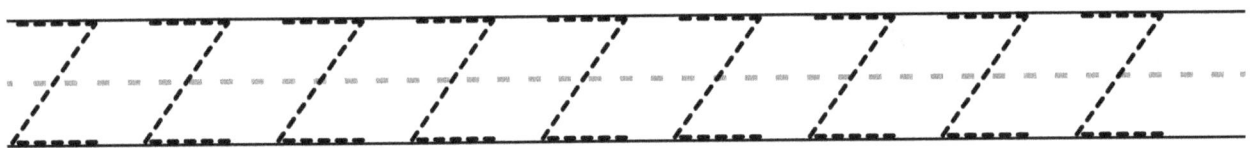

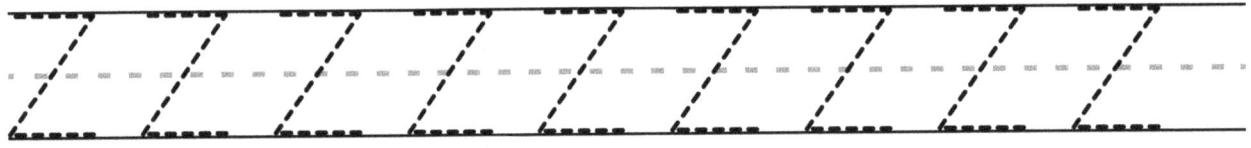

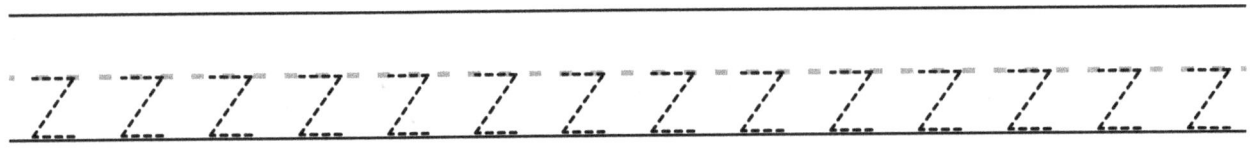

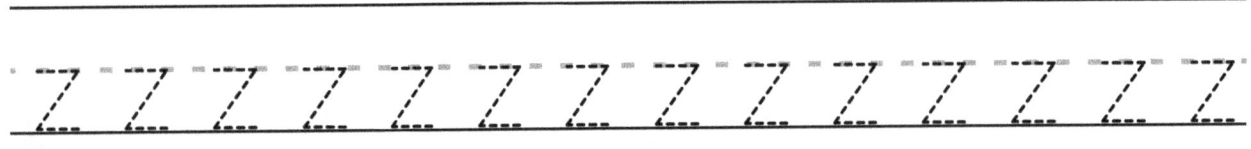

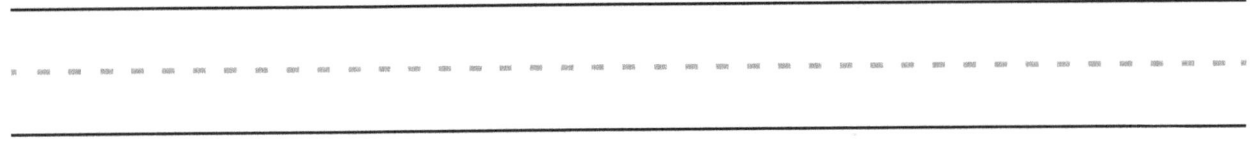